The Research Process

OXFORD
UNIVERSITY PRESS

Oxford University Press is a department of the University of Oxford.
It furthers the University's objective of excellence in research, scholarship,
and education by publishing worldwide. Oxford is a registered trade mark of
Oxford University Press in the UK and in certain other countries.

Published in Canada by
Oxford University Press
8 Sampson Mews, Suite 204,
Don Mills, Ontario M3C 0H5 Canada

www.oupcanada.com

Copyright © Oxford University Press Canada 2019

First Edition published in 2009
Second Edition published in 2012
Third Edition published in 2016

Library and Archives Canada Cataloguing in Publication
Bouma, Gary D., author
The research process / Lori Wilkinson, Gary D. Bouma, Susan Carland.
– Fourth Canadian edition.

Includes bibliographical references and index.
Issued in print and electronic formats.
ISBN 978-0-19-902979-2 (softcover).–ISBN 978-0-19-902983-9 (PDF)

1. Social sciences–Research–Textbooks. 2. Social sciences–Research–
Canada–Textbooks. 3. Social sciences–Research–Methodology–Textbooks.
4. Textbooks. I. Wilkinson, Lori, 1972-, author II. Carland, Susan, author
III. Title.

H62.B675 2019   300.72   C2018-904229-X
                                                             C2018-904230-3

Cover image: Ainsley Duyvestyn-Smith/EyeEm/Getty Images

Cover design: Sherill Chapman
Interior design: Sherill Chapman

Oxford University Press is committed to our environment.
This book is printed on Forest Stewardship Council® certified paper
and comes from responsible sources.

Printed and bound in the United States of America

1 2 3 4 — 22 21 20 19

Fourth Canadian Edition

The Research Process

Lori Wilkinson

Gary D. Bouma

Susan Carland

OXFORD
UNIVERSITY PRESS

Contents

Phase 3   Analysis and Interpretation   269

Acknowledgements

To Donald H. Bouma

This book is dedicated to my father—sociologist, community leader, and opinion shaper. I learned research as a child. I learned the importance of having evidence to support an argument and how evidence-based argument could be a powerful tool for liberation. For my father, this was used in support of the black civil rights movement in the United States. For me, it has been used to advance other liberations and for the analysis of the shape and management of religious diversity in postmodern societies.

We would like to thank all those who have attended workshops and seminars on "research methodology." The questions you raised, the ideas you shared, and the enthusiasm you had for the topic led to the writing of *The Research Process*.

We are grateful to the hundreds of students who have taken the research process course at Monash University. Their comments on both the strengths and the weaknesses of the text have greatly helped to shape the progress of new editions.

I am deeply indebted to the many PhD, masters, and honours students who have come to me for supervision. I hope that they have learned as much about research from me as I have from them.

I also wish to thank the thousands of people who participated in the research projects I have conducted. Whether it was quantitative or qualitative research, I depended absolutely on their willingness to tell me about themselves in some way.

It has been a pleasure to work with Susan Carland on the revision and refreshment of *The Research Process* for the fourth edition. Susan was a student of mine many years ago and has just been awarded her PhD. She claims she found this book very helpful and was delighted to have the chance to bring it into the twenty-first century.

—*Gary D. Bouma*

I am incredibly grateful for Professor Bouma's generosity in bringing me onto this project. From that packed undergraduate sociology lecture when I first heard him speak, until today, he continues to be the kind of academic I hope to emulate in more ways than one. I am indebted to him.

Thanks, and big squeezy hugs to Aisha and Zayd for their patience while I edited this book. And, as always, my deepest thanks and love goes to Waleed.

—*Susan Carland*

The most important work I do as a professor is teaching students. I have learned from all my students, both graduate and undergraduate, and every edition of this textbook has benefitted from the interactions I have had with them over the years. I would also like to thank some individuals, starting with my students

Farzana Quddus, Fadi Ennab, and Nicole Palidwor for providing assistance in preparing the book for editions one and two. Sally Ogoe has assisted with some of the preparation of the third edition. Abdul-Bari Abdul-Karim helped with parts of the fourth edition. Lance Roberts, Tracey Peter, and Jason Edgerton, my colleagues at the University of Manitoba, have continued to provide me with great academic support and have encouraged me to become a better, more critical methods professor. Jennifer Charlton and Jodi Lewchuk at Oxford University Press are commended for their attention to detail and for their understanding of the delays brought on by a broken arm late in the writing stages of the second edition. Amy Gordon has shepherded me through the third and fourth editions—once again battling a (different) broken arm after a massive bicycling accident. Her patience, kindness, and understanding have made this process more bearable. Rhiannon Wong and Michelle Welsh also helped with the production of the newest edition of this book.

I am appreciative of the comments made by the anonymous reviewers in all four versions of the text; their suggestions have greatly strengthened this work and have changed my ideas about research. My sincere appreciation goes to Pamela Erlichman for her careful copy editing of the manuscript for the second edition—you made my job much easier! Many thanks to Jennifer McIntyre for her careful editing of the third edition of the book. My deepest thanks to Joanne Muzak, who copy edited the fourth edition—and corrected the mistakes we missed the first three times! I thank Joanne for pointing out the fabulous book *Elements of Indigenous Style* and the revisions to the TCPS2. Her attention to minute details has made this version of the book even stronger.

My sincerest appreciation goes out to my family, colleagues, and numerous friends who have always supported me throughout my academic endeavours. Finally, I would like to acknowledge the support of my spouse, John Sorensen, who, despite being a chemistry professor, keeps his copy of this book prominently displayed on his desk at work.

—*Lori Wilkinson*

Preface

If you want to know what social science research is all about and how to do it, this book is for you. In accessible language, it will lead you into the world of research and give you confidence that you know how to design a research study, how to carry it out, and how to report on your research. You will become aware of the range of possible approaches and what each offers. You will learn how to decide what approach suits the issue you want to study, and the question you want to answer. You will also become aware of some of the pitfalls, as well as learning a few key "tricks of the trade."

The logic of research is presented in such a way as to enable the novice to prepare research proposals and to conduct research. The essential logic of scientific research is the same for physicists as it is for sociologists. It is the same for beginners as for masters of the art. This book introduces the essential logic of research—that is, the kind of disciplined thinking that scientific research requires. Designing and conducting a research project also requires clear and disciplined thinking, and this book is intended to serve as a brief, easy-to-digest introduction to the research process. More advanced students are strongly encouraged to consult other methodological texts, particularly once they have decided on a research design, mode of sampling, and method of data analysis.

While there are many kinds of research, and research projects seem at first to take many forms, it is a mistake to assume that there is no pattern to the process. A second mistake is to mindlessly follow one pattern.

This fourth Canadian edition of *The Research Process* is aimed at post-secondary students who are enrolled in an introductory research methods course or who want to learn how to do the kinds of research required for jobs in marketing, social policy, social work, politics, communication, or community work. It assumes that readers have only an introductory understanding of "social science" and little knowledge about doing research. The text begins in a leisurely way, introducing concepts one at a time with examples. It takes a non-statistical approach, presenting the essentials of the research process in an understandable manner. Quantitative, qualitative, and mixed methods are introduced, along with discussions of recent innovations in social science research methods. While quantitative and qualitative methods differ in some ways, there are many issues common to both of these important ways of gathering evidence for understanding the social world we live in.

The past few decades have witnessed hotly contended debates about the aims, the achievements, and the very possibilities of the sciences. In the meantime, researchers have carried on with their basic task of describing the way aspects of our world work and testing theories by relating evidence to propositions about the state, nature, and operation of the universe. While this is not a book on the philosophy of science, the essential philosophical questions apply to all researchers—chemists, physicists, social psychologists, demographers, and others.

The Approach

We approach research methodology as a process involving a sequence of activities, each step preparing students for the next. When doing social science research, some questions are best answered before others are raised. The reasons for this sequencing of questions are explained to readers and several common pitfalls are pointed out. The process of social science research is divided into three phases.

Phase 1 involves

1. selecting a problem (including narrowing and clarifying the problem) and restating it as a hypothesis for quantitative research or as a research objective for qualitative research;
2. defining variables and determining ways of measuring them;
3. choosing a research design;
4. choosing a sample.

Phase 2 is the data collection stage. This book includes a discussion of researchers' ethical responsibilities; understanding these will be helpful in securing the approval of a human research ethics committee to conduct your research.

Phase 3 involves the analysis and interpretation of data and writing the report.

Several examples in each chapter demonstrate how the research process progresses. Case Study boxes provide relevant examples from various academic disciplines, and In Focus boxes provide further insights and handy tips for conducting research. In addition, each chapter ends with a list of key terms, a list of web resources, and questions to test your comprehension of the material and encourage critical thinking questions to help you take the content further.

This Canadian edition also contains critical coverage on ethical policies including the Tri-Council (2010) Policy Statement on Ethical Conduct Involving Humans, ethical and secure storage of data and personal information, Canadian examples of ethical oversight, and guidelines on obtaining informed consent and what to do if an ethical dilemma occurs when conducting research, and new suggestions for respecting power dynamics when conducting research. Our aim is to give students a good understanding of how to navigate the ever-changing contexts of ethics. This edition also contains more examples, more on developing a theoretical framework for your research, more on mixed methods, more qualitative coverage, more on internet-based research, and up-to-date Canadian statistics.

The Research Process is designed to develop research skills important for living and working in our world—a world in which information is becoming one of the most valuable commodities and in which the ability to handle information is not only one of the most valued and marketable skills, but one that is critical to getting a job today.

Lori Wilkinson
Gary D. Bouma

Susan Carland
April 2018

Introduction

1 How We Know What We Know and How We Know We Know

Have you ever had an argument with someone? She said one thing, and you said another. She claimed she was right because she read it in a book. You defended your position by pointing out that a doctor told you and a doctor should know. So, arguments go. But how do they stop? How can these points of view be tested to determine which is correct? How do we know when we are right or wrong? How do we know what we know?

We are confronted by questions all through life. What is the best diet for weight loss? What is the impact of job loss on the rate of marital breakdown? What is the solution to child poverty or homelessness? Is post-secondary education worthwhile? Is coeducation better for males than it is for females? We may spend a lot of time debating the issues raised by these and similar questions, but how do we find reliable answers to our questions? How do we get the knowledge we seek?

Knowledge can be defined as a description of the state or operation of some aspect of the universe upon which people or groups are prepared to act. If I "know" that it will rain, I am likely to take my umbrella or wear a raincoat. If I "know" that completing a post-secondary education is reliably associated with higher levels of income, I am more likely to make some effort to attend and graduate from a post-secondary institution.

Knowledge does not hang in space; it is a product of social processes. The production of knowledge usually begins when the public, governments, or groups of experts recognize that the state of knowledge in a particular area is inadequate. Next, funding bodies, corporations, and universities accept research proposals and decide which are the most relevant and deserving of support. Successful proposals are created by teams of researchers who produce findings through their combined experience and skills. Research findings are communicated and endorsed by professional organizations that decide what research should be published and how it should be presented. Finally, communities and governments have a say in how new knowledge is applied by debating and legislating for its appropriate uses. In this way, knowledge is both a product and the property of social groups.

Research as a Way of Life

Students might be saying to themselves, "Why should I care about research? I'm not interested in becoming a researcher or professor. This information seems irrelevant as I prepare to enter the job market." I tell my students that almost every professional job involves research in some capacity. Some students will find employment that requires them to research every day. Jobs with titles such as policy analyst, research analyst, journalist, lawyer, or consultant all require some degree of research. Other jobs, at first glance, may not appear to require research as a skill set, but once you begin work, you will quickly discover that research is a central component. For example, did you know that teachers have to research? They may have to learn more information about a student's particular health needs, for instance, and they also have to be up to date with current curriculum and pedagogy, meaning that researching these issues is a necessity. People in other jobs such as police officers, corrections officers, nurses, physicians, dentists, business owners, community service providers, those who work in non-profit organizations or government positions, and even fiction and nonfiction writers, all conduct research in some form as part of their jobs. If they are not conducting the research themselves, they likely need to read other peoples' research and make judgments about its quality and validity. For instance, if you are working for a government department, you might be asked to read many published research papers and to provide advice to your supervisors about the quality of those papers. Governments use this information to make important program and policy decisions, so the ability to assess the quality of research results is very important, particularly when public funds and continuation of programs are at stake.

Additionally, in a society where information is more readily available than ever before, people find themselves becoming researchers by necessity. Which daycare is most appropriate for my child? Should I ask my physician about a new medication I found on the internet? Should I select the defined benefit or defined contribution plan for my pension? Finding the answers to these questions requires you to do research. This likely means you find yourself sorting and evaluating large amounts of information that you gather to answer these questions. An understanding of research methods allows you to determine the quality of the information you obtain so you can place more emphasis on good, scientific information and to be able to identify and discard the poorly designed and subjective information you collect. No matter what you do in life, in terms of both your career and your everyday life, you are likely to use the skills you learn in your research methods course to assist you.

Answering Our Questions

One of the first issues facing us is whether to answer questions ourselves or rely on others for the information we need. If we want to know whether it is raining outside, we can look for ourselves or ask someone else. If we want to know what Canadians think about politicians, we can either ask Canadians ourselves or look at the recent polls. Whatever the question, we are faced with roughly the same choice. We can do research—that is, collect the evidence ourselves—or consult an authority.

Consulting an Authority as a Way of Knowing

Usually when we have a question, we look up the answer in a textbook, search the internet, ask a friend who knows, or ask an expert—a medical practitioner, a professor, a religious leader, a police officer, a lawyer, or an umpire, as appropriate. We refer to articles in journals or newspapers or look for a book or a website on the subject. The most common way by which we get answers to our questions is to consult authorities. As long as the authority consulted knows the answer, this is the most efficient way to answer a question.

People can have at least two kinds of authority: authority based on position and authority based on knowledge. The kind of authority most useful for answering our questions about the nature and operation of the world—particularly the social, biological, and physical world—is authority derived from knowledge.

The main problem with consulting authorities is selection. On what basis do we select authorities? When we are looking for an answer to a question or problem, the essential guideline should be that the authority has the knowledge we need. However, other factors sometimes influence our choice.

For example, we are sometimes influenced by people's position, popularity, or appearance. The critical point is that no matter how prominent people are, no matter how much authority or power they have, their opinion on a subject is of no more value than any other person's unless they have expertise in the area. A bishop, a physician, a judge, or an Olympic gold medalist may hold opinions about unemployment, taxation, the way families should be raised, or the role of government in foreign aid. These opinions, however, unless based on special knowledge of the issue in question, are no more valid than those expressed on the same topic by anyone else.

Another problem arises when (almost inevitably) two or more recognized authorities in the same field disagree. For example, it is very common to encounter conflicting opinions regarding the extent of unemployment, gender discrimination, and racial discrimination; the benefits and costs of domestic welfare programs, foreign aid, and affirmative action policies; and the incidence of infections and work-related injuries. Authorities also fail us when they cannot answer questions with assurance. Sometimes their opinions are unconvincing. On many issues that are or appear to be new, there may be no authorities at all.

Research as a Way of Knowing

To evaluate the opinions of authorities, we review their research. For this, we need to understand the *research process*—the generally adopted approach to doing research. Then we can make informed inquiries and judgments of authorities. Has the authority chosen the most appropriate research method? Have all stages of the research been conducted properly? Does the authority's research address the relevant aspects of the question? Has the authority made a valid interpretation of the research findings? What are the limitations of the research?

When authorities cannot answer our questions, or we are dissatisfied with their opinions, we conduct research ourselves. To obtain findings in which we can have confidence, we must be familiar with the research process.

The research process is guided by rules and principles for making confident statements about knowledge of the world based on our observations. As the rest of this book will show, the research process is not an activity that we know intuitively and can just go and do on our own. It is an activity that others have spent much time developing through practice and critical discussion. You will not become familiar with the research process unless you study and practise it.

The following list contains examples of the types of important questions that face groups in today's societies. To pursue valid answers to such questions, it is essential that you have knowledge of the research process.

- Corporations need to have an informed idea of public preferences for products or services. Will the public accept changes in packaging or product performance?
- Social workers need to know what it is like to live under certain conditions, with certain levels of ability, or in certain ethnic groups and subcultures, in order to design appropriate service delivery systems. Do immigrants from China have the same access to an English as an Additional Language Program as immigrants from other countries?
- Professionals such as doctors need to assess the validity of theories that have consequences for the way they practise. Does taking a low-dose estrogen birth control pill increase the incidence of reproductive cancers?
- Governments need to know about the effects of policies. What have been the consequences of the economic policies of the past two decades? What are the consequences of prison terms for juvenile offenders?

If the subject of the research is controversial, it will come under considerable scrutiny. The researchers will be challenged to provide solid and carefully collected evidence. If the results of their research are clear, they may be able to settle the controversy, not by appeal to authority, but by appeal to the evidence they have collected and are able to show to others.

It is also important to understand that one way of knowing is not the only way to locate information. Our way of evaluating, accepting, and discrediting information is also based on our culture. We learn what is acceptable and unacceptable through our culture: what might be an acceptable practice in one culture may be unacceptable in another. For example, one of the authors lived for an extended period in India. She has observed that personal space has a different definition there. In her home country, there is a significant amount of space between individuals as they are walking, talking, and interacting with one another. In India, however, people stand closer together. Similarly, among Indigenous Peoples in North America, the oral tradition—passing information by telling history rather than writing it down—is also a cultural norm. In both cases, the way we see, interact with, and learn about one another is greatly influenced by our culture. We will have many opportunities to discuss cultural context as a way of knowing throughout this book.

In Focus

Credibility and Internet Sources

As you begin work in this course, you will be required to perform research such as a literature review (see Chapter 3), some of which may require research on the internet. The World Wide Web is a wealth of information, both true and false. It is easy for students and new researchers to be intimidated by the amount of information that is available. One of the questions we are often asked is "How do I know that the information I find on a website is accurate?" Another question we are asked regards the authenticity of the author or the webpage. Determining the authenticity of the data or information on a webpage can be difficult, but we suggest a few tips.

1. Use only data from websites of reputable academics, universities, or governments. A good rule to follow is that if the webpage's author is someone you haven't heard of or if the webpage looks unprofessional or out of date, the data are likely not very reliable either. This does not mean that information found on "reputable" sites is 100 per cent trustworthy, but you can feel more assured when using these data than when you use information from a personal webpage that may be based on opinion and not fact.

2. Corroborate data with other sources. You might locate some interesting information from a webpage that you wish to use in your report. It's best to see if others have found or reported similar information. In other words, you can feel more confident in using data if others have reported or found similar information.

Continued

3. Look for sources and/or references on the webpage. You can feel more assured about the information located on a webpage if there are citations provided. If the webpage indicates where the information was located, then you can look up and confirm the original information yourself.

4. Be careful when using newspaper sources. Major newspapers and news websites strive for accuracy in their reporting. However, newspapers can make mistakes too, especially as they compete with one another to be the first to publish stories. Be sure to check the accuracy of a story by accessing versions from multiple newspapers.

5. Avoid using editorials from websites. This information is mainly based on opinion and may not contain much useful factual information. Furthermore, the opinion of the author may be heavily influenced by political, religious, or other kinds of associations. Sometimes, editorials are very "one sided," meaning that they do not present opposing yet valid viewpoints.

6. Be cautious when using Wikipedia. Wikipedia is a good source for general information, but it is not the best source for material in a research report or term paper. This is because it is an open-source page, which means that any user can edit the material at any time. In many cases, particularly with the pages for famous people, malicious editing introduces false or even libellous information. Readers may be unable to ascertain whether or not the information provided is correct or biased. Even the management at Wikipedia suggests that the material that is provided on their websites be checked for accuracy. Sandra Ordonez, a former vice president at Wikipedia, says,

> Wikipedia is the ideal place to start your research and get a global picture of a topic; however, it is not an authoritative source. In fact, we recommend that students check the facts they find in Wikipedia against other sources. Additionally, it is generally good research practice to cite an original source when writing a paper or completing an exam. It's usually not advisable, particularly at the university level, to cite an encyclopedia. (Cited in Jaschik, 2007)

When in doubt, either do not use Wikipedia at all, or ask your professor for advice.

Summary

Research is done to settle disputes about the nature and operation of some aspect of the world we live in. The research process is a disciplined way of coming to know something about our world—and about ourselves.

Questions for Review

1. When is research carried out?
2. In what ways is the expertise of an authority limited?
3. Discuss some of the problems involved in consulting authorities in order to answer questions. Who would you consult about child-raising techniques? Who would you consult about the impact of explicitly violent television on the play routines of children?
4. List the authorities you regularly consult. How do you know they know? What characteristics of these authorities are important to you? Gender? Age? Social position?
5. Is it possible to live without accepting the word of authorities?
6. What are some tips for selecting good and reputable sources of information?
7. Prepare one or two researchable questions of your own. Can you think of resources that would help you answer these questions?

Source

Jaschik, S. (2007, January 26). A stand against Wikipedia. *Inside Higher Education.* Retrieved September 19, 2015 from www.insidehighered.com/news/2007/01/26/wiki#ixzz2hAWSQjaI

Suggestions for Further Reading

Booth, W. C., & Colomb, G. G. (2016). *The craft of research* (4th ed.). Chicago: University of Chicago Press.

Cochran, P. A. L., Marshall, C. A., Garcia-Downing, C., Kendal, E., Cook, D., Mccubbin, L., & R. M. S. Gover. (2008). Indigenous ways of knowing: Implications for participatory research and community. *American Journal of Public Health, 98*(1), 22–8.

Denzin, N. K., & Lincoln Y. S. (Eds). (2000). *Handbook of qualitative research* (2nd ed.). London: Sage.

Suggested Web Resources

Cullins, F. (2013, November 8). *Finding accurate information on the internet.* Retrieved March 22, 2018 from http://msue.anr.msu.edu/news/finding_accurate_information_on_the_internet

Georgetown University. (2018). *Evaluating internet resources.* Retrieved March 22, 2018 from www.library.georgetown.edu/tutorials/research-guides/evaluating-internet-content

Research as a Way of Knowing

Science can be defined as a discipline that collects, weighs, and evaluates the empirical evidence for accepting a particular **theory** or explanation. The *goal of science* is to produce a widely acceptable description of the nature or operation of some aspect of the universe. Science, whether social, psychological, biological, or in the field of physics, does this by collecting and analyzing sensory evidence in such a way that others looking at the same evidence in the same way would draw the same conclusions or at least understand that it is possible to see what the researcher was examining. *Scientific research* involves the attempt to collect evidence in such a way that others can see why particular evidence was gathered, how that evidence was gathered, and what the findings were; observers can then draw their own conclusions on the basis of that evidence.

This chapter explores the practical meaning of this definition of science. How does scientific research go about trying to produce knowledge that is supported by empirical evidence—that is, by physical, tangible evidence? What are the several kinds of disciplined activities involved in the research process?

Scientific research is done to find ways of understanding, describing, and making more predictable, or controlling, the behaviour of some aspect of the universe. The results of research may be used to develop remedies for problems, strategies for projects, and plans for action. Problems such as youth homelessness, projects to improve levels of education, and plans to combat or contain diseases such as West Nile virus all require information that does not exist and must be researched.

We also engage in research to settle conflicting claims or differences of opinion or to test ideas about the world we live in. Take the following simple case:

Georgina: Diets high in cholesterol cause heart disease.
Frank: You are wrong. Coronary heart disease is not influenced by dietary cholesterol. There are other factors that are more significant in predicting the incidence of heart disease.

The conflict between Georgina and Frank can be settled by scientific research. They both have theories about the causes of heart disease. It is possible to collect evidence to test their competing theories. This example will be developed throughout the chapter.

Research as a Process

Doing research involves a process or a series of linked activities moving from beginning to end. The research process is not absolutely rigid, but it will be weakened or made more difficult if the first steps are not executed carefully.

Those who have done a lot of research develop their own style of going through the phases of the research process. Researchers will be able to describe a pattern or a regular way in which they do their research. When their patterns are compared, a "normal" sequence begins to emerge—not in the sense of a strict set of steps but as an order of basic phases, with related issues considered at each phase.

The following outline of the research process has helped many students to learn the necessary skills and avoid the major pitfalls involved in research. It is not the only way of doing research, however, but just one useful way.

Outline of the Research Process

Phase 1: Essential first steps
The researcher clarifies the issue to be researched, creates a question, and selects a research method.

Phase 2: Data collection
The researcher collects and evaluates evidence related to the research question.

Phase 3: Analysis and interpretation
The researcher relates the evidence to the research question, draws conclusions about the question, and acknowledges the limitations of the research.

Phase 1 of the research process involves five essential steps, each concerning a separate issue. Failure to satisfactorily address these issues will render the rest of the research process more difficult or impossible—therefore, the steps are essential. While **qualitative** and **quantitative research designs** both follow these steps, there are differences in the way they do. These differences will be noted as we go along.

Phase 1: Essential first steps
1. Select, narrow, and formulate the question to be studied.
2. Select a suitable research design.
3. Design and devise measures for **variables** or research concepts.
4. Set up tables for analysis, if required.
5. Select a **sample** and/or identify participants.

In Focus

Qualitative and Quantitative Research: Understanding the Difference

Often students and those new to research will ask for advice about conducting research for the very first time. They usually have a discretely identified problem they need to have answered, and often they have predetermined that they will conduct their research in a particular way. Even experienced researchers can make biased assumptions about the way they will answer their research question. It is very important to understand, however, that the nature of the research question—the way that question is phrased—determines the methodology that is employed to answer it and dictates the order of the research procedures.

Qualitative and quantitative research methodologies are designed to obtain very different kinds of answers. Qualitative research, the kind of methodology that uses non-numerical information, is used to address questions of how or why things happen. In this type of research, we are interested in deeper meanings of experiences. For example, we might be interested in learning more about the experience of being bullied in elementary school. Asking principals to provide numerical information about the number of bullying instances at the school during the year provides useful information, but it doesn't tell us why or how bullying happens. Instead, we need to dig deeper to find out why and how this happens. One way to get an understanding of the experience of being bullied is to interview victims of bullying. We might have to do this over a long period of time, particularly because those who are traumatized by bullying may not trust the researcher. We might have to ask different kinds of questions of each participant because the experience of bullying is very different for each individual involved. Maybe we would like to do some participant observation about the interactions between youth on the playground, so we can obtain information in a more natural setting. This is a powerful research design because the data obtained are rich, often in the participant's own words, and provide a holistic overview of the experience.

Quantitative research, the kind that uses numbers, formulas, and statistics to make inferences or predictions, is used to produce descriptive research. We are interested in describing the phenomenon. For instance, if we were interested in predicting how long it will take a student to finish a bachelor's degree at university, we could examine the administrative databases at the university. We could use information about date of entry, number of courses taken per semester, field of study, grade point average, and other characteristics such as sex, birth date, and secondary school grades. We could use a set of formulas to predict their time to completion based on the information available in the database.

Step 1: *Focus and narrow the research problem.* Initially, a research problem may start with an observation such as "Most people who are unemployed seem to be young." One approach to developing a research problem from this observation would be to ask, "What is it like to be young and unemployed?" This would probably lead to qualitative research guided by a **research objective**. Another approach would be to test the validity of this observation. To do this, it is necessary to be clear about what has to be tested. The observer claims that there is a relationship between two varying aspects (variables) of his general social experience, "unemployment" and "age." The observer is really saying that, according to his general observations, "The lower a person's age, the more likely the person is to be unemployed." This is one way of moving from the observation to articulating a relationship to be tested. Each of these approaches clarifies the focus of the research. At this point, it is important to review the literature on youth unemployment. This will assist you in identifying the major findings and the research questions asked by other researchers. It is also the first step in situating your own research findings within the existing research debates. More will be said about the literature review in Chapter 3.

Step 2: *Select a research design.* The first choice here is between qualitative and quantitative research. Your observation might motivate you to ask, "What is it like to be young and unemployed?" or "Is being unemployed different for young men compared with young women?" Such questions are usually answered using qualitative research methods rather than quantitative methods.

Conversely, you might want to test a more quantitative question, such as "What percentage of youth are unemployed?" or "Is youth unemployment greater now than in the 1980s?" or "Is youth unemployment more prevalent in Vancouver than in Victoria?" The first question about the relationship between age and unemployment could be tested in a single social environment, such as a social club or a suburb. The results would be based on information gathered in that one environment. The subsequent questions would require that the relationship be examined in several social environments, such as different clubs or suburbs, and that the results for each be compared, providing the desired results.

Step 3: *Design and devise measures for variables or research concepts.* If you choose to take a quantitative approach, you will select variables and find measures for them before you gather evidence. For example, to measure changes in unemployment, you might select the government's official unemployment rate. However, if you take a qualitative approach, you will decide which prompts to use to enable your interviewees to tell their stories or select certain aspects of human behaviour to observe and record. Consulting the literature is an important step here as well. How have other researchers defined unemployment? How have other researchers defined youth? Does the existing literature define youth as being between the ages of 15 and 24, or do other researchers define youth differently? This is an important aspect to consider when situating your research and is further discussed in Chapter 3.

Step 4: *Create an analysis plan.* If you choose to take a quantitative approach, you will design tables to be used in summarizing your data in a manner that makes later reporting and analysis straightforward. If you have more time and funding, you may create your own survey and collect large amounts of numerical data. If you take a qualitative approach, you may have a set of tentative themes in mind that you expect to explore, but you remain open to various data collection methods to shape the approach and in analyzing your observations or interview transcripts.

Step 5: *Select a sample or identify participants.* Research is almost always done on a small number of people who represent a larger group; very rarely is everyone included, even in quantitative research. The extent to which you wish to generalize your findings will shape your selection of a situation or a group of people for your research. In qualitative research, situations or people are selected to represent dimensions of interest to the researcher. To learn what it is like to be young, unemployed, and female/male, it makes sense for you to talk to some young males and females who are unemployed. Conversely, if you wish to test the relationship between age and unemployment in your local area, you will want a sample that represents the population of the area; a more systematic sample that includes both employed and unemployed youth is required.

These five steps provide a basis for the successful conduct of the research in three ways. First, they articulate the problem and narrow the focus of the research. This allows the researcher to undertake the practical aspects of the project with a clear awareness of what has to be tested or studied. Second, they immediately introduce discipline to the research procedure. This discipline is necessary to keep the project focused and to maintain rigour in data collection and analysis. Finally, they provide a structure to evaluate the progress of a research project. If something goes wrong or the project is delayed, revisiting the steps will probably tell the researcher where changes can be introduced to resolve research problems.

A quantitative example

We now return to the argument about whether or not dietary cholesterol causes heart disease. Both Georgina and Frank have a hunch, or a *theory*, about the relationship between dietary cholesterol and the development of coronary heart disease. Let's test these theories. We commence with step 1 of Phase 1 by focusing the question and narrowing it to a specific set of circumstances.

Phase 1: Essential first steps

For this particular problem, consideration must be given to the following issues:

- Do participants need to be diagnosed with heart disease or can they be identified as "at risk of developing heart disease"?
- Will both males and females be considered for inclusion in the study (since the causes of coronary heart disease might be different for male and female patients)?

- What will be the geographical context of the study? All Canadians? Only those living in a particular province? A particular city? Those visiting a physician? Those who are in a hospital database?
- What will be the age of participants? Do they have to be young? Old? What is our definition of elderly? Age 60? Age 65? Age 70?
- How do we define "coronary heart disease"? How many symptoms must participants have to be included? Do they have to have all symptoms before they are included or only a few?
- How long must the patient have lived with coronary heart disease before being considered for inclusion in the study? Six months? One year? Five years? Ten years? Does it matter?
- What aspects of coronary heart disease will be considered? Physical fitness? Stress and depression?
- Will other aspects be taken into consideration (e.g., marital status, ethnic group)?
- Will any allowances be made to consider the effects of patient history, such as previous accidents and hospitalization, on the development of coronary heart disease?

Step 1 requires us to focus, clarify, and narrow the research problem. Let's say that the study is limited to adults ages 65 years and older who have been previously diagnosed with coronary heart disease in the past six months. This will be a national study, so participants may be drawn from samples collected in any city or province in the country. It will include all ethnic groups, and marital status is not an issue (so all persons can be included), but we will exclude men because the causes of coronary heart disease for them are slightly different than for women. Since diet is our main area of interest, other contributing factors to heart disease will not be considered (e.g., smoking, physical fitness). We should, however, still ask about these outside factors to learn more about the relationship between them and the development of coronary heart disease. As with qualitative studies, it is imperative that we consult the existing research literature on the subject. It will help us to formulate the appropriate research questions and to situate our findings within the existing research debates.

The research question is no longer simply "What is the relationship between dietary cholesterol on the development of coronary heart disease?" It has become "What is the relationship between dietary cholesterol on the development of coronary heart disease among Canadian women ages 65 and older?"

We also define our variables. The first variable is development of coronary heart disease. A number of studies have tested questions dealing with the onset of coronary heart disease. We select some recent research to see what kinds of questions were asked of patients and note the findings. The second variable is dietary cholesterol. How will we acquire this information? This information can be obtained by asking the women to record their daily food intake—what they ate and how much—in a diary or log. This is one way of collecting the data needed to answer the research question. Alternatively, we could conduct a series of physical tests on blood and fluids, for example, which would be important indicators if we had reason to believe the participants may not be truthful about their diets.

In step 2, we select a research design. We are going to use a basic research design in which we compare the coronary heart disease incidence among women by means of a simple survey and daily nutrition diaries. Here an examination of the research literature may be helpful in determining an appropriate research design. Research design also entails the way the research question is phrased. This topic is discussed further in Chapter 7.

In step 3, we select the measures for each variable. The measure for coronary heart disease is relatively straightforward once we agree upon the necessary criteria. Since coronary heart disease has been defined by the medical profession, this part of the data collection involves asking the women a series of previously known questions relating to their disease. If we don't feel confident that the subjects can adequately identify coronary heart disease, perhaps we ask for permission to contact their family physicians regarding their diagnosis or a provincial health database. Based on their answers (either from the women themselves or their physicians or a provincial health database), some women will be identified as suffering from coronary heart disease while others will be identified as "healthy." Dietary cholesterol is measured by asking respondents to complete food diaries and answer some questions in a survey. Again, consulting the literature is important. Other researchers have likely studied this phenomenon, and it will be important to review their findings. They may have asked questions or defined the variables in a similar way, which may be useful for your research.

In step 4, we design a table for easy analysis and data collection, such as Table 2.1.

Table 2.1 • A simple table designed for easy collection and analysis of research results

	Diet Is High in Cholesterol	Diet Is Low in Cholesterol
Presence of coronary heart disease		

In step 5, we select a sample. In this case, we need to select a random sample of adult females over the age of 65 and living in Canada. We discuss sampling strategies in Chapter 8. For now, let us assume that we have a list of 40 women who fit the criteria for our study (being age 65 or older and living in Canada). Let's say that half (20) will have high cholesterol in their diets while the other half (20) will have low cholesterol in their diets.

Phase 2: Data collection
1. Collect data.
2. Summarize and organize data.

Data collection is a major enterprise in research but not the only factor in producing a good research study. Preparation (Phase 1) takes the most time, and drawing conclusions and writing the report often take more time than data collection. Data collection may not be time-consuming, especially in quantitative research. The time we spend in the early procedures will likely result in better and more accurate research results than had we rushed through the preliminary planning activities.

In step 1, we collect data from the women with regard to their history of coronary heart disease and daily cholesterol intake. Let's say that 12 of the women who have high levels of cholesterol in their diets have been diagnosed with coronary heart disease, whereas only 8 of those with low levels of cholesterol in their diets have been diagnosed with heart disease. A discussion on calculating the findings can be found in Chapter 11.

For step 2, we summarize the data (see Table 2.2).

Table 2.2 • Completed table

	Diets High in Cholesterol	Diets Low in Cholesterol
Presence of coronary heart disease	12/20	8/20

Now we are ready for Phase 3, analysis and interpretation. In this phase, we relate the data collected to the research question and draw conclusions. It is really quite simple, as long as the research problem is articulated and made clear in Phase 1.

Phase 3: Analysis and interpretation
1. Relate data to the research question.
2. Draw conclusions.
3. Assess the limitations of the study.
4. Make suggestions for further research.

In step 1, ask yourself, "How do the data relate to the research question? What can the data tell us about the relationship between dietary cholesterol and coronary heart disease?"

In step 2, we draw conclusions. Given the data in Table 2.2, what would you conclude? Is Frank right in his assertion that dietary cholesterol is not higher among those diagnosed with coronary heart disease, or is Georgina's belief correct that diets high in cholesterol cause heart disease?

In step 3, we acknowledge the limitations of the research. You may be able to see some limitations in our study. It applies only to women above a certain age living in Canada. Measurements were taken at one point in time, so changes occurring over months and years were not quantified. The outcome might have been influenced by the way we selected our sample. Maybe we located women who were waiting in emergency rooms. Perhaps we contacted physicians in certain cities or in particular neighbourhoods. Research on coronary heart disease reveals that place of residence has an influence on the development of the disease. What might have happened if we had collected data on cholesterol levels and heart disease using different methods? Would we have obtained the same results? What other limitations should be mentioned in the research report?

In step 4, we suggest further research that should allow us to answer the research question in more detail. You should propose and plan another piece of research that would clarify any questions raised by the limitations. For example, the research was conducted with only 40 women. This raises the question "Would the results be the same with a larger number of women participating?" To answer this question using valid research methods, the test should be repeated among a larger sample of women.

At this juncture, a return to the literature review is important. How do your findings differ from the existing research on this topic? Do your findings support certain aspects of the debate or refute them? It is important for you to present the ways in which your results are both similar and different to what is already in the literature. This helps us advance knowledge in the area and helps readers understand the impact of your research.

As shown in this quantitative example, research is a process by which ordinary questions are focused upon and in which data are collected in such a way that the research questions are answered on the basis of observable evidence.

Most research projects raise new questions, and in this sense the research process is a continuous one, with the end of one project becoming the beginning of another. The steps for conducting qualitative research are similar. The following section outlines the process.

A qualitative example

Phase 1: Essential first steps

The first step in qualitative research requires that we decide what to observe and state what it is in the form of a research objective. This is necessary to focus our attention and to screen out what is of only incidental or passing interest. In practice, we all tend to get distracted by things that have some personal interest and it is important not to let this impinge on our research work.

For example, let's look at the observation mentioned earlier about youth and unemployment. You might decide to take as your research objective "Are the experiences of unemployed young men different from those of young unemployed women?"

In step 2, you decide to do an in-depth interview study involving young men and women from one post-secondary educational institution such as a local college. This will keep a number of background characteristics similar (such as age and educational background) while allowing access to both genders. This is a case study, so our goal is to select participants who have similar characteristics.

In step 3, you decide to ask interviewees to tell you about being unemployed. What is it like? How do other people respond when they learn of their situation? Do they try to pretend to be employed? If one topic gets them going, let them follow it—it is probably important to them.

Step 4 involves identifying themes for analysis. These might include self-esteem, parents' reactions, friends' reactions, dealing with employment agencies, and other themes. For the most part, you will wait until all of your informants have told their stories before you code the responses.

Step 5 involves selecting those whose stories you will collect. This will depend on who is available and willing to participate. It will also depend on characteristics that you may have identified as potentially important—length of unemployment, marital status, or whether the participants live at home or on their own.

Phase 2: Data collection

You go to the local college and put up a poster saying you want to talk to people about their experiences of being unemployed. You sit in a corner and people talk with you. You may audio-record what they say, or you may make notes and summarize them afterwards. Whichever way you choose, your data will be conversations with unemployed young people, male and female.

Phase 3: Analysis and interpretation

This is where the really hard work begins in qualitative research. You pore over the interviews and begin to code them and identify themes. As you read and reread the interviews, you will begin to appreciate and understand what it is like to be young and unemployed. You will also begin to detect differences between males and females. These may not be what you expected, but that is why we do research—to find out what we do not already know. The process is time intensive and very detailed. Chapter 13 and Chapter 14 discuss analysis and interpretation more thoroughly.

Research as a Discipline

Research requires discipline, clear thinking, and careful observation. The first and probably the most difficult step in the research process is learning to ask the right questions. The problems that motivate us to do research are often enormous. How to prevent nuclear war? How to save the economy? How to prevent sudden infant death syndrome? How to improve the quality of life for all people? The first task is to move from these "global" questions to researchable questions.

 ### Creating a Research Question

Researchable questions have two basic properties. First, they are limited in scope to certain times, places, and conditions. A researchable question is usually a small fragment of a larger question such as the ones we discussed above. One of the most difficult tasks for a researcher is to confront a large issue by tackling only one small, manageable part of it. Failing to take a focused approach to an issue, of course, would doom the work to failure because the researcher would not have the time, energy, or other resources necessary to take on the larger issue. Think of how difficult it would be to conduct research on "saving the economy." That is a very large task. It is better to answer a small question than to leave a large one unanswered. Perhaps by piecing together a number of small answers, a large answer may be discovered.

For example, the question "What factors affect decision-making within Canadian families?" is very broad. Many factors are involved, and these factors may vary depending on the type of family observed. A more manageable question would be "Among single-parent families in Halifax, is selection of school influenced by the parent's income?" Similarly, in order to be researched, the question "Does parents' education affect scholastic achievement of children?" would have to be focused, narrowed, and limited.

The best and probably only way to learn the skill of narrowing and focusing a broad issue so that it becomes a research question is to practise. Try limiting the question "Does parents' education affect scholastic achievement of children?"

To help you get started, let us look at the question just mentioned. As it stands, it looks like a simple question requiring a "yes" or "no" answer. To become a research question, it needs to be made more specific. It helps to ask, "What are the main things, ideas, or activities in the question?" The question asks something about the *relationship* between parents' education and scholastic achievement. What do we mean when we use the term "parents' education," and in what aspects of "parents' education" are we specifically interested?

- The type of education attained (secondary school diploma, technical diploma, college certificate, or university degree)?
- Their grades or academic achievement at school, technical college, or university? (Were they the top students, average students, or mediocre students?)
- The types of schools (public/private) they attended?
- The prestige of the schools or universities they attended?
- What if they have only one parent? How does that "count" in our research?

Similarly, we should ask what we mean by "scholastic achievement":

- Final grades in all subjects?
- Consistency in high grades across subjects? Overall grades? Only the top three grades?
- Level of participation in important school activities, such as student councils and sports?

The process results in some focused research questions that incorporate the focused versions of our original concepts, "parents' education" and "scholastic achievement":

- Does the type of education attained by parents affect children's final grades?
- Does the academic standing of parents affect children's overall place in class?
- Do parents' levels of academic achievement affect the quality of children's school report cards?

Now try your hand at limiting the following questions:

1. What factors are important in family decision-making? (Hints: Try listing some factors—for example, economics, social life, extended family commitments. Limit the area of decision-making.)
2. Can we promote the development of a positive self-image among teen-agers with disabilities? (Hints: What do you know about self-image? What are key factors that lead to a healthy self-image or to a negative self-image?)

The first property of a researchable question is that it is limited in scope—it must be narrowed in focus and confined to a certain time, place, and set of conditions. Although it is frustrating and difficult to draw up such an inquiry, the discipline required to focus the research question is one of the most important factors in the research process.

The second property of a researchable question is that it identifies some observable, tangible, countable evidence or data that can be gathered. There must be something that can be observed by you and others. That is, the question must be answerable through observation of some aspect of the universe we live in. Some refer to this as empirical research. Empirical research can deal only with the observable, measurable aspects of the questions we want to answer. For example, questions about morals are not answerable by the kind of research we are talking about, nor can it determine whether an action is right or wrong. For example, the question "Is it morally right to allow terminally ill patients to die?" is not answerable by empirical research. **Empirical** research can be either qualitative or quantitative. Empirical research seeks only to answer those questions that can be answered by reference to sensory data, which are data that can be seen, heard, touched, recorded, measured, or counted. It cannot deal with questions of morality or ethics such as assisted suicide.

While empirical research cannot answer the moral question "Is it right or wrong to allow terminally ill patients to die?" it can answer the question "How many students in a particular university seminar think that it is right or wrong to allow certain types of terminally ill patients to die?" One of the disciplines associated with doing research is learning to ask questions to which there are measurable, sensory, countable answers—that is, questions that can be answered in terms of observations and experiences.

There are other kinds of questions to which there are no empirical answers—for example, questions of beauty or faith. Are the Rocky Mountains more or less beautiful than the Gatineau Hills in Quebec? Is St John's, Newfoundland, more beautiful than Montreal? Is the Canadian Museum of History in Ottawa more interesting than the Hockey Hall of Fame in Toronto? Does God exist? These are questions of aesthetics, taste, and spirituality, not empirical questions.

Of course, they can be turned into empirical questions. For example, we can make up an empirical question relating to one of the preceding aesthetic questions. And while empirical research cannot answer questions of religious faith, it can answer questions such as "How many professors at Dalhousie University believe that God exists?" or "What social characteristics are found among believers in God?"

The same issues can be raised about other questions of taste, fashion, etiquette, morality, religion, and political ideology. Empirical research cannot determine which table setting is "most tasteful" or which jacket is "most fashionable." These are not empirical questions. Empirical research can, however, answer such questions as "Which table setting is judged the most tasteful by a sample of interior decorators?" or "Which museum is more interesting for young people?"

In summary, the first discipline required by the research process is to ask the right kind of questions. Researchable questions are limited in scope and very specific. It can be a real challenge to devise a clear, specific, narrow question. This skill can be learned. You can learn to take a general question and formulate a research question from it. You will get more practice in doing this in Chapter 3.

Honesty and Accuracy

The second major discipline required by the research process is to be honest and accurate. Honesty and accuracy should be characteristics of any intellectual enterprise, and they require a degree of self-control. We often have in mind an outcome we wish to arrive at. For example, we might think that a majority of university students believe that vaccinating their children causes autism. But discipline in doing research compels us to be as objective as possible; we must make sure that there is no bias in the way we ask questions and ensure that we correctly record the data and are honest in reporting the results. The following are biased questions asked in a fictitious research project. What is wrong with these examples?

- "Recent research has indicated that vaccinations do not cause autism. You really don't believe that, do you?" Write an unambiguous version of this question.
- "Only 70 per cent of those asked thought that childhood vaccinations cause autism." Write an unbiased statement of this research finding.

If we are disciplined and accurate in our reporting of research findings, then we increase the reliability of the research process. Some research has fallen into disrepute because researchers have not been disciplined, accurate, and honest.

Have you ever read about controversy over scientific work in which bias was suggested? An example is Hwang Woo-Suk's research on cloning human embryos. His research was published in the prestigious research journal *Science* in May 2005 and claimed he had created new stem cells from 11 human patients. Seven months later, Korean researchers reported that they were suspicious about the findings because they could not be replicated.

CASE STUDY

....

Evolution of a Research Question

Creating a concise research question is challenging, even for experienced investigators. The following is a synopsis of the development process.

My research interests centre on the settlement experiences of immigrants who come to Canada in their childhood or teenage years. "Settlement experiences" is a good topic but a very broad one. To narrow the topic down, I must ask myself what aspect of settlement I am most interested in. For researchers who specialize in this area, the key points of academic achievement and the transition to paid employment are most significant because success in these two areas tends to predict successful settlement in other areas, including family life, health outcomes, and civic participation. Still, embarking on a research project examining all aspects of educational attainment and work experiences would be too big, requiring a significant amount of time and financial resources to complete.

One way to narrow the topic even further is to consider the purpose of the project. If you are applying for a research grant, most agencies have a strict set of criteria that define the studies that they are interested in funding. If this is the case, these criteria can assist you in moving your subject from a broad topic to a researchable question. In a recent project of mine, the granting agency required that the subject focus on the settlement experiences of migrants in the first four years in Canada. This criterion meant that my interest in youth must focus on the early years of settlement in Canada. If the persons coming to Canada were still in their teenage years, then their education experiences might be a good area on which to focus my investigation since most of them would not be old enough to enter the labour market. In your own case, perhaps you are writing a research paper for a class and the professor limits the number of pages. The size of the final product (i.e., the word count), the number of graphs and tables, and the expectations of the research funders and audience reading the report can also determine the scope of your research question.

Using some of the authors' own research as an example here, the topic of educational experiences remains too large for any reasonable-sized research project. I must then ask myself what aspects of educational attainment I am most interested in learning about. Am I interested in their grades? Their friendship networks? The challenges they face in a new school? Or maybe I am interested in the process of having their education credentials accepted at their new school. I have learned from other research I have conducted that many newcomer youth have experienced being bullied at their new school. Using evidence from previous research projects (your own or what you know from other subjects) may also assist you in narrowing your research project. Now I am on my way to determining a discrete research question—but I need to turn the topic into a research question.

Continued

One way to do this is to think about cause and effect. Who are the students that are most likely to experience bullying in school? This is an important question to ask because it may have policy or procedural implications if it is answered. For instance, if teachers knew that young immigrant boys were more likely than girls to be bullied, they might be willing to watch more closely for symptoms among this group. If school administrators knew that those newcomers who arrive in Canada as refugees are more likely to be victimized by bullying, they might consider creating a program that assists refugee students to integrate into the school system.

So how do we turn this into a research question? It might be helpful to look at the known research on bullying as experienced by students born in Canada. We know from the literature that boys are more likely to be bullied than girls. We don't know much about the experiences of refugee students and bullying because there are no studies on the subject, but we do know by examining the research on refugee youth in schools that they often have more difficulty adapting. With this in mind, it may be fair to predict that refugees could be more likely to be victimized by bullying than other types of immigrants who come to Canada under very different circumstances, such as newcomers arriving in the family or economic classes. We can then phrase the research question by considering cause and effect (we will discuss cause and effect in more depth later in this text). At this point, we know that the chances of becoming a victim of bullying differ according to gender. We also know that refugees often have more difficulty adapting in school. Let's now embed these ideas into the question.

Our topic (or "effect") is victimization from bullying. Our influences (or "causes") are sex and refugee status. We will use these as the starting points of our research question. Research questions tend to take two forms:

- To what extent do _____ affect (influence) _____?
- To what extent are _____ associated with _____?

We can insert the influences into the first blank and the topic into the second blank. Our research question now becomes "To what extent do sex and refugee status influence immigrant youth's victimization from bullying?" Alternatively, we could ask, "To what extent are sex and refugee status associated with immigrant youth's victimization from bullying?"

As well, research questions can be phrased as thesis statements. Generally, thesis statements are used when the researcher is confident about the direction of the relationship. Since we know that boys are more likely to be victimized than girls and we have a fairly good hunch that refugees are more likely to be bullied based on their other experiences in the school system, we can phrase the research question as a thesis statement: "Among newcomer youth, boys and refugees are more likely to experience bullying than girls and those arriving in other immigrant classes do."

Some people have forced their data to fit their theory by falsifying results, by not recording data accurately, or both. Research is useful only to the extent that the researchers have been disciplined, accurate, and honest. In Professor Hwang's case, the falsification of data and misleading information published in the two papers cost him his job, and he was convicted of fraud, embezzlement, and bioethics violations in 2009, for which he now has a criminal record (see Normile, 2009). This event tarnished his research career, one that included a major and valid scientific achievement, the first cloning of a dog known as Snuppy (see Normile, 2009). Another outcome of this incident was that scientific journals have begun to scrutinize data collection procedures and results more vigorously. We will discuss research ethics in greater detail in Chapter 9.

Recordkeeping

The third discipline is recording what was done in such a way that someone else can see exactly what was done and why. There are two reasons for this kind of discipline. First, it safeguards the reliability of the research process. If what was done is reported accurately and in adequate detail, then another person can repeat the research. If they get the same results, then what was originally found becomes even more certain. If they do not get the same results, then the original findings are less certain.

The second reason for this discipline is to provide a record for yourself. It is amazing how quickly we forget what we did and why. At the end of a research project, you need to be able to refer to your research notes and refresh your memory. This is a great help when you are writing about the limitations of the study.

Assessing Limitations

The fourth and final discipline of the research process involves assessing the limitations of the research. If you study only one family, you cannot apply your findings to all families. If you study a group of 10-year-old boys, your findings apply to that group and that group only. It is a great temptation to overgeneralize, to make claims that apply beyond the data collected.

Similarly, if you did your research on an empirical question derived from a non-empirical question, your conclusions apply only to the empirical question. For example, if your initial question was "Does childhood vaccination cause autism?" but your research question was "How many university students believe that vaccinations cause autism?" the data you collect will answer the empirical question but not the question of interest. Keeping your conclusions at the level of the question asked is part of the discipline of accepting the limitations of the research process.

In summary, doing research requires discipline. First, the right kinds of questions must be asked. Questions must be narrowly defined, because only empirical questions can be answered by empirical research. Second, honesty and accuracy in asking questions and reporting findings are required. Third, careful recordkeeping and accurate reporting are needed. Finally, you must assess the limitations of the research process and your particular research question.

Theory and Data

A research question can come from anywhere. We may just be curious: I wonder how that works? I wonder why some people do this or that? Does it make any difference? Curiosity can begin the research process.

Conversely, a problem may motivate us to ask a researchable question. How is the problem of teenage malnutrition best handled? How can I make my father understand me? How can I improve my health? How can the incidence of drunk driving be reduced? Problems such as these, and many others, motivate people to ask researchable questions. Some of these questions become careers for many people.

Arguments are a frequent starting point. The example of Georgina and Frank is typical. I might have one idea about how things are, and you might have another. It may be possible to design a piece of research to see whose idea is supported by evidence.

Research is often started by controversy. Magellan sailed around the world. Was this uniformly accepted as proof that Earth was not flat and that sailors who ventured too far would not fall off the edge? No. Even after Magellan's circumnavigation of the Earth, many people continued to believe that it was flat. Perhaps satellite photographs of Earth taken from a great distance provide the most compelling evidence available to date that the Earth is not flat. There are some people even today who continue to believe the world is flat.

As with Magellan and the flat Earth theory, evidence does not always stop the controversy that motivated the research. Some people do not accept the evidence. Some argue that the research was not properly conducted. Some argue that the research questions were not properly defined. In such cases, the research process usually continues, with more evidence being collected to test more carefully defined questions. Part of the fun of doing research is to see how each question leads to more questions. The research process is continuous.

The research process is a disciplined process for answering questions. Another way of putting this is to say that the research process is a disciplined process for relating theory and data. At this point, we will try to clarify and simplify the terms "theory" and "data."

Theory

Put most simply, a theory is a guess about the way things are. Georgina had a theory about coronary heart disease among Canadian women ages 65 and older. A theory is an idea about how something works, or what it is like to be something, or what will happen if. . . . It may be an idea about what difference will be made by doing or not doing something. Theories are ideas about how things relate to each other.

There are many ways of expressing theories. Some are very formal, while others are informal. Some theories are very elaborate and complex, yet simplicity and clarity are often desirable features of theories. Put simply, theories are ideas about the way other ideas are related. Theories are abstract notions about the way concepts relate to each other. This will become clearer as you proceed through this book. Here are some examples of crude theories:

- a hunch that refugee students might be more vulnerable to being bullied at school
- a guess that the more reassurance you give to small children that they are valued, cared for, and wanted, the more likely they are to develop healthy self-images
- the idea that more education produces more reliable, more productive, and more contented people

A theory asserts a relationship between concepts. It states that some things are related in a particular way. It is a statement of how things are thought to be. A theory is an idea, a mental picture of how the world might be.

In Focus

What's the Difference between an Educated Guess and a Theory?

It is very important to understand the difference between an educated guess and a theory. An educated guess is likely only a guess because we don't know much about that particular topic. For example, we know very little about how artificial intelligence may affect the future of work. An educated guess would suggest that as robots become more intelligent and mobile, they will begin to do more of our jobs—so the number of jobs in certain sectors may decline. This educated guess is "educated" based on the role that robots already play on some assembly lines in car and appliance manufacturing plants. Theories, in contrast, are developed based on mountains of evidence. They are more than educated guesses about the way something works. The evidence collected is so plentiful that experts can identify a pattern and connections between two or more variables. For example, Einstein's special theory of relativity suggests that the speed of light in a vacuum is not influenced by other variables. The theory is a theory because it is based on thousands of experiments that all reproduced the very same findings.

Theories are developed in the social sciences in the very same way—by amassing significant amounts of data showing the same relationship between two or more variables. More developed theories have years of data and research that support the viewpoints. For example, labelling theory is popular in criminology and other disciplines. It states that once someone is labelled in one way, they are more likely to be treated in a certain way. Labels can be lifelong and detrimental to people. In this way, someone who has committed a crime is labelled as criminal. That label can follow the person throughout

Continued

his or her life, making it difficult for them to find work, international travel or access certain resources. Even though the person labelled as "criminal" may have never spent time in jail, or committed the crime many decades ago (in some cases as a young person), that label follows them. In this case, the label "criminal" can affect life chances in many areas and can have irreversible, damaging effects on an individual. There is significant research to support this theory. The two linked concepts here are the label of criminal and life outcomes. This detailed identification of concepts and how they are linked, backed with research evidence, separates a theory from a hunch or educated guess.

The research process is a disciplined process for answering questions. It is a way of testing theories, a way of determining whether there is any evidence to support a mental picture of the way things are. The evidence collected in the research process is called **data**.

Data

Data are facts produced by research. Data, like facts, by themselves are meaningless. They acquire meaning as they are related to theories. For example, the fact that a woman living in Winnipeg has high levels of cholesterol in her diet and does not develop coronary heart disease and a woman living in Hamilton has low levels of cholesterol but still develops coronary heart disease is meaningless. The fact takes on meaning when it is related to the two theories about how dietary cholesterol influences the development of coronary heart disease. The fact becomes part of the data by which these theories can be tested. From the theory and by examining the quantitative connections between data, we can ascertain that dietary choices and not city of residence, influences cholesterol levels. The theory helps explain this relationship and why diet is important but not city of residence.

Data are empirical facts. They are scores regarding a number of questions (amount of cholesterol in diet). They are counts (100 students thought that vaccinations cause autism in children). They are tapes of conversations or transcripts of interviews. They are written observations. Data are records of the actual state of some measurable aspect of the universe at a particular point in time. Data are not abstract: they are concrete; they are records of events; they are measurements of the tangible, countable features of the world. While theories are abstract mental images of the way things may be, data are measures of specific things as they were at a particular time.

Two kinds of data are used in social science: quantitative and qualitative. We know from our earlier discussion that quantitative research tends to answer questions such as "How much?," "How many?," and "How often?" Quantitative data are usually expressed in numbers, percentages, or rates. In contrast, qualitative research tends to answer questions such as "What is it like to be a member of that group?," "What is going on in this situation?," or "What is it like to experience this or that phenomenon?" Hence, qualitative data tend to be expressed in the language of images, feelings, and impressions; they describe the qualities of the events under study. The research process is somewhat different for each type of research. Quantitative styles of research are dealt with first because they require the most preparation during Phase 1, while the efforts in qualitative research are concentrated in the data collection and interpretation phases.

The challenge of the research process is to relate theory and research in such a way that questions are answered. Both theory and data are required. When we are faced with a question, we formulate a theory about its answer and test it by collecting data—that is, evidence—to see if our theoretical answer works. Data cannot be collected without some theory about the answer to the question. Theories alone are unsatisfactory because they are unproven, untested. To answer our questions, we need both theory and data.

The result of the research process is neither theory nor data but knowledge. Research provides answers to researchable questions with evidence that is collected and evaluated in a disciplined manner. This is how we know. We ask questions, propose answers to them, and test those answers. We ask what it is like and go and find out. Doing research in a disciplined way is "how we know we know."

Key Terms

Data 28	Research objective 13
Empirical 21	Sample 11
Qualitative research design 11	Theory 10
Quantitative research design 11	Variable 11

Questions for Review

1. Why do we undertake research?
2. It is claimed that research is a process. What is a process?
3. What is the normal sequence of the research process? In what way is it normal?
4. What are the essential first steps of the research process? Why are the first steps so important?
5. What is done in Phase 2 of the research process?
6. List the four major disciplines involved in the research process.
7. What are the two major properties of a researchable question?
8. What are theory and data? What role does each play in the research process?

9. What are the two major kinds of research? What is the main difference between them?
10. Find a newspaper article or an article in a recent magazine that reports a controversy over research findings. What was the nature of the criticism of the research?
11. How is a theory different from a hunch or educated guess?
12. What kind of data is collected using qualitative research? Contrast that to the data collected using quantitative research. What kinds of questions can qualitative and quantitative methods answer?

Sources

Normile, D. (2009). Scientific misconduct: Hwang convicted but dodges jail; Stem cell research has moved on. *Science, 326*(5923), 651.
Scientific misconduct: Timeline of events. (2009). *Science, 326*(5923), 650.

Suggestions for Further Reading

Babbie, E. R., & Roberts, L. W. (2016). *The fundamentals of social research*. Toronto: Nelson.
de Vaus, D. A. (2013). *Surveys in social research* (6th ed.). St Leonards, NSW: Allen & Unwin.
Giddens, A., & Sutton, P. W. (2017). *Sociology* (8th ed.). Cambridge, England: Polity Press.
Murray, J. (2013). *Labeling theory: Empirical tests*. New York: Routledge/Taylor Francis.

Suggested Web Resource

Glanz, K. (2018). Theories and why it is important. In *Social and behavioral theories*. National Institutes of Health, Office of Behavioral and Social Sciences Research. Retrieved March 22, 2018 from www.esourceresearch.org/tabid/724/default.aspx

Phase 1

Essential First Steps

3 Selecting a Problem

The first step in Phase 1 of the research process is selecting and focusing on a research problem. This step involves decision-making, sorting, narrowing, and clarifying. It requires clear thinking and at times the discarding of favourite topics for more focused ideas. This chapter describes the skills involved in developing an initial question into a practical research problem.

Starting Points

The research process begins when our curiosity is aroused. When we want to know something, we begin formally or informally to engage in research. An observation, something we read, a claim someone makes, a hunch about something—each may be a stimulus to begin the research process. This chapter presents several examples to develop your skills for moving from starting points to focused researchable questions.

Here are some examples of starting points for research projects.

An observation
Some students get better grades than others.

An observation like this may prompt someone to ask the following questions: Why? Which students? Is it the way papers are marked? An observation may trigger the inquiring mind to ask questions, and the research process has begun.

An important family decision
The Khan family has to decide whether to send their daughter to a public school or a private school.

Someone who knows of this situation might be prompted to ask questions such as, What difference would it make? Is there a difference in terms of her chances of being accepted into university? What kinds of factors do the Khans consider important as they arrive at their decision? A situation like an important family decision may stimulate the asking of questions, and the research process is underway.

A news report
News reports often raise questions for research. Read your daily newspaper (in print or online), or tune into radio and television news, and pay attention to headlines that may lead to research projects: "Divorce Rate Steady for a Decade," "Crime Rate Increasing," "Single Moms in Poverty Trap," "1 in 10 Unemployed Seriously Depressed," "Teenage Suicide Rate Increases," "Plight of Homeless Worsens," "More Females Studying Law." Each of these headlines could lead to a research project to expand knowledge about some aspect of social life or to test some idea about what is happening in the world.

News reports usually contain a lot of "facts" about patterns in society but few clear and explicit interpretations or explanations of those "facts." You may be prompted to ask questions: How does the pattern presented in this report compare with the situation 5, 10, or 15 years ago? Why is this pattern developing? What factors might be affecting changes in things such as the career choices women make, the teenage suicide rate, age at first marriage, or the effects of unemployment? Questions like these, prompted by your reading of news reports, can be the start of research projects.

A policy issue
The provincial government is concerned about the provision of proper care in homes for elderly people.

Think about this issue. What questions does it raise? What is the current state of affairs in homes for elderly people? What do elderly people need? Again, the inquiring mind is prompted to ask questions that might lead to research.

It makes little difference where you begin the research process: the first step is to narrow the focus and clarify the issues involved in the problem. None of the preceding starting points provides a sufficiently focused research question. The first step in the research process is to move from an ordinary, everyday question to a researchable question by focusing on one aspect of the issue arousing your interest. Experience tells us that this step can be the most difficult in designing any research project. A narrow, researchable question, although it may take some time to create, will determine the quality of your research project from start to finish.

The Literature Review

An important step in the research process is embedding your research question and your subsequent findings within the existing literature. The literature review has several purposes. At the **conceptualization** phase, it can assist in identifying and preparing a good research question, be helpful in identifying appropriate theoretical and research design approaches, and assist in defining central variables. At the data analysis stage, it is important for embedding your findings within the larger research debates and in advancing knowledge on a particular topic. It can also assist policy-makers in determining new directions for existing programs. The literature review is a central component of the research process, and it is worthwhile to examine some of its uses here.

At the beginning of the research, when you may not yet have a clearly de-fined research question, the literature review will assist you in identifying the studies that have been conducted. It is best to become familiar with these stud-ies to get a sense of the research results and to identify the prevailing debates in the literature. This process can take a while, especially for topics that have been subject to a large number of studies. However, it is a crucial first step. It is not worth your time to replicate a study that has already been conducted, and funders will not want to support research questions that have already been an-swered. For this reason, becoming familiar with the existing literature will save you time and money. Throughout the literature review process, look for gaps in the literature. What questions have not been asked? This information is import-ant because it increases the chance that your research will receive funding and it increases the value of your research findings, since you will be contributing new knowledge to our understanding of existing social problems.

Reviewing the literature can also assist in the selection of theoretical ap-proaches. A good deal of social science literature utilizes the major theoretical approaches. What is your theoretical approach? How can it help you to answer your research question? What does your theoretical approach have to say about the problem you are investigating? This review of theoretical approaches will help you to identify important factors to consider in your study. Similarly, it may give you clues about an appropriate research design. How have others con-ducted research on similar questions? What research designs best capture the answers you need to answer your research question? Perhaps there are new re-search designs that you can use to answer your research question. From a theor-etical and research design standpoint, the literature review is a useful tool. We discuss selecting a theory in the section right after this one.

The literature review can be central to identifying factors that you may not have considered including in your research project. Reconsider the planned research on the causes of youth unemployment. A small but growing part of the literature on this topic reveals that family contexts, such as the presence of both father and mother and the birth order of siblings, are a major determinant of post-secondary school attendance. Youth who live in two-parent-headed households and who are the youngest siblings have the greatest chance of attending and completing university. If you do not review the existing literature on youth unemployment, you may forget to include questions about family context and birth order, making your research open to criticism and much less valuable once it is completed.

Once your data have been collected and analyzed, return to your literature review. How do your findings contribute to existing research? Say, you discovered in your study of youth post-secondary education completion that birth order of siblings matters only if they live in families headed by a single father. In families headed by a single mother or those headed by two parents, birth order does not determine university completion. Knowing about this debate makes it easier for you to discuss your research findings and make a valuable contribution to the literature on a particular topic. Since you have already done all the hard work prior to collecting data, the literature review at this stage is more easily accomplished. All you need to do is update yourself on the research literature that may have been published between the time you conducted your initial review in Phase 1 and the analysis of your data in Phase 3.

In short, while it may seem as though you are not accomplishing much by reviewing the literature at the beginning of the research project, a good knowledge of the existing literature on a topic is essential to research planning and dissemination. It also saves you from doing unnecessary work in your research project!

Identifying a Theoretical Framework for Your Study

Identifying a theoretical framework is essential for all research projects. The process may seem daunting, particularly to novice researchers. They often ask, "How do I select the right theory?" "Does this theory belong to my discipline?" "Does this theory adequately explain the issues I will witness and the data I collect?" These are important questions to ask—and the answers to these queries are found below.

How does theory connect to the research process? First through the research question, second through the literature review, and finally in the interpretation of the results (we discuss how this is done in more detail in Chapter 14). In terms of the research question, we need to ask ourselves the nature of the question that shapes our research project. Remember that qualitative research focuses on questions involving how something is done or how something happens or why something happens. Quantitative research focuses on the extent of the problem (how big or small it is), who is most affected by the problem, and how we might better understand the nature of the problem. This gives us a clue to which theory we select and how the theory is used in the project.

In qualitative research, the theory plays a central role. Qualitative research needs theories that are more explanatory, that give us guidance about what kind of information we need and what data we need to answer the research question. The theory, by nature, is more amenable to one kind of data or another. For instance, critical race theory is very popular in studies of discrimination and racial inequality. It is a theory that suggests that the organization of society is fundamentally flawed to the point where racialized people are disadvantaged in all aspects, including getting a job, a scholarship, or even equal health care. (Think of the recent cases in Canada where Indigenous Peoples have died waiting for care in hospitals. This would be one example where critical race theory could be used. See the In Focus box for more.) If we read more about the theory, we learn that the theory relies on narrative analysis and storytelling—relying on the reports of individuals who have lived these experiences. This is a clue to the type of data we need to collect. If we need narratives of peoples' histories and life experiences, then we should be doing some form of qualitative data collection if we were to use this theory. Furthermore, the theory would give us clues about the questions we should ask in an interview setting or a focus group setting (if those were the modes of data collection we chose). In this example, both the theory and the research question help us to identify the kind of data we need to complete the research project. In some cases, we build upon existing theories, adding new ideas and hunches for future researchers to explore. In this way, qualitative research can also contribute to theory building (though novice researchers are advised not to attempt this until they are more comfortable with the research process and their discipline).

In Focus

Critical Race Theory as Applied to Health Care

Critical race theory suggests that the way society is organized is fundamentally unfair to racialized peoples. The rules, the regulations, and the way we conventionally do many things in our society mean that some people have more access to social resources than others. Take the very sad case of Mr Brian Sinclair. In 2017, an inquiry led by physicians and academics across Canada found that Mr Sinclair died as a result of racism (Brian Sinclair Working Group, 2017). Mr Sinclair entered the emergency room of a hospital in downtown Winnipeg one day in 2008. He was found dead, 34 hours later, still waiting for his turn to be seen by an ER physician. The physical cause of his death was a bladder infection, an illness treated by simple antibiotics. The health care system, and the biases held by the people who worked at the hospital, were the social reasons behind his death. According to the inquiry, ER staff assumed that Mr Sinclair "was drunk and 'sleeping it off,' had been discharged previously and had nowhere to go, or was homeless and had come to avoid the cold" (CBC News, 2017). Imagine waiting for 34 hours in an emergency room in pain and being ignored. The fact that the staff thought that Mr Sinclair was drunk or homeless are assumptions

Continued

that were made because he was an Indigenous man. No one bothered to check on his health and well-being until he died, with dozens of other people around him. Two waiting room patients pointed out to ER staff that he had vomited and that he had passed out but they still did nothing. Mr Sinclair's untimely death at the age of 45 can be understood using critical race theory to identify and rectify the factors that led to it. The ER was overcrowded and mismanaged to the point that someone could die waiting for care. The racist stereotypes held by some staff members meant that Mr Sinclair was ignored until he died.

In qualitative analysis, the theory helps us to categorize and make sense of the results, an issue we discuss in Chapter 12.

In contrast, the theory plays a slightly different role in quantitative research. Like qualitative research, your research question will help you decide the kinds of theories you would like to use. Unlike qualitative research, however, the theory plays a more central role earlier in the project. The purpose of quantitative research is to test theories. We are interested in collecting data that either supports an already established theory or debunks it. The kind of theory we use in quantitative data is focused on questions of what or who. A theory about the connection between diet and cholesterol, like the example from Chapter 2, would give us clues about who is most affected and what factors increase or decrease cholesterol. It would not tell us how men or women feel about having high cholesterol, but it would give us some information about the questions we should ask participants in our study. In short, the theory gives us guidance on who participates, the questions we ask, and how the variables are linked together with one another (we discuss this last aspect in Chapters 11 and 13). Once we have analyzed and interpreted our results, we can determine whether or not the data we collected supports the theory or rejects the theory. Either way, we are advancing knowledge about a particular problem.

It is important that, once you have identified a theory, regardless of whether your research is quantitative or qualitative, you are aware of its limitations. There is no "perfect" theory explaining everything, particularly in the complicated social, economic, and cultural lives of human beings. Being aware of the theory's limitations and honestly reporting them not only helps readers understand the role theories play in interpreting your results but also gives readers the knowledge and understanding of the gaps in the theory and therefore the ways in which the theory may not address all of the findings in your project.

Many times, students will try to use too many theories in a research project to try to deal with all the limitations of a particular theoretical framework. They use one theory to explain one set of results and a different theory to explain other findings. The use of two or more theories is complicated. Even the most seasoned researchers use only two or three theories in their research projects. We suggest that novice researchers use only one theory when embarking on their first research projects.

Narrowing and Clarifying the Problem

Our goal in this step in the research process is to produce a clear statement of the problem to be studied. A statement of a problem must explicitly identify the issues on which the researcher chooses to focus. How do we do this? There are no rules or recipes. The skill is best learned by practice.

Once we examine most starting points, we quickly realize that they suggest research problems that are too unclear and unfocused for practical research. To clarify and focus a problem, we have to "unpack" it—that is, list the issues that make up the problem. We can then choose the issues on which to focus our attention.

The following general questions can be used to unpack a problem:

- What are the major concepts?
- What is happening here?
- What are the issues?
- Is one thing affecting, causing, or producing a change in something else?
- Why is this so?

Such questions may isolate issues of interest. As an example, take the observation "Some students get better marks than others." Begin with the question "What might lead to this observation?" Here are four possible explanations:

1. Some students are smarter than others.
2. Some students study more than others.
3. Some students eat better meals than others (nutrition has a link to academic success).
4. Some students enjoy studying more than others.

Relying on your own experience, identify four other possible reasons for some students getting better marks than others.

Did you think of factors such as exercise, parents' education, social life, family income? If so, you have begun to unpack the issue. You have begun to isolate factors and possible explanations.

You now have eight possible factors. You can begin narrowing the research question by selecting just one. However important other factors may be, it is usually necessary to focus on very few.

Our general observation of the differences in student marks can now be focused to create a variety of research problems. These problems can be described in direct questions about the issues they address:

- Are students' marks affected by the amount of time spent studying?
- Are students' marks affected by the nutrition of the meals they eat?
- Are students' marks affected by their enjoyment of school?
- Are students' marks affected by the status of their parents' occupations?

Another way to narrow and clarify a problem is to consult research relevant to issues raised by the starting point—in other words, review the literature. What have others found? Look at previous research for factors and approaches to the problem that you have not considered.

In unpacking the observation "Some students get better marks than others," you might also consult your professor. A reference librarian might be able to suggest a few articles or books for you to read. This documentation may include reports of previous research in the area. More ideas will come to you. Reading about the topic of your research will help to clarify your thinking.

Since this step in the research process is so important, let us take another example. Remember, the goal is a clear question for research. To do this, you unpack your starting point. List everything that comes to mind about the subject. Do some reading. Consult some people who know—the more ideas, the better. Then select one factor, one idea, and one small problem for your research.

Take the example of an important family decision. The Khan family has to decide whether to send their daughter to a public school or a private school. Remember that the aim is to isolate a question for research, not necessarily to find an answer to the problem facing the Khan family. What issues are suggested? There are no right or wrong answers here. You are working towards a research question.

Here is a list of some of the issues raised by this particular starting point:

1. Is one system of education (public or private) demonstrably better than another
   - in terms of student test results?
   - in terms of excellence of teachers?
   - in terms of social life?
   - in terms of availability of sport and cultural activities?

2. How do families make decisions like this?
   - What factors do they consider?
   - Do the children participate in decision-making?

3. Do socio-cultural factors shape these family decisions?
   - Is gender an issue?
   - Do ethnic groups differ in these decisions?
   - Is social class a factor?

What issues, further questions, and factors occurred to you? Write them down. What resources do you have that might help you with this question? Do you know someone who might have ideas on the subject? You could ask your librarian for material on family decision-making, or you could ask for information on public versus private education. Are there other things you can use to help identify the issue here? List some other resources.

At this point, the key tasks are to identify issues, select one to pursue in depth, and leave the rest behind.

We have seen that there are many issues, ideas, and factors involved in the decision to send a daughter to a public school or a private school. You will probably be able to direct your research to only one of them. The rest must be left for other studies. The mark of a clear thinker and a good researcher is the ability to identify and note the many issues and to choose to study one. People reading your report will recognize that you are aware of the complexity of the issues involved but are sufficiently disciplined to address only one.

Stating the Problem

The next task is to restate the issue as a researchable question. This is a skill in itself. Two basic forms will be discussed: **hypothesis** and *research objective*. Most other forms can be seen as variations of either a hypothesis or a research objective.

The Hypothesis

Used only in quantitative research, a hypothesis is a sentence that tells us about a relationship between two **concepts**. A concept is an idea that stands for something, or that represents a class of things or a general categorization of an impression of something. If we watch a chess game and decide that chess is an "intellectual activity," we are describing, both to ourselves and to others, our impressions of chess in terms of the concept "intellectual activity." Concepts are categories or descriptions of our world and experience. We use concepts to make sense of the world for ourselves and others.

The key feature of a hypothesis is that it asserts that two concepts are related in a specific way. Usually a hypothesis takes the form "Concept X causes concept Y" or "Concept X is related to concept Y." Return to the example of students' grades that we have been using. We began with the observation "Some students get better grades than others." We have unpacked this observation by listing issues that come to mind. We thought of the possible impact of factors such as amount of study, nutrition, and students' enjoyment of particular subjects. We talked to our professor and read material given to us by the librarian. When all that was done, we decided to do some research into the influence of number of hours of study on grades. We have two concepts: "hours of study" and "grades." We also have an idea about how these two concepts are related. We suspect that the longer somebody studies, the better her grades will be.

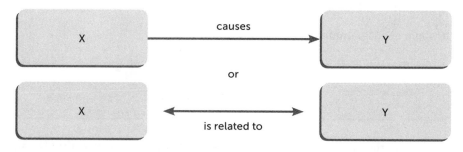

The usual form of a hypothesis

Having done our preparation, we are in a position to write a hypothesis to guide our research. For example:

The longer a student studies, the better the student's academic performance will be.

Note that a more general concept, "academic performance," has been selected in place of "grades." Our observation was of a difference in grades, but the general issue or problem is variation in "academic performance." It sometimes helps to become more general before focusing on concepts. In our example, this will enable you to consider a wider variety of measures of academic performance.

This hypothesis states that two concepts—namely, hours of study and academic performance—are related in such a way that more of one (study) will produce or lead to more of the other (academic performance). This hypothesis could be represented or "diagrammed" as follows:

The two concepts are in boxes. The boxes are linked by an arrow going from one concept to the other. The arrow indicates that one concept (amount of study) does something to the other concept (academic performance). The plus sign indicates that the relationship is seen as a positive one—that is, that more of the one will lead to more of the other.

Diagramming hypotheses is a very useful device to promote clear thinking. If you cannot diagram your hypothesis, it may be because it is not yet clear to you.

Take a different example. We have diagrammed a positive relationship between two concepts. How about a negative relationship—that is, when more of one concept leads to less of the other and vice versa? Look over your list of factors that might affect academic performance. Would you say that increases in any of them may lead to lower academic performance? How about the number of parties attended? The hypothesis would be stated thus:

The more parties a student attends, the lower the student's academic performance.

It would be diagrammed as follows:

A hypothesis states that there is a relationship between two concepts and specifies the direction of that relationship. The preceding hypothesis states that there is a negative relationship between parties attended and academic performance. The greater the number of parties attended, the lower the academic performance.

Continue with the "factors affecting grades" example. Suppose that in doing your literature review on the factors affecting grades, you came across an article that claimed that the kind of breakfast students ate had an effect on their academic performance. Write a hypothesis derived from this article.

Now diagram this hypothesis in the form below:

*Is the relationship proposed by the hypothesis positive or negative? If it is positive, place a plus sign in the blank. If it is negative, place a minus sign in the blank.

The best way to develop skill in deriving hypotheses is to practise. Do the following exercises, and then derive hypotheses relevant to other topics and issues.

1. Here is a hypothesis: "As fewer people purchase audio CDs, there will be an increase in the number of people purchasing their music online." What are the concepts?
   • purchasing rates of audio CDs
   • purchasing rates of music online

What relationship between these concepts does this hypothesis assert? Diagram the hypothesis here:

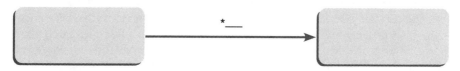

*Is the relationship proposed by the hypothesis positive or negative? If it is positive, place a plus sign in the blank. If it is negative, place a minus sign in the blank.

2. Suppose you decide to compare the self-perception of overall health between married and unmarried individuals. You might propose the following hypothesis:

People who are married have higher perceptions of their health than those living alone.

In this example, the relationship between the concepts cannot be described as positive or negative because the independent concept, "marital status" (married or single), is a special type, the categorical concept. A **nominal variable or concept** is one that is rigidly divided into two or more exclusive categories. Examples of categorical concepts include

- marital status (formal marriage versus common-law marriage versus unmarried);
- gender or sex (male versus female—see In Focus box below);
- social class (upper class versus middle class versus lower class);
- occupational status (white collar versus blue collar);
- school education (public school versus private school);
- wealth (poor versus rich); and
- spiritual belief (atheist versus believer).

Changes in categorical concepts are not described as "more" or "less" of the variable but as "one category" or "another category." You don't usually classify people as "more married" or "less married" but rather as either "married" or "single" or "widowed" or "divorced" or "separated" or "cohabiting."

In the preceding example, we cannot say that more or less of the independent concept "relationship" leads to more or less "self-perceived health." The independent concept does not vary in terms of "more" or "less." It takes the form of either of its categories, "formally married" or "single."

In Focus

Measuring Gender

Social science and medical science researchers have known for a very long time that sex is not binary. Human beings are not simply just "male" or just "female." Instead, sex exists in a continuum and takes dozens of different forms. These identifications cannot be based on examination of genitalia or sexual orientation. Yet our surveys and the way we often discuss sex differences assumes that only two categories of sex exist. How does good research allow participants to express themselves in a way that is true to their identity? The answer is quite simple. Instead of asking the same old survey question, "What is your sex?" followed by two forced choices ("male" or "female"), we can ask the question differently. Instead, we can ask, "What is your gender affiliation?" Instead of forcing participants to select one of two options, we leave a blank line at the end of this question. That way, people can answer using a category they feel most comfortable with. For these reasons, most researchers use the term "gender" to refer to the multitude of ways humans may express themselves. It is the preferred approach in the twenty-first century.

Some less open-minded researchers will argue against this approach because it takes more time to code the data. That might be true, but the human right to identify as one chooses outweighs any extra time and money that it may take to code an open-ended response. Put simply, it is simple human respect that should override any extra "work" entailed by coding data.

Diagram this hypothesis here:

3. If you read some of the literature on health status, you will discover that there are many factors that influence an individual's perception of his or her health. Some of these factors are

    *   emotional health;
    *   physical health;
    *   number of friends;
    *   economic security;
    *   age;
    *   gender;
    *   job security.

One hypothesis that could be derived from these factors is this:

People with more friends have higher perceptions of their health than those with few friends.

Diagram this hypothesis:

4. Derive another hypothesis from the above list of factors and write it out concisely.

As you can tell from doing these exercises, developing a hypothesis requires that you identify one concept that causes, affects, or has an influence on another concept. The concept that does the "causing" is called the **independent variable or concept**. An independent concept "causes," produces a change in, or acts upon something else. The concept that is acted upon, produced, or "caused" by the independent concept is called the **dependent variable or concept**.

Writing a hypothesis requires that you identify an independent concept and a dependent concept. In the examples where we examined students' grades, the factors amount of study, parties attended, and nutrition were independent concepts. These concepts were seen as "causes" of changes in academic performance.

List the independent concepts in the exercises you have just done. For example:

Exercise 1: rate of CD purchase
Exercise 2: marital status
Exercise 3:
Exercise 4:

In terms of the diagram, the independent concept is the one from which the arrow is drawn.

The dependent concept is the thing that is caused, acted upon, or affected—the thing in which a change is produced by the independent concept. List the dependent concepts in the exercises you have just done. For example:

Exercise 1: online music purchases
Exercise 2: self-rated health
Exercise 3:
Exercise 4:

In the pattern of diagramming introduced above, the dependent concept is the one to which the arrow is drawn:

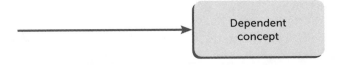

Hence:

In its usual form, a hypothesis states that something about the independent concept produces a change in the dependent concept.

Some of the confusion about independent and dependent concepts arises from the fact that it is possible for the same concept to take the *independent* role in one hypothesis and the *dependent* role in another. Just because a concept is independent in one case does not mean that it should always be treated as independent. For example, here are some concepts:

- academic performance
- nutritional adequacy of breakfast
- study
- party attendance
- intention to go to university

These concepts can be linked in a variety of ways. Many hypotheses can be derived from this list. We can ask the following questions:

Which of the above concepts is the independent concept? Which is the dependent?

We have also seen that

Which of the above concepts is the independent concept? Which is the dependent?

But it also makes sense to derive the following hypothesis using two of the concepts in the above list:

The greater the academic performance of a high school student, the more likely it is that the student will intend to go to university.

This hypothesis would be diagrammed as follows:

In this case, what had been a dependent concept (academic performance) in one hypothesis becomes an independent concept, because going to university is dependent on academic performance, whereas, earlier, academic performance was dependent on study. Whether a concept is independent or dependent depends on your theory. Focusing and diagramming hypotheses help to clarify theories.

The Research Objective

Not all research is best guided by a hypothesis. Some research, particularly qualitative research (see Chapters 4 and 12), is done to find out what is "going on" in a situation. Sometimes it is not possible or desirable to specify the relationship between concepts before making observations. There are times when developing a **research objective** is a more desirable way to focus a qualitative research project. For example, if the general area of your study relates to child development or skill acquisition, you might use the following research objective to guide your research:

> **Objective:** To observe a particular child, four years of age, for a specified period of time, in order to observe patterns of skill acquisition through play.

When the goal of the research is descriptive rather than explanatory, a statement of an objective can serve to guide the research. Consider this example:

> **Objective:** To describe what factors the Khan family took into account in deciding whether to send their daughter to a public school or a private school.

The intent of this research is to describe what happened, not to explain what happened. At the end of the study, the researcher will be able to specify the factors that emerged in this family discussion. Who raised which issues? Who responded and in what ways? These observations can lead the researcher to formulate an answer that attempts to explain the family's actions, to be tested later. The goal of qualitative research is not to provide an answer about how everyone would respond to the Khan family situation. Instead, it is to understand the personal situation. In other words, we are not trying to explain how everyone makes decisions, just how the Khan family makes decisions.

A starting point dealing with the policy issue of care for the elderly might prompt research that is primarily descriptive. When you want to describe what is "going on," an objective will help to focus your efforts. Here are some examples of research objectives related to care for the elderly.

> **Objective:** To determine the number and percentage of elderly people in a particular community who require special accommodation.

The goal of this study is to ascertain a community need. There are no influencing factors under study. There is no attempt to test the impact of anything or to ascertain whether special accommodation is needed.

CASE STUDY

....

Canadian Youth and Identity

A recent qualitative study conducted by one of the co-authors was interested in learning more about what young people know about politics and how they view their lives in three Canadian cities. At the onset of the project, instead of formulating hypotheses, the team stated research objectives because we felt that it was important for youth to define their identity in their own voices. Not surprisingly, this was a qualitative research project so it was not appropriate to pre-define concepts prior to collecting data. Some of the objectives we identified included

- to determine how youth define themselves in terms of their ethnic identity, particularly in relation to Canadian identity;
- to identify public and private places in the cities where youth feel safe and unsafe, included and excluded in order to get a sense of their spatial mobility; and
- to identify their consumer habits.

Objective: To discover the existing policy on admission to homes for elderly people.
Objective: To discover the government's policy on funding for homes for elderly people.

As long as your aim is to describe what is, rather than to test explanations for what is, a research objective is the preferred guide to your research. Chapters 5 and 6 show how to convert a research objective into a statement that can guide your research effectively, whether you adopt a qualitative or quantitative approach. Chapter 12 describes the way that qualitative research is done.

Summary

The research process may be started from many points. Curiosity, claims of others, reading, problems—all these can begin the process. Once research has begun, the first step is to clarify the issues and to narrow your focus.

For your research to succeed, a clear statement of the problem or issue must guide it. The two most common forms of such statements are the hypothesis and the research objective. A hypothesis is developed to guide research intended to test an explanation. A research objective states the goal of a study intended to describe. Without a clear statement of the problem, the research will be confused and ambiguous. It is impossible to satisfactorily proceed to the next stage of the research process without such a statement.

Key Terms

Concept   41
Conceptualization   35
Dependent variable or concept   45
Hypothesis   41

Independent variable or concept   45
Nominal variable or concept   43
Research objective   48

Questions for Review

1. List six common starting points for the research process.
2. What are the reasons for reviewing the literature on a particular subject?
3. Why is it essential to identify the issues or factors involved in a subject, topic, or problem being considered for a research project?
4. Why is conceptualization so important to consider prior to collecting data?
5. Why is it necessary to select one issue from among the issues identified?
6. What is a hypothesis? Give an example. Diagram a hypothesis.
7. What is a negative relationship? Give an example. How is it diagrammed?
8. What is a positive relationship? Give an example. How is it diagrammed?
9. What is an independent concept? What is a dependent concept?
10. What is used instead of a hypothesis in qualitative research? Why isn't a hypothesis used in qualitative research?
11. What role do theories play in the development of a research question? Why do we need a theory?
12. Compare and contrast the role of theory in a qualitative and a quantitative research project.

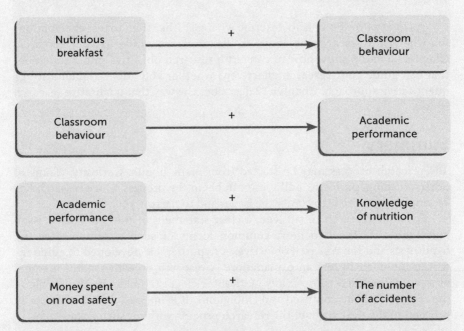

13. Fully write out each of the above diagrammed hypotheses.
14. Diagram the following:
    - The greater the proportion of sweets in the diet, the greater the incidence of dental cavities in children.
    - The introduction of a module on management theory will improve the quality of decision-making among students.
    - The greater the age gap between parents and children, the greater the degree of difficulty in communication they experience.

Sources

Brian Sinclair Working Group. (2017, September 15). *Out of sight: Interim report of the Sinclair Working Group*. Retrieved March 24, 2018 from http://ignoredtodeathmanitoba.ca/index.php/2017/09/15/out-of-sight-interim-report-of-the-sinclair-working-group/

Ignored to death: Brian Sinclair's death caused by racism, inquest inadequate group says. (2017, September 18). *CBC News*. Retrieved March 24, 2018 from http://www.cbc.ca/news/canada/manitoba/winnipeg-brian-sinclair-report-1.4295996

Suggestions for Further Reading

Palys, T., & Achison, C. (2014). Sources of research ideas. In T. Palys & C. Achison, *Research decisions: quantitative and qualitative perspectives* (5th ed.). Toronto: Thomson Nelson.

Remler, D., & Van Ryzin, G. (2011). Research in the real world. In D. Remler and G. Van Ryzin, *Research methods in practice: Strategies for description and causation* (pp. 3–24). Los Angeles: Sage.

Taylor, S. J., Bogdan, R., & DeVault, M. (2016). *Introduction to qualitative research methods: A guidebook and resource*. Hoboken, NJ: Wiley.

Suggested Web Resources

Brikci, N., & Green, J. (2007). *A guide to using qualitative research methodology*. Médecins Sans Frontières. Retrieved April 2, 2018 from https://cloudfront.ualberta.ca/-/media/science/research-and-teaching/teaching/qualitative-research-methodology.pdf

USC Libraries. (2018). *Organizing your social science research paper: Writing a research proposal*. Retrieved April 2, 2018 from http://libguides.usc.edu/writingguide/researchproposal

4   Qualitative or Quantitative Research? Where Do I Begin?

We have spoken a bit about the difference between qualitative and quantitative research in earlier chapters. In this chapter, we investigate these differences in greater detail. A significant debate exists in the social science literature with regard to the relative value of qualitative and quantitative data collection strategies. In our opinion, much of this debate is false. A guiding principle of all good research is to let the research question determine the data collection strategy rather than the other way around. Good researchers will use the method that best answers the research questions posed. It is our belief that researchers who declare themselves as strictly qualitative or quantitative methodologists do a disservice to their research agendas. It is important for all researchers, no matter what they are studying, to approach their research questions critically, with the aim of obtaining the best possible answers. This means being flexible in your data collection approach. Even if your career does not involve much research, it is important to be able to distinguish between qualitative and quantitative research and to become knowledgeable about the benefits and problems associated with each method.

This chapter examines the differences between qualitative and quantitative research to give you an overview of each method. This may help you to review existing studies more critically and to determine an appropriate approach to your own research projects.

What Is Qualitative Research?

Qualitative research sets out to provide an impression: to tell what kinds of "something" there are; to tell what it is like to be, do, or think something. Qualitative researchers exercise great discipline to find out "what is going on here" from the perspective of those who are in the situation being researched. By comparison, quantitative research sets out to find numerical results that can be reported in tables and graphs. It answers questions about situations in terms of "how many?" or "what proportion?" Drawing an absolute line between qualitative and quantitative research projects is never satisfactory, because they have similarities, and researchers often combine the approaches.

For example, one of the co-authors of this book is conducting a study of the job-search experiences of racialized youth in Winnipeg, in conjunction with a similar study conducted by colleagues in Vancouver, Hamilton, and Toronto. First, the researchers wanted to know how many first-generation youth and racialized youth live in Winnipeg compared with the other three cities. They also wanted to know about their educational attainment and employment rates. Most of this information could be gained from the census and other government statistics. However, the researchers also wanted to find out "what it is like" to be a racialized first- or second-generation young adult looking for work in Winnipeg or Vancouver. This could not be ascertained by reference to census data or other available data sources. To find out "what it is like" to be a racialized youth in Canada, it was necessary to listen to these young people describe their lives.

The fundamental obstacle was that the co-author could not assume that she perceived or appreciated the most outstanding issues in the lives of people of a different age, ethnicity, or sex, and with migration backgrounds different from her own. If she had already understood the dimensions of living as a member of a racialized minority in Canada, she might have been able to construct a questionnaire along the lines of those described in Chapter 6. But she had only limited experience (and there was limited existing research to guide her), and many of the issues that were important to her were not important to racialized youth living in Canada. If she had embarked on the research with preconceived ideas, she would not have found out what it is like to be young and racialized in Canada, because she would have been appreciating their lives in the context of her own experience.

Although it helps to declare preconceptions at the start of a project, it also helps to share them with others in order to uncover potential biases that the researcher may not be aware of. In designing this study, the co-author declared her preconceptions to members of a community liaison group, who then directed her attention to their concerns and their view of things.

She chose to use two qualitative techniques, **semi-structured interviews** and **focus groups**, so that the subjects of the research would feel free to tell her what was important to them, free to tell their stories and to describe their perceptions and their feelings. She did not attempt to take a random sample, nor would it have been relevant to do so. Rather, people were selected as "windows" into, or "listening posts" on, some aspect of racialized youth in Canada. Male and female youths from a variety of ethnic backgrounds, who had been in Canada a short time, a moderate length of time, or a long time, or who were born in Canada, were interviewed. The interviews, each of which took around one hour, were conducted by university students who were the same age as the target group. These interviews were conducted according to an interview schedule that essentially helped to produce an "employment biography" for each participant.

This research used both qualitative and quantitative research techniques because the research was designed to answer both "what is it like?" and "how many?" questions.

Once the data were collected, further questions of "qualitative versus quantitative research" arose. The data could be analyzed in a qualitative way or a quantitative way. It is important to remember this when discussing the differences between qualitative and quantitative research. These issues arise at each phase of the research process, and decisions are made at *each phase* about which

---

CASE STUDY

Focus Groups

Focus groups are qualitative interviews where groups of participants answer a series of questions in a conversational format. Groups usually comprise between 4 and 12 people. Larger groups make it difficult for all voices to be included in the conversation while fewer people may make it difficult to engage in a conversation. A facilitator directs the proceedings. The facilitator welcomes the participants, helps with introductions, and ensures the list of discussion topics or questions is completed in the session. The facilitator usually takes a role in transcribing the conversation for later analysis—though professional transcribers may be hired to complete the initial transcriptions. Focus group participants usually share common characteristics, which are determined by the research objectives. Some examples of selection criteria may be age, gender, occupation, political persuasion, or diagnosis of disease. Focus groups are a popular method of data collection. They allow researchers to collect information from several people at the same time; the group dynamics may cause the conversation to change course—uncovering topics that the researchers may not have anticipated. Focus groups are used in many disciplines and professions, including market and entertainment research.

A series of focus group interviews were conducted in the summer of 2009 in four cities across Canada. The research objective was to learn about the experience of being unemployed among recent university graduates. It was an interesting time to conduct this research because the economic recession had caused the highest rates of unemployment among university students for several decades. In the course of the research, the researchers discovered that despite the pessimistic economic outlook, young people had optimistic career aspirations, seeing the recession as a temporary stumbling block or as an opportunity to upgrade their education. The researchers transcribed the focus group interviews and compared the results across the four cities to identify similarities and differences in experiences and learned that in Hamilton, youth had lower expectations and were more pessimistic about their life chances than were those living in the other three cities.

to use. Sometimes quantitative options will be used at one phase and qualitative at another. It is possible to collect qualitative data and to subject them to quantitative analysis, just as it is possible to collect quantitative data in a way that makes it possible for them to be analyzed qualitatively.

When to Use Qualitative Research

As with all decisions that arise during the research process, deciding whether to use qualitative or quantitative approaches is based on what the researchers want to know—that is, it depends on the questions they are asking. If the researchers want to know how many first- and second-generation youth live in certain neighbourhoods of Winnipeg, it will be necessary to do quantitative research. Counting households, citizens, adults, women, men, and children and recording ages may be some of the tasks involved in the census required to answer "how many?" This is why the census is conducted every five years in Canada (and many other countries). If there were no census, researchers would have to rely on sample surveys to estimate features of the population. Qualitative approaches will not answer questions such as "how many?," "how often?," or "what proportion?" because qualitative research is not concerned with such questions.

Qualitative approaches, such as visiting a neighbourhood, may give an impression, provoke a feeling about the place, or enable the researcher to describe the look of the neighbourhood. For instance, while driving through certain commercial districts in the Vancouver suburb of Richmond, a researcher will see many shops with Vietnamese and Chinese signs offering foods from Southeast Asia and may form the impression that this is a Vietnamese and Chinese neighbourhood. The shopping strip gives that impression, but it does not reveal how many Vietnamese and Chinese people live in that area or what proportion of the businesses are owned or run by Vietnamese and Chinese people. However, asking "What impression does a particular shopping area give?" is a perfectly valid research question. It may also be a very important question for market or ethnic-relations research. And that question cannot be answered by information about how many people of a particular ethnic background live in the area.

In addition to providing impressions and feelings about a particular situation, qualitative research often seeks to answer the question "What is going on here?" Often, the aim of qualitative research is to describe in detail what is happening in a group, in a conversation, or in a community—who spoke to whom, with what message, with what feelings, with what effect.

Sometimes researchers apply qualitative methods as a preliminary to quantitative research. For example, you may want to know how many or what proportion of users of a particular service are satisfied with it. You could ask a simple "yes/no" or "much/some/little" question of each user over a few days. This would give a lot of quantitative information about levels of customer satisfaction, but it is probably not all you really want to know. You would soon become curious about the aspects of the service the users do and do not like, what users expect, and why they use the service. Unless you already know why people use the service and what their problems are, you will find that you need some qualitative research to answer your questions.

In this case, you may wish to interview a range of users to learn what they expect from the service and their range of perceptions of its performance. Having listened to users of the service, you will know what using the service feels like because respondents will have told you "what is going on here." You will be able to appreciate the range of reactions to the service, and you will have gained impressions about the users. You may even be able to identify types of responses to the service, themes in the comments, or other patterns in the users' responses. But you will not know how many or what proportion of users react in each way or how many come away with certain types of feelings. In order to answer such questions, you will need to survey representative samples of the clients with a quantitative measure. Having already identified certain types of users and certain perceptions or themes in the users' responses in the qualitative research, the quantitative survey will enable you to discover the frequency with which these types of themes occur.

What separates qualitative from quantitative research is its approach to the study of human nature. For qualitative methodologists, there is no single unified truth. The search for truth is meaningless, since truth is shaped by individuals. What I believe is true differs from what you believe is true. This is part of being human. For this reason, qualitative research is very focused on the individual rather than on generalized social trends. To understand a phenomenon, it is best to take a lived-experience approach. For example, how do people with a terminal illness such as cancer make sense of their mortality? This would be a difficult question to research with a quantitative approach. Qualitative researchers value the individual voices of the participants in their study. In a study of cancer patients in palliative care, for instance, researchers would be interested to hear the stories of both cancer survivors and cancer sufferers in order to better understand their life outlook. Asking cancer survivors and sufferers a battery of impersonalized questions intended to generalize the "cancer experience" would be demeaning and would not shed light on the experience of living with terminal cancer.

The idea that individuals have a voice and that their stories should be central to understanding a social issue is called **phenomenologism**. According to Palys and Achison (2014), "Any effort to understand human behaviour must take into account that humans are cognitive beings who actively perceive and make sense of the world around them, have the capacity to abstract from their experience, ascribe meaning to their behaviour and the world around them, and are affected by those meanings" (p. 8). Approaches that try to assign numbers to people's opinions are artificial and do not fully explain the human experience. To fully understand the issue, researchers must work hard to learn about all aspects of a social problem. In the study of terminal cancer patients, good researchers would not only interview cancer sufferers but also get to know their family, friends, and caregivers to get a full picture of the end of life. In the process of talking with all stakeholders, researchers often uncover other questions and ideas that they had not previously considered. This process is called **inductive** understanding. By building on information provided by all informants and stakeholders, the researcher obtains a fuller explanation of the phenomenon. We discuss inductive reasoning in greater detail later in this chapter, once we have introduced its cousin, deductive reasoning.

In Focus

Types of Qualitative Data Collection Strategies

The beauty of qualitative research methods is that there are numerous ways to collect information about people, problems, and social phenomena. For the most part, we are limited only by our imagination in how we collect these data. The following are brief descriptions of some of the most commonly used qualitative research strategies.

Interviews come in several forms but they can be classified into three categories: **unstructured**, semi-structured, and **structured interviews**. Structured interviews are used in quantitative research so they are not relevant here; see the box below on structured interviews. Unstructured interviews are a type of method where researchers ask questions to participants but there are no pre-determined questions. The rationale is to allow the participant to determine what information is relevant to their story or version of events. The idea is to give the participant a "voice" to describe their experiences without the researcher predetermining their descriptions of events. Semi-structured interviews work the same way, though the researcher has perhaps six to ten questions that may or may not be asked of all participants. Researchers using semi-structured interviews have a list of topics that must be covered during the data collection phase, but the order or type of information collected doesn't matter.

Participant observation is a type of qualitative methodology where the researcher observes activities within a group or social setting. The researcher does not become a member of the group but has to be accepted and authorized in order to collect information. This kind of research involves taking extensive **field notes** (a notebook or electronic file of observations, impressions, etc.) and may use other methods such as focus groups and interviews, information that all becomes part of the data used to understand the situation, event, or phenomenon.

Content analysis is a data collection strategy that uses written or archived information. Content may include reports, books, newspaper articles, diaries, autobiographies—anything that is written down. It may be historical. For instance, a social scientist wishing to understand the civil war in Finland at the conclusion

Continued

of the First World War may need to rely on newspaper accounts, government documents, and other written resources as it is unlikely that anyone still alive can provide useful information and personal reflection about the conflict. The data are organized according to theme, and the analysis can take some time, but it is a very powerful and useful methodology we can use to understand historical and current events, along with government and civilian understanding of such phenomenon. Content analysis can also be a quantitative method; see Chapter 6 for instructions.

Photovoice is a newer method of collecting data. Participants are given cameras or asked to provide their own photos, and asked via interviews, diaries, logs, or other methods of data collection to describe their thoughts and feelings about the photos that they take. This is a very powerful method of understanding human life that proves the adage "a picture is worth a thousand words." One of the textbook's authors has used this methodology to identify places where students feel unsafe and intimidated in major Canadian cities. The students could better identify these areas to the researcher, could better talk about their feelings when visiting these areas, and were better able to recall events that had happened in these places when they had pictures in front of them. The angle, lighting, and viewpoints of the photos can also provide thoughtful information about the photographers' experiences. Photovoice is often combined with interviews or other forms of data collection to help researchers better understand social phenomenon.

Often, the best and most innovative research uses both qualitative and quantitative approaches. Well-executed qualitative research is often essential preparation for worthwhile quantitative research and vice versa. This does not mean that qualitative research should be regarded as secondary to quantitative research. In many cases, the relationship between the two is symbiotic. Quantitative research presumes that the researcher knows "what is going on." Having discovered the range of issues confronting certain people, it is often highly desirable to find out how these themes or issues are distributed among those people, demonstrating the close relationship that exists between quantitative and qualitative research techniques.

What Is Quantitative Research?

In contrast to qualitative research, the purpose of quantitative research is to describe trends and large-scale social processes using numbers as data. Sample sizes in quantitative research are much larger than in qualitative research. Sometimes the studies include millions of people, such as in the Canadian national census. In 2018, just over 37 million people (or their proxies) participated in the survey. Its goal is to give the government and researchers access to a large pool of data from which to draw conclusions—such as an assessment of the size of the city of Winnipeg or the number of females living in the Yukon. But sample sizes may be much smaller, some as small as 20 people. The idea is to draw a representative sample from which to draw conclusions about social trends. For example, the General Social Survey, conducted annually by Statistics Canada, surveys a few thousand people about such issues as their use of time, reported victimization, and internet usage. In this case, the idea is to collect information about a small number of people in order to understand more about a particular social phenomenon. It is not necessary to survey all the people; a small sub-sample of the population is usually enough to reveal accurate, truthful information about a particular phenomenon.

A common concern of quantitative research is the way the sample is selected. One of the issues that differentiates quantitative from qualitative research is the sampling method. Quantitative research is concerned with generalizing the results to a larger population and does not involve asking everyone for their opinion (which would be too time-consuming and costly), so samples must be selected using random means. Sampling is discussed in Chapter 8 and we will not go into detail here. For now, we will simply say that the idea of sampling is to give every person in a population an equal or near-equal chance of being selected to participate in the study.

In contrast to qualitative research, quantitative research designs cannot give detailed in-depth information about a social problem. They can only provide data on general trends and patterns. This is because participants are asked only a small number of questions that are closed-ended. For example, researchers might ask participants whether they support the building of a hydro power line along the eastern shore of Lake Winnipeg. They ask the participants a series of short questions, such as "How likely or unlikely are you to support the construction of a new hydro power line along the shore of Lake Winnipeg?" This may be followed by five choices (very unlikely, unlikely, neither likely nor unlikely, likely, and very likely). At no time are participants asked to say why they feel this way. For instance, one participant may be very likely to support the initiative because she believes that it will create more jobs for people working in the construction industry. Another respondent may also support the initiative, but for different reasons, such as favouring hydroelectricity over nuclear-powered generators. Unless the surveyors ask, we will never know why the respondents feel the way they do. It is tempting to ask respondents "why?" in large-scale quantitative research, but such questions are generally avoided because they prolong the research process and cost too much in terms of recording and analyzing the answers. Remember that surveys are large, aimed at capturing information from hundreds or thousands of participants.

Another difference between the quantitative and qualitative approaches has to do with perspective. Most quantitative researchers feel that the social sciences should adopt scientific methods to mirror the kind of research conducted in the natural sciences. In this regard, quantitative methodology encompasses a **positivist approach**. Positivists believe that there are real and truthful answers to any social questions. The purpose of social research, according to this paradigm, is to uncover facts and truth. The best way to accomplish this, according to most positivists, is to measure the attitudes, beliefs, and experiences of as many people as possible. Using scientific methods, such as statistical modelling,

In Focus

Structured Interviews

One quantitative method of collecting data is called the structured interview. In this method, the researcher is present and asks the participants questions directly from an interview guide. Well-trained interviewers ask the questions in the order in which they appear using the words exactly as they are printed. In this way, the interviewer can ensure that the participant does not miss any questions (although participants always have the right to refuse to answer some questions) and that participants answer the questions in the order they are intended, and the interviewer can address any concerns or questions the participants may have. This method produces some of the most detailed and precise information in quantitative studies because a trained interviewer is present to collect the data. There are many benefits to the structured interview. Typically, response rates are higher because it is more difficult for a participant to refuse an invitation when it is presented in person. The data are usually (but not always) more precise because the interviewer is there to answer questions and provide clarification if the participant has any confusion. There are some important limitations, however. This method is the most expensive way to collect data because even the most experienced interviewers require extensive training. Participants often require honorariums to participate as these interviews tend to be lengthy. Sometimes, depending on the subject, participants may feel compelled to lie or embellish the truth to please the interviewer or to mask their shame regarding a particular topic.

One of the book's authors was part of a large longitudinal study examining the health and well-being of immigrant children and their families. Our questionnaire was very complex and lengthy, and had been translated into 18 different languages. One of the sections asked participants if they had vaccinated their children against many common childhood diseases. The words and phrases physicians use to describe certain diseases may not translate into some languages, or may be terms some participants had never heard of before. Take rubella, for example. How many of you know what rubella is? You might not know because this disease has been officially eradicated from North, Central, and South America. Rubella is the word physicians use to identify what Canadians commonly call "German measles." Neither rubella nor German measles translates very well into most languages. When these questions were asked of participants, our well-trained interviewers were able to describe the disease to participants and had information about the age at which this vaccination is typically given to children. By using structured interviews, the researchers were able to collect more precise (but maybe not 100 per cent accurate) information about the vaccination history of immigrant children.

researchers can begin to understand social causes and effects. Although social science does not directly deal with cause and effect, those following the positivist paradigm want to follow the model as closely as possible. Students interested in learning more about positivism and quantitative standpoints should consult Palys and Achison (2014) or Neuman and Robson (2009).

Unlike qualitative researchers who use the inductive approach to collecting data, quantitative researchers use the **deductive approach**. As a form of organization, this approach organizes research "from the top down." This means that this type of research design relies heavily on the findings of previous studies as a guide to build on our existing knowledge. As well, it relies on extensive reviews of the academic literature to identify appropriate theoretical frameworks to frame researchers' studies; to create a bank of questions that have been asked of similar research participants for comparative purposes; and to attempt to replicate previous findings to provide further evidence supporting or refuting existing research.

Understanding Inductive and Deductive Reasoning

As we mentioned earlier in the chapter, inductive reasoning is an approach to research that tries not to make assumptions about the answer to the research question. This means that by its nature, inductive reasoning deeply prioritizes the words, thoughts, ideas, and preferences of the individual participants. The idea behind this type of approach is that the researcher is not the expert on the topic, rather the participant is. The purpose of data collection using the inductive approach is to listen and learn about the experiences and perspectives of research participants because only they can truly understand the experience. Even if the researcher has had experience in this area, her job is to allow the participants to share their experiences, histories, and stories unfettered by theories and previous research.

Let's return to the previous example of the study of what it is like to be a cancer survivor. Perhaps the researcher is a cancer survivor herself. Perhaps she has also worked for many years in this field studying the social context of the cancer survivor community. Her research, knowledge of the existing literature, and her previous personal experience as a cancer survivor is important background for her to have. It will help her to empathize with participants and to ask appropriate questions to gather the information she needs to conduct her study. She cannot, however, let this previous knowledge determine how she proceeds with the project or how she interprets and analyzes the data. What do we mean by this? Despite all her personal knowledge and experience, she has to let the participants speak and share their experiences without her biases filtering their words. She must not let her prior knowledge of theories and research to "direct" or "guide" the participant in the sharing of her experiences. She must let the participants' words and experiences be the focal point of her research and the reports she writes. The objective of inductive research is to give privilege to the voices of the participants, not to let theory or knowledge from the scientific literature to override or hide the voice of the participants.

This can be tricky work for researchers, particularly those who do have personal experience or with years of knowledge in the subject area. Researchers **bracket** their previous personal experiences and knowledge, meaning they push these aside during the interview and analysis process so as to allow the experiences of the participants to take centre stage.

What role does theory play in inductive research? Although theory has some influence on determining some of the questions asked in focus groups and interviews, its main role is in helping the researcher make sense of the data she collects. In her study of cancer survivors, the researcher may use a theory to help explain the patterns in themes and ideas she encounters as she compares the responses of the participants in her study. She may locate a theory that helps explain why women may be more likely to participate in weekly meetings with other cancer patients while male cancer survivors may not. She may also contribute to creating a new theory or refining an existing theory based on the information she has gathered in her study. For example, she may find that existing theories are unhelpful in explaining why survivors of a particular form of cancer, say liver cancer, are less optimistic than those surviving other types of cancer. She can use this information not only to inform other studies and other research; she may use it to create a new theory. We call this process inductive reasoning because we are interested in developing new approaches to a problem or subject and are not interested in having the results affected by existing theory or research.

In contrast, deductive research is more connected to theory and past research from the beginning. Often, researchers use the vast amount of research already published in the field to inform their own research in an attempt to advance our knowledge and understanding of a particular problem even further. If we maintain the experiences of cancer survivors idea for the moment, approaching the problem in a deductive manner has an influence on the entire project from start to finish. Unlike the efforts to bracket our personal experiences as discussed earlier, researchers depend on the findings of other research to inform their own projects. This means replicating questions from surveys that have already been conducted with cancer survivors. It means leaning greatly on existing theories to tell the researcher what kinds of questions and what to look for in their research. It has an effect on how we develop the research question, too. We lean on the existing research to give us clues as to what influences we should look for and how information about participants is connected. These activities are hallmarks to the deductive approach—we let the existing research and theory guide us in our decision-making and understanding of the data we collect. In other words, we rely on the words and knowledge of other experts in the field as we draw conclusions about our findings.

You might have heard the terms "top-down" research and "bottom-up" research. These are the non-technical terms for deductive and inductive approaches, respectively. In the top-down approach, theory plays a significant role in determining all aspects of the project, from the selection of a data collection method, to designing the data collection instruments and how we analyze and make sense of the results of the research. This is why the top-down approach is linked to deductive reasoning. By contrast, inductive research is all about privileging the experiences, opinions, and ideas of the people involved in the problem. The idea is to allow them to speak freely and for the researcher to report their findings in a way that is unencumbered by the rules and expectations of deductive research. Our hope in inductive research is to give more power to the participants than is normally allowed in deductive research.

The deductive/inductive didactic is then tied to understanding some fundamental differences between qualitative and quantitative research. Most quantitative research is deductive given that the purpose of such research is to test existing theories our knowledge of social, cultural, health, and other problems. Inductive reason is tied closely to qualitative research given the importance placed on situating and understanding the experiences of the people who experience these problems. Neither form of research is better or worse than the other; each just gives us different and equally valuable information, an issue we discuss below.

When to Use Quantitative Research

As you have likely already surmised, research is done for very different purposes. In qualitative research, we are very interested in exploring questions of "why" something happens or explaining phenomenon in greater detail. Sharing the life experiences or histories of groups and individuals is also a purpose of qualitative research.

But there are times when the nature of the research question is distinct and requires different data to address the problem. Often, governments, businesses, public institutions, and academics want to know information about what happens to people "in general" or "on average." For instance, pediatricians will want to know at what age does the "average" male enter puberty? The answer to this question will assist physicians in treating the health problems of their patients more accurately. A city planner will want to know at what time of the day (and what days) is a particular traffic intersection the busiest or when do the most accidents occur? The answer to that question will help the city to determine how many seconds they should add to the green light and in what direction that additional time should be given. A sociologist would be interested in identifying the factors that influence young people to join street gangs. The answer to this question will help us to better identify early warning signs and perhaps prevent youth from entering a world of crime. These are all questions that are best answered using quantitative data. We use quantitative data when we are interested in knowing the "average" or the "typical" situation. We use quantitative data when we want to identify the factors that influence a certain kind of behaviour or result. This type of data will allow us to identify patterns of activity and social trends that assist policy-makers, governments, planners, and other professionals to address social problems and perhaps even prevent them from occurring in the first place. This kind of research cannot tell us much about what it "feels" like to be in a traffic accident or to undergo puberty or to join a street gang—but it can tell us a lot about when accidents happen, what might cause puberty to happen, and why someone might join a gang—all very important when we care about social issues, health, and public safety.

Which Is Better: Qualitative or Quantitative?

By now, it should be clear that the difference between qualitative and quantitative research is not a matter of "better" or "worse" but rather of appropriateness to the question. However, since the mid-1960s, when the importance and value of qualitative research became more widely used in the social sciences, some people have taken staunch ideological positions on the relative merits of quantitative and qualitative research. This has resulted in an artificial and politicized conflict between those who practise one method and those who subscribe to the other. Fortunately, this conflict is subsiding as it becomes increasingly obvious that such polarized views do not coincide with what researchers are actually doing or how social, economic, or political problems develop. However, some traces of the conflict persist, and some people still resolutely cling to one side or the other.

For example, some argue that each individual, family, or situation is unique, so it is impossible—indeed immoral—to group them for purposes of analysis and **generalization**. To do so, they contend, is to fly in the face of reality. For them, the only valid research is individual case studies, in which the uniqueness of each subject or group is appreciated. This is a difficult position to maintain because someone will eventually begin to identify patterns within and between groups: for example, the stories of women share certain themes, as do those of people with a common lifestyle or of a particular age group; villagers recount different experiences from those of urban dwellers. The original careful attention to the details of individual stories is valuable in itself, but through these details it may be possible to begin to see patterns that can be tested by quantitative approaches, demonstrating again the need for both qualitative and quantitative research methods. It's best that students remember that the nature of the problem and the type of data needed to answer the research question dictates the methods used to collect information, not the other way around. While we can correctly assess our own skill sets as stronger either in qualitative or quantitative methods, it is a poor research procedure to only practice one or the other.

Mixed Methods Research

Now that you have a good idea of the difference between qualitative and quantitative research, we can combine them! Some of the best research uses both qualitative and quantitative methods to address the research question. The reasoning for this is that quantitative research can provide a different set of data and a level of detail that qualitative research cannot—and vice versa. This lets the researcher get the best of both worlds and helps address some of the limitations

In Focus

A Note on Primary versus Secondary Research

Not all research involves you going out and collecting your own data. Many very successful research projects use data that someone else has collected. It's worth your time and money prior to beginning your study to find out whether or not the information you need to answer your research question has already been collected. This will save you time, frustration, and money. You might also find that the information that has already been collected is better than what you could collect on your own.

We've been talking mostly about **primary research**, or collecting your own data. These are the type of data most people are familiar with. The researcher goes out and interviews people, sends them a survey to complete, or watches a social event as an observer who takes notes. There are many ways we can collect data and we've identified many of them in this chapter. Sometimes we use a combination of data collection strategies to obtain information to answer our research question. This is all primary research because the data are generated by the researcher for a specific research project. Most of this book details the steps needed in primary research.

Secondary research is the use of available data and information to answer a research question. Instead of the researchers collecting the data themselves, they locate and use data that are already available. You might be asking yourself, "How can there be data available to answer my research question?" You might be surprised how much information is available today. Newspaper articles, diaries, blogs, and internet chat rooms are some examples of qualitative data that can be used to answer research questions. Administrative databases, government databases, censuses, publicly available surveys, and statistical tables are examples of quantitative data that can be made available to researchers to answer their questions.

All of these data require reorganization and manipulation to answer the research question. For example, reading and classifying hundreds or even thousands of blog posts on a particular social issue will take time and significant organizational skill, but you would have enough information to write an entire book on a particular subject. A popular research method used by many graduate students today is to read, categorize, and analyze anonymous comments from newspaper articles to answer deep social questions such as whether anonymity gives people the licence to be racist, or whether people feel that euthanasia is a worthy social program. This is called content analysis, a method we discuss in Chapter 6. Similarly, quantitative datasets provide important information about the thoughts, beliefs, and actions of thousands of people. Even though these may arrive to you in a neat computer file, the data require reorganization and analysis, which also take time. You might find that you still need to collect some new information, such as conducting interviews with people, but that newspaper articles, databases, and existing tables can be used as secondary sources for your research.

of each method. For example, a major limitation of quantitative methods is that they lack personalized information. When we conduct a study about (as an example) poverty using quantitative methods, we will find very interesting and important information, such as the number of people in Sherbrooke who rely on food banks in a given month, or the number of people who receive rental supplement so they can afford their housing, or the shelter-to-income ratio (the percentage of total income a family spends on their monthly housing). This is very important information and is very helpful for governments to make decisions about how much they should spend on social housing in Sherbrooke. But this information tells us nothing about what it is like for a family to live cheque-to-cheque, using food banks and worrying about increases in their monthly rent. The quantitative data can provide information about how many people this problem affects but not how it affects *them*. This is where a qualitative study could provide valuable information.

Adding a qualitative component to this study could address this gap. Let's say, for example, that the researcher had funds and could identify 40 low-income families in Sherbrooke who were willing to be interviewed. The researcher would prepare a list of topics to discuss, and an unstructured interview could take place. The researcher would tape-record and transcribe the interview and, at the end of the study, would code the interviews and prepare an analysis. This analysis would be included alongside the quantitative data on the number of food bank users, the number of people who received rental income supplements, and other information to gain a more holistic picture of vulnerable people in Sherbrooke. This would provide very valuable contextual and personal information that would help policy-makers and programmers to perhaps create programs that better serve the needs of this group of people. It is a very powerful form of research.

It is, however, very expensive and very time-consuming. Rarely can researchers get the funds they need to collect the data using one method. As the time collecting data increases, so does its cost. In a time where research funding in most areas is on the decline, very few researchers are able to obtain the funds needed to conduct a good mixed methods study. In fact, obtaining funding to do mixed methods research is often beyond the ability of even the most experienced researchers.

As well, combining the research results can be very difficult. Very often, mixed methods research reports look like two separate reports—first reporting one set of results then ending with another set of results. Novice researchers often have difficulty adequately embedding the findings within one another (something that is called **triangulation**, which is very tricky to do correctly).

In sum, using mixed methods is a good idea when it is done correctly, but we are often faced with lack of funding, time, and expertise to really do a good job of such projects. It is possible to do and when such projects are done with care and precision, the information is extremely valuable. However, we have seen many poorly conducted mixed methods projects and would advise novice researchers against attempting such projects until they become comfortable in both methods of research.

Summary

Both qualitative and quantitative approaches are absolutely essential to the research process in the social sciences. They require some common and some different skills. Neither approach sets the standards for the other, because each has its own rules of practice and requires various disciplines on the part of the researcher. Neither is easier than the other, nor is one more creative than the other. Using both together is possible, but difficult, and requires familiarity with both methods for success.

Key Terms

Bracketing   62

Deductive approach   61

Field notes   57

Focus group   53

Generalization   64

Inductive approach   57

Phenomenologism   56

Photovoice   58

Positivist approach   59

Primary research   65

Secondary research   65

Semi-structured interview   53

Structured interview   57

Unstructured interview   57

Triangulation   66

Questions for Review

1. How do the questions asked in qualitative research differ from those asked in quantitative research?
2. What kind of information is obtained from qualitative methodologies?
3. What kind of information is obtained from quantitative methodologies? How is deductive reasoning linked to quantitative research?
4. Is inductive reasoning linked with qualitative research? Why or why not?
5. What is the difference between inductive and deductive reasoning? Can you give some examples?
6. Why can't data from focus groups be used quantitatively?
7. Why is it not helpful to ask whether quantitative or qualitative research is better or which is more important?
8. When is it appropriate to use primary data collection methods? When is it appropriate to use secondary data to answer a research question?
9. Compare and contrast three different methods of data collection.
10. Describe how theories are connected to research questions in both qualitative and quantitative research.
11. What are the difficulties in conducting mixed methods research?

Suggestions for Further Reading

Hesse-Biber, S. N., & Leavy, P. (Eds.). (2004). *Approaches to qualitative research: A reader on theory and practice*. New York: Oxford University Press.

Neuman, W. L., & Robson, K. (2009). *Basics of social research: Qualitative and quantitative approaches* (2nd Cdn ed.). Toronto: Pearson.

Palys, T., & Achison, C. (2014). *Research decisions: Quantitative and qualitative perspectives* (5th ed.). Toronto: Harcourt Brace.

Suggested Web Resources

Centre for Innovation in Research and Teaching. (n.d.). *When to use quantitative methods.* Retrieved April 15, 2018 from https://cirt.gcu.edu/research/developmentresources/research_ready/quantresearch/whentouse

London School of Economics. (2010). *FAQ1: When is it better to do qualitative or quantitative research?* Retrieved April 15, 2018 from www.lse.ac.uk/media@lse/research/EUKidsOnline/BestPracticeGuide/FAQ01.aspx

5 Selecting Variables and Concepts

As you will recall from Chapter 2, the act of doing research involves reducing conceptual problems to empirical questions—that is, questions about "things" that can be measured, counted, recorded, or in some way observed. Finding ways of measuring concepts demands creativity and skill. It is one of the more challenging aspects of doing research.

Concepts and Variables

Concepts are categories into which ideas, impressions, and observations of the world can be placed. Concepts are used in both qualitative and quantitative research. So far, we have dealt with concepts such as academic performance, study, nutrition, and health. Although concepts are critically important in the initial stages of research, they have limited use when they are difficult or impossible to measure. Some are elusive to define, mean different things to different people, and lack definite boundaries. Often, concepts are not perceived by touch, sight, smell, or hearing, and direct measurements are not possible. For others, there's no consensus as to what defines a particular concept.

Take the concept "happiness." How could you define or describe the essential aspects of happiness? The problem is that an infinite number of experiences, observations, and impressions are included in the concept. A simple definition that includes all your impressions of happiness is impossible to produce. This task becomes even more difficult to imagine when you attempt to account for other people's impressions of happiness. Finally, what are the boundaries of happiness? When does happiness become its opposite, unhappiness? Often, we feel that we are neither happy nor unhappy. If we don't know which we are, then there must be "in-between" emotional states in which we cannot be sure whether we are measuring happiness or unhappiness.

It is clear that the concept of happiness has a wide range of meanings, is not readily measurable, and is difficult to observe in both qualitative and quantitative forms. How, then, can happiness be observed and measured in a way that is acceptable to you and to most other people? The same problems are encountered when you try to research most concepts.

Variables

If we are going to do empirical research that others can follow and evaluate, we have to make our abstract concepts observable and measurable. The conventional procedure for doing this is to replace abstract concepts with measurable concepts, referred to as variables, a procedure we use in quantitative research. A variable is a type of concept, one that varies in amount or quality. A variable is something that it is possible to have more or less of, or something that exists in different "states" or "categories." The variables that interest us are those that not only vary in amount or kind but are also measurable.

For example, the concept "heat" can be calculated by measuring the variable "temperature." To measure temperature, we read a thermometer and document the measurement it indicates. We generally take the measurement of temperature to be an indicator of the level of heat.

Someone might say that "love" is a variable—you can have more or less of it, and there are different kinds of love. However, love is not directly measurable. If we want to measure love, we have to find suitable and measurable variables to use. Some might choose such measurable variables as the number of kisses received from their partner or spouse, the frequency and quality of flowers or gifts received, the number of hugs, or the failure to remember important dates such as birthdays and anniversaries. Although love itself is not directly measurable, we can use measurable variables to assess whether we are loved or not.

Specifically, the primary function of any variable is to enable measurement of changes in its corresponding abstract concept. When we pose a hypothesis, we argue that changes in one abstract concept occur as a result of changes in another. When we test a hypothesis, we use variables to allow us to measure changes in the abstract concepts. To be measurable substitutes for abstract concepts, variables must have the following characteristics:

1. Variables must validly represent an abstract concept being studied. This means that changes in variables validly represent changes in abstract concepts. A valid variable for the concept "academic performance" is "final grades," because most people would be confident that changes in final grades represent changes in academic performance. Generally, though, the concept of academic performance does not extend to "batting average" or "popularity rating," which, in this case, would not be valid variables for detecting changes in academic performance. We will expand on this point later in the chapter, in the section titled "The Question of Validity."

2. Variables must have at least one range of possible states. For example, a range of possible states for the variable "final grades" is "distinction," "credit," "pass," and "fail." (Another range is 0–100 per cent. Some educational institutions use the range A, B, C, etc.) Because a variable has a range of states, it can change, and these changes can be taken to indicate change in the abstract concept represented by the variable. A positive change in a student's final grades (variable), from credit to distinction level, indicates a positive change in academic achievement (abstract concept).

3. Variables have "states" that are observable and measurable. You can detect changes in a variable only if you can observe and measure it. For example, the variable "final grades," which represents the abstract concept "academic performance," can be observed and measured by checking students' reports or asking their teacher. If you cannot observe and measure a variable, then you cannot detect changes in the variable, and you cannot detect changes in the abstract concept it represents. Say the abstract concept "happiness" is given by the variable "inner peace." This would be unsatisfactory, because you cannot observe or measure "inner peace." Consequently, it would be a useless variable for the concept "happiness."

The activity of finding measurable variables for concepts is called **operationalization**. An operational definition of a concept goes beyond a usual dictionary definition. It defines a concept in terms that can be measured—that is, it defines a concept in empirical terms.

The basic question that guides this activity is "How can I measure that?" That is, what can I take as an indicator of what is going on? Let's continue our sample hypothesis about academic performance. When we last left it, it looked like this:

This hypothesis says that two concepts, "study" and "academic performance," are related in such a way that the more there is of one (study), the more there will be of the other (academic performance). The question we now face is, "How shall we measure study and academic performance?" or "What measurable, tangible, observable things can we take as indicators or variables of study and academic performance?"

Take academic performance first. We are so familiar with ways of measuring academic performance that we often forget the concept being measured. The measures with which we are most familiar include

•   final grades,
•   test results,

- essay marks,
- professors' and teachers' reports,
- project assessments.

Academic performance, then, is the abstract concept. Grades and test results are variables related to the concept of academic performance.

What about study? How shall we measure study? What variables can be taken as indicators of study? It is hard to measure such things as concentration or the absorption of material. But we can measure the amount of time a student spends "studying." Hence, an operational definition of the concept "study" might be

- time spent studying, or
- time spent practising.

It is now possible to state our hypothesis in two forms: a conceptual form and an operational form.

Conceptual form of the hypothesis

In its conceptual form, the hypothesis describes a relationship between the concepts "study" and "academic performance." Study is the independent concept, and academic performance is the dependent concept.

Operational form of the hypothesis

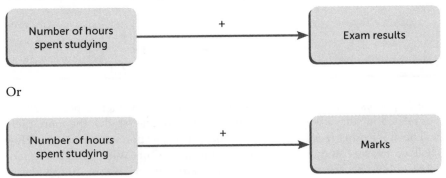

Or

The operational form of the hypothesis asserts that there is a relationship between variables—that is, the number of hours spent studying and exam results or grades. Number of hours spent studying is the independent variable, and exam results, or marks, is the dependent variable.

Any hypothesis can be stated at both the conceptual (abstract or theoretical) level and the operational (empirical or measurable) level. At the conceptual level, a hypothesis asserts a relationship between concepts, and at the operational level it asserts a relationship between variables. We will practise deriving variables as appropriate measures of concepts, and then we will discuss the problem of the relationship between concepts and variables.

Finding Variables for Concepts: Hypotheses

There are no set ways or even useful guides for finding variables that are appropriate measures for concepts. This is an area for creativity and experimentation. Doing research involves a great deal of inventiveness and a willingness to think in new ways. You have to search for variables. Variables must be measurable and relate in some accepted way to the concept in question. Beyond those two rules, the task (or fun) of finding variables is up to you. Here is another conceptual hypothesis:

Better nutritional status leads to better academic performance.

Diagrammed, the hypothesis looks like this:

If we are to test this hypothesis, we must find a variable that relates to nutrition and another that relates to academic performance. We already have some ideas about academic performance—test results, marks, examiners' reports, etc. What variables might give an indication of a student's nutritional status? What about

* how many meals per week include vegetables;
* whether breakfast includes fruit;
* the percentage of recommended daily allowance of nutrients in foods eaten each day?

List others you can think of. Then, taking one of the variables associated with nutrition and one of those associated with academic performance, restate the hypothesis in operational form.

Higher nutrition of meals leads to higher final grades.

Now in diagram form:

In this case, what is the independent variable, and what is the dependent variable?

For further practice, take two other variables, one related to nutrition and another related to academic performance. Develop an operational hypothesis and write it out. Then diagram it.

Now let us try an entirely new hypothesis relating to the area of family life. We are concerned about the relationship between the abstract concepts "family resources" and "family happiness." We may have the theoretical hypothesis:

> The more resources that are available to a family, the happier that family will be.

Diagram this theoretical hypothesis:

Think of variables that might be useful indicators, or specific measures, of family resources—things such as

- family income;
- relatives;
- time;
- social status;
- quality of housing.

Now, what variables might be taken as indicators of family happiness? Happiness is one of those concepts that are not directly measurable. But we can get some indication. How? What about

- absence of divorce;
- presence of observable signs of affection—hugs, kisses;
- self-reported happiness;
- the result on a test of marital happiness?

Think of other indicators of family happiness. One operational hypothesis that can be derived from the above lists of variables is as follows:

Greater family income leads to less divorce.

This would be diagrammed as follows:

Note that although some conceptual hypotheses assert a **positive relationship** between two concepts, this operational hypothesis asserts a **negative relationship** between two variables. This is not a problem. Divorce is taken as a negative indicator of marital happiness. Here is another possible operational hypothesis:

The more time a family spends together, the more likely members of the family are to report that they are happy with the family.

This hypothesis would be diagrammed thus:

Gain some practice by deriving other operational hypotheses from the preceding lists of variables, and diagram them.

Let us take a final example, this time with a categorical variable. Some family researchers believe that intimacy between parents and their infants is a very important factor in successful infant development. The independent concept in this example is "parent–infant intimacy," and the dependent concept is "infant development."

A variable for "parent–infant intimacy" could be "feeding intimacy," which is a categorical variable with two states, "breastfed" and "bottlefed." The first half of a diagram of an operational hypothesis, the part showing the independent variable, would look like this:

The problem now becomes selecting some measure of "infant development." Infant development is a very wide concept. To arrive at a suitable variable, let's consider some "sub-concepts" of infant development that might be affected by feeding preference:

- infant growth
- motor development
- physical health
- emotional health

Add some of your own.

Let's take "infant growth" as a substitute for infant development. The developed conceptual hypothesis would be:

Greater feeding intimacy leads to increased infant growth.

This would be diagrammed:

But this is still at the conceptual level. It is now necessary to think of variables that are indicators of infant growth. What variables might be associated with infant growth? There is weight accumulation. You can have lower or higher weight accumulation. "Weight accumulation" is a variable. The operational hypothesis could now be phrased as follows:

Feeding intimacy influences infant weight accumulation.

This hypothesis would be diagrammed:

Alternatively, you might have preferred to use the sub-concept "physical health" instead of "infant development." In that case, the conceptual hypothesis would be stated as follows:

Parent–infant intimacy influences a baby's physical health.

How can this hypothesis be operationalized? What variables can you think of that relate to physical health? Here are a few:

A Note for Qualitative Research

There are two essential points where qualitative research diverges from quantitative research when we are discussing conceptualization: the creation of variables and the hypothesis.

First, there are no "variables" in qualitative research. Instead, we talk about concepts. Because qualitative research aims to let the participants "speak for themselves," defining and operationalizing a variable would reduce the power of their voice in the study. For this reason, in qualitative research, conceptualization usually leads to data collection (through a qualitative means such as interview or focus group). The operationalization of the concept occurs after the data has been collected so that the participants' words can be used to determine the definition of the variable. We discuss this issue in more detail in Chapter 6.

Second, when we talk about directional hypotheses (either negative or positive) we are discussing quantitative research. In fact, when the word "hypothesis" appears in any research monograph, you can be sure that the research was conducted using a quantitative method. Since hypotheses are not used in qualitative research, we don't have a predefined expectation about the outcome. This doesn't mean we don't have "hunches" or an opinion (based on what we already know about a topic) when we are undertaking a qualitative study, but we don't want to prejudice the results. This is why we have research objectives that guide the research process in qualitative research instead of hypotheses.

- absence of colic
- absence of infectious disease
- normal growth pattern
- appropriate development
- physician's report

Add to this list.

To gain more practice in selecting variables, look through your notes, identify some issues, formulate conceptual hypotheses, and then try to identify appropriate variables.

Finding Variables for Concepts: Research Objectives

When developing research to meet our objectives, it is still necessary to clarify our concepts and to select variables appropriate to these concepts. For example, the research objective might be:

To learn about infant growth and development.

"Growth" and "development" are the concepts. The question that needs to be answered is "What variables relate to growth and development?" Growth is fairly easy—weight, height, and length of limbs are all variables that relate to growth. By observing changes in these variables, we can measure growth.

What variables relate to development? We can now see that the above objective is still very broad. What kind of development? Social? Behavioural? Psychological? For each of these and other kinds of development, there are well-established variables to observe. Specific abilities or patterns of behaviour are taken as evidence of certain kinds of development.

Research objectives are used to guide research that seeks to *describe* rather than *explain* what is happening. Although this means that there will not be independent and dependent concepts and variables, it is still necessary to operationalize the concepts in the research objective. Variables must be selected to serve as indicators for the concepts being studied.

An objective presented in Chapter 3 was:

Objective: To discover the existing policy on admission to homes for elderly people.

"Policy" is a fairly general concept. How might admission policy vary from home to home? How do policies relate to

- age?
- health?
- financial status?
- family status?

All of these are variables related to the concept "policy." Put differently, they are aspects of admission policies of homes for the elderly, which can vary. By thinking through these issues before beginning your data collection, you ensure that the research is focused and clarified. Some background reading—reviewing the relevant literature—will help you to identify variables that might be related to the concepts being studied.

Another example of a research objective may help to further demonstrate the idea that both hypotheses and research objectives deal with concepts.

Objective: To observe the classroom behaviour of school students.

What aspect of the concept "classroom behaviour" is to be observed? What are some variables related to the classroom behaviour of students? Some of the following might be considered:

- attention span of each student
- noise level in the classroom
- frequency of discipline
- attention span of the whole class

- frequency of disruptive behaviour
- length of time taken to settle down at the beginning of a lesson

Before beginning an observational study, it is necessary to decide what is to be observed. This involves selecting a few variables related to the concepts being studied.

The Question of Validity

The most critical consideration in choosing variables is **validity**. When measured, does the variable adequately reflect our understanding of the concept? This is the issue of validity. We must question all the variables we use to provide indicators of our theoretical concepts. How good is a possible indicator? Does it adequately represent our concept? Is it not quite the same thing?

Many arguments arise over the issue of validity. Take the case of IQ testing. Are such tests valid indicators of intellectual ability? Or do they test something else? Take the issue of academic performance. Do exam results validly reflect academic performance? Or do they measure something else? Can the absence of disease be taken as an indicator of health, as one of our hypotheses suggested? Can the absence of divorce be taken as an indication that a family is happy? Were you satisfied with the variables suggested as measures of love—number of kisses or hugs, flowers, and anniversaries remembered?

Whenever we feel dissatisfied with the variables chosen to measure a concept, we raise the issue of validity:

- Is a low noise level a valid indicator that a class is learning? Or is the class just well disciplined?
- Is the fact that a baby gains a great deal of weight quickly a valid indicator of the baby's health, or does it simply indicate the kilojoule content of its diet?
- Is an expressed opinion a valid indicator of the way a person will act?
- Is church-going a valid indicator of depth of spirituality? Or is it an indicator of conformity? Or of something else?

These are examples of issues regarding the validity of chosen variables. Such issues are inevitable, because the act of choosing variables involves finding a concrete expression of abstract (i.e., conceptual) ideas. Not everyone will agree with your choice of variables. Some people will question your research based on your variable choices.

Another problem raised by questions of validity is that concepts are often multi-dimensional and impossible to represent with a single variable. For such concepts, a single variable has to be chosen on the basis of its being the "least inadequate" option. For example, "social class" is a concept with a range of dimensions—income, wealth, education, ownership/control of the factors of production, etc. When choosing a variable for "social class," you can generally select only one of these factors. Obviously, any single factor is inadequate as a

In Focus

Types of Validity

Validity is a serious issue in the research process for both quantitative and quali-tative methods. Let's think of the variable "happiness." It seems like a straight-forward concept, right? How do we know that someone is happy? Perhaps they smile a lot. Maybe they give lots of compliments. But how do we measure hap-piness? Let's look at the different types of validity using happiness as a variable as an example. The validity of a measure can be questioned in several areas:

- External validity refers to how closely your variable produces scores or to observations that are consistent with what we observe in real life. Put simply, we can ask ourselves the question "Does this variable appear to measure what we believe it is measuring?" For example, if our variable is "happiness," is it actually measuring "happiness" or something else? At face value, do the questions we ask appear to reflect the variable "happi-ness" or are they referring to some other sort of feeling such as euphoria or mania?

- Internal validity refers to the absence of errors in the research process. Projects fraught with errors are less valid than those that pay more atten-tion to detail. In our study of happiness, for example, there could be a number of threats to internal validity. Something bad can happen, such as the start of a war in the country where you are intending to conduct the study. This event would seriously affect the outcome of your study of hap-piness. Perhaps a variable that you have neglected to measure is affecting your participants' happiness. This could mean you aren't measuring hap-piness at all or you are missing a very important element that might inter-fere with your understanding of happiness. These are just some of the threats to internal validity in any study. There are issues related to cause and effect with this kind of validity problem. What if we have the rela-tionship wrong? If we have reversed the independent with the dependent variable, then we have a problem with internal validity as well.

- Construct validity refers to the relationship between the variable and the theory. The variable must adequately reflect the theory used in the re-search project. Psychologists are particularly concerned with this type of validity. In this science, much work has gone into devising indices that measure all sorts of psychological phenomenon such as depression, anx-iety, and obsessive compulsive disorder. Taking our "happiness" variable example from above, construct validity here would lead us to ask the question "To what degree have the questions we asked participants about happiness actually link to the theory of happiness we are using in our study?" Put another way, we hope that the questions we are asking ad-equately address the aspects the theory believes is important for under-standing happiness.

- Content validity refers to the degree of match between the definition of your variable and the range of possible values of that variable. In other words, are we capturing all the aspects of happiness? Detecting error in this variable is fairly easy. When you examine the question, are all the ranges of feeling included in your response categories? Is it possible to rank an answer as being unhappy as well as very happy? When you examine all of the questions you've asked about happiness, are all the possible indicators of happiness included? These are questions the researcher must ask themselves when considering whether or not the survey includes all the questions that could measure happiness.

variable. Therefore, you have to choose the variable that is the "least inadequate." The inadequacy of your chosen variable is a limitation of your research. The only thing that can be done about it is to describe the inadequacies of your chosen variable in your research report.

Usually, you cannot find the "perfect" variable for a given concept. There are no perfect variables. Variable selection is a matter of finding an adequate variable and being honest about its shortcomings.

Understanding Independent and Dependent Variables

Remember the issues of cause and effect that we introduced in Chapter 3? We return to this discussion here. Now that you have an idea of what a variable is and how to define or operationalize it, we need to be able to determine or differentiate the causes from the effects. This can be a tricky proposition for many new researchers. How do I know one variable causes something? Maybe it is the other way around? This is where we need to differentiate between independent and dependent variables.

The easiest way to separate the two is to think of the dependent variable as the problem part of the research question. It is the problem that originally led you, the researcher, to do the research in the first place! Let's return to a problem we've discussed earlier: "Does the number of hours studying affect academic performance?" Can you guess what "problem" we are investigating here? If you said "academic performance," you are correct! Because academic performance is the problem we are concerned about, it would be considered an "effect." In the language used by quantitative researchers, academic performance is then identified as the dependent variable.

"Hours studying" then becomes known as the independent variable. We want to know, does studying *cause* better academic performance? Although social science researchers are very careful about the use of the word "cause" (since it implies there is a direct relationship between an independent and a dependent variable—and we know that the social world is far more complicated

In Focus

Control Variables

Now that we know about independent and dependent variables, it's important to understand what a control variable is. Humans are complex. Our social environment, our biology, our culture, and other aspects of life combine in myriad different ways to affect all aspects of our life. Unlike the natural sciences, we cannot confine humans to one or two stimuli to uncover the condition of cause and effect. Imagine volunteering for a study where the experiment forced you to be exposed to a virulent strain of the flu, remain in a box for a month being fed a strict diet of crackers and water, and being exposed to light for only one hour per day to allow scientists to discover whether or not a new vaccine to prevent the common cold actually works? Not only is this impossible; it is inhumane and unethical experimentation.

So how do scientists control for outside influences when they want to study humans? One way is to use a control variable (or set of control variables). When researchers collect data from many people (think thousands of people), they need to have a way to "control" some aspects of their demographic characteristics and social and economic situations to examine cause and effect. Luckily, statisticians have devised a way to do this without resorting to isolation experiments! When using a control variable (or more likely a set of control variables), the researcher examines people who have similar conditions and economic and social situations in order to "control" the influence of these forces. This allows them to gain more confidence in their results. In the above example, if the researcher "controls" age, health condition, and other aspects of the participants' lives, they will have more confidence in their research results. The statistical methods behind how this works are a bit beyond this textbook, but what they do statistically is that they hold certain characteristics constant while they look for relationships between the independent and dependent variables. In our example of the creation of a new vaccine for the flu, the researchers "hold constant" several characteristics of participants. Often you will read that the experiment was carried out only in men. This is because there could be sex differences in how the vaccine is tolerated. The ethics of excluding women from such studies is extremely problematic and also beyond the scope of this book, but the idea is to remove the influence of biology (think how different hormone combinations might influence vaccine uptake) on whether or not the new vaccine works.

This is, in essence, the idea behind the control variable. Most often, researchers want to control many things such as sex, age, socioeconomic status, place of birth, etc., in order to examine the effects of one or two independent variables on the dependent variable. In the social sciences, this is done all the time using statistical measures, which we hope you will learn in your next research methods class.

than that), it is helpful at this stage for novice researchers to remember the difference between independent and dependent variables. We can remember that one type of variable (independent) may "cause" a change in the problem (dependent variable) we are studying. Since social scientists know that the world is complicated and rarely does one action "cause" something else, we use the language of independent and dependent variable.

In most research, there is only one dependent variable but many independent variables. Think of our previous example. We know that studying likely increases academic performance. We also know, however, that there are other variables that also affect academic performance. Can you think of some? We have already listed a few. Can you think of more? How about parents' educational attainment? There's research to suggest that children who live with parents who have university degrees are more likely to have higher academic performance than children who live in families without university-educated parents. But that's not the only influence on a student's academic performance. Availability of books in the child's household also is connected to academic performance. More access to books equals better academic performance.

In the above paragraph alone, we have identified parents' educational attainment and number of books in the household as two possible independent variables to include in our research project. In a quantitative research project, there are typically one or two "main" independent variables and many other "less important" independent variables. The main independent variables appear in the research question; the lesser variables do not. In our example above, this is why hours of studying is part of the research question but parents' highest educational attainment is not. We advise students to make a list of all the independent variables they wish to include in their study before embarking on data collection so that they do not forget to include an important variable in their research!

An Overview of the Research Process

What have we learned so far? It is important that we keep the various threads of development together.

When we encounter a problem, or a question about which we want to do some research, we first try to express that concern in a research objective or a hypothesis. This activity focuses our attention. It clarifies our interest. When stated as a hypothesis, our focal question or statement of concern asserts a relationship between two or more concepts. When stated as a research objective, our focal question defines, using concepts, our area of interest. We examined sample hypotheses such as:

> More study leads to better academic performance.
> Better nutrition leads to better academic performance.
> Greater family wealth leads to greater family happiness.

These hypotheses are all stated at the conceptual level. Each hypothesis states a relationship between ideas.

By now we can see that regardless of whether our research is guided and focused by a hypothesis or by a research objective, we select variables as observable indicators for the concepts we are studying. One of the more challenging and creative tasks in the research process is the discipline of finding measurable, observable, sensory variables that relate to the concepts that concern us. The following may help to clarify the steps in the research process that we have learned so far:

Step 1

Select, narrow, and focus the problem to be studied.
State the problem as either a hypothesis or a research objective.

Step 2

Select variables that relate to the concepts in the hypothesis or research objective.

As we go along, we will fill in the additional steps that have to be taken. Table 5.1 lays out some of the examples we have developed.

For each concept, we have identified several related variables. For each idea, we have suggested two or more measurable, observable indicators.

If a variable relates appropriately to the concept being studied, it is said to be a valid variable. The problem of validity deals with the success of our efforts to find measurable indicators of our theoretical concepts. One of the limitations usually discussed in research reports is the validity of the variables selected. How valid is this variable as an indicator of that concept? For example, how valid are test results as indicators of intelligence? How valid are changes in height and weight as indicators of growth, or the contents of someone's lunch as an indicator of the nutritional adequacy of their diet?

Table 5.1 • Concepts and their related variables

Concept	Variables Related to Concept
Academic performance	Grades
	Exam results
	Essay evaluations
	Examiner's reports
Nutritional adequacy	What is eaten for breakfast
	Contents of lunch
Growth	Height
	Weight
	Length of limbs
Classroom behaviour	Attention span
	Degree of disruption

Key Terms

Negative relationship 75

Operationalization 71

Positive relationship 75

Validity 79

Questions for Review

1. What is a concept? Give three examples.
2. Why aren't variables used in qualitative research?
3. What is a hypothesis?
4. Why doesn't qualitative methodology use hypotheses?
5. What is a variable?
6. What is the difference between an independent and a dependent variable?
7. Why are variables selected?
8. Table 5.2 lists a number of concepts. For each one, think of at least two variables.

TABLE 5.2 • **Finding variables for concepts**

Concept	Related Variables
Health	
Marital happiness	
Nutritional adequacy	
Maturity	
Socio-emotional development	

9. What is the difference between a hypothesis and a research objective? Why must variables be selected for both?
10. To what does the question of validity refer?
11. What is an operational definition? State the following hypothesis in an operational form:

    The better a student's nutritional status, the better that student's classroom behaviour will be.

Suggestions for Further Reading

Connelly, R., Vernon, G., & Lambert, P. (2016). Modelling key variables in social science re-search. *Methodological Innovations Online, 9*(1), 1–2.

Chambliss, D. F., & Schutt, R. K. (2010). Conceptualization and measurement. In D. F. Chambliss & R. K. Schutt, *Making sense of the social world: Methods of investigation* (3rd ed., pp. 73–106). Los Angeles: Pine Forge.

Roberts, L. W., Kampen, K., & Peter, T. (2009). *The methods coach: Learning through practice.* Don Mills, ON: Oxford University Press.

Suggested Web Resources

24/7 Science. (2017, April 4). *Part 1: Identify the independent and dependent variables with the MythBusters!* [Video file]. Retrieved June 28, 2018 from www.youtube.com/watch?v=l0jTMDtX4WY

Wiley, D. (2012, October 4). *Social complexity and scientific validity* [Video file]. TedX Bedford. Retrieved June 28, 2018 from www.youtube.com/watch?v=QwV07-xR43k

6 Finding a Variable's and Concept's Measurements

The general task of empirical research is to observe for changes in variables or in concepts. When testing hypotheses as we do in quantitative research, we observe for changes in at least two variables to see whether they change together in the manner we predict. When pursuing research objectives, we focus our attention on certain variables, observing either how they appear or how they change. In qualitative research, we do this in a similar way. We are looking for changes, but instead of having a predetermined list of variables, we are examining concepts that are usually named by the participants themselves. So how do we know whether variables have or have not changed? In quantitative research, we "measure" variables in different situations, such as two points in time. If the measurements are different, then we recognize that a change has occurred. If the measurements produce the same results, then we recognize that no change has occurred. But how do we "measure variables"? In qualitative research, we are not interested in quantifying change but looking at links between concepts. That is the main subject of this chapter, where we examine both the quantitative and qualitative methods of measurement.

The Logic of Measurement

The logic of measurement is something we take for granted. For instance, we frame many of our everyday perceptions in standard systems of measurement—thinking of distances in kilometres, the outdoor temperature in degrees Celsius, and the cost of gas in cents per litre. Also, we constantly use measuring instruments such as watches, speedometers, thermometers, rulers, and gas meters. Generally, we don't question the validity of these measuring systems and instruments—we tend to take their validity for granted.

In a quantitative research situation, where we set out to measure variables, we need to be more conscious of the logic of measurement. In deciding how variables should be measured, we face three major issues that require careful consideration:

1. What is it that varies in the variable?
2. By what instrument are we going to measure the way(s) the variable varies?
3. In what units are we going to report our measurements of this variation?

Table 6.1 uses the example of physical growth to show the relationship among concept, variable, measuring instrument, and units of measurement. This relationship is basic to all empirical research. To measure a variable, we need both a **measuring instrument** and **units of measure** in which to report variations in measures taken of the variable.

Table 6.1 • Measurement: The example of physical growth

Concept	Variable	Measuring Instrument	Units of Measurement
Physical growth	Length	Metre stick, ruler, tape measure	Metres, centimetres
	Weight	Scales	Kilograms, grams

Figure 6.1 clearly shows the order in which the problems facing you, as a researcher, should be handled. First, clarify the problem by defining the concepts to be studied. Second, identify variables associated with each concept. Select one or two variables for each concept. Third, for each variable, devise or select a measuring instrument. Fourth, select or devise units of measurement.

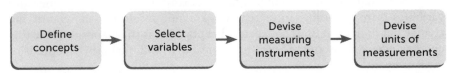

Figure 6.1 • The logical order of issues to be decided in measurement

Some additional examples may help to clarify the logical flow of the issues related to measurement. As you look at the examples in Table 6.2, try to think of other ways of measuring each variable or of other units of measurement.

Table 6.2 • Examples of the logical order of issues to be decided in measurement

Concept	Variable	Measuring Instrument	Units of Measurement
Physical growth ⟶	Height ⟶	Ruler ⟶	Centimetres
Physical growth ⟶	Weight ⟶	Scales ⟶	Kilograms
Heat ⟶	Temperature ⟶	Thermometer ⟶	Degrees Celsius
Fever ⟶	Temperature ⟶	Thermometer ⟶	Degrees Celsius
Vehicle performance ⟶	Speed ⟶	Speedometer ⟶	Kilometres per hour
Drunk driving ⟶	Level of alcohol in blood ⟶	Breathalyzer ⟶	Percentage by volume of alcohol in blood
Tire performance ⟶	Pressure ⟶	Pressure gauge ⟶	Kilopascals

Variable and Concept Measurement in the Social and Behavioural Sciences

For most variables studied in the natural sciences (physics, chemistry, and biology), there are generally accepted units of measurement and measuring instruments. Length is measured in metres; volume of sound, in decibels; time, in seconds (or fractions of seconds); and the strength of an electric current, in amps. Clocks are standard instruments for measuring time, speedometers commonly measure speed, and so on. This is because natural scientists have established widespread agreement on the nature of many of their common variables, such as velocity, current, and salinity. Since they generally agree on *what* they are measuring, they have general agreement on *how* variables are to be measured. Other researchers follow suit by using these units to take their measurements.

Agreeing on what is to be measured makes agreement on how to measure easier. For example, if you and your friends generally agree that the variable "height" is the physical distance from the floor to the top of a standing person's head, then agreeing on how to measure "height" is not so difficult, because at least there is general agreement on what has to be measured to obtain a value for "height."

In the social and behavioural sciences, however, researchers do not enjoy the same level of agreement about the nature of common variables such as class, status, and poverty. Consequently, they have not reached general agreement on how certain common variables ought to be measured consistently.

For example, any two social researchers will probably agree that there is such a variable as "educational attainment." However, many would disagree about the nature of this variable. One researcher might think of "educational attainment" in terms of a scale of the highest level of formal education a person has completed (none/primary/secondary/post-secondary schooling). Another might think of it in terms of the number of years in full-time education. Each measurement is valid. Different ideas about the nature of the variable would lead different researchers to adopt different measures, because they would have different notions about what they were measuring. In qualitative studies, instead of being called a variable, we would call "educational attainment" a concept. In these kinds of studies, the participant themselves would likely have their own idea as to what "educational attainment" meant to them. For example, one student might think that educational attainment refers to their mastery of a particular subject matter, such as their research methods course. Mastering the material in research methods could be considered "educational attainment."

Life as a researcher would be simpler, although perhaps less interesting, if there were generally accepted and standard ways of measuring the following common social and behavioural variables:

- social class
- academic performance
- political preference
- quality of teaching
- marital satisfaction
- sexuality
- ethnicity
- motivation
- race
- racial tension
- status
- social integration

Given this situation, researchers need to take great care when devising their own measures for variables. This process is one of the challenging aspects of doing research in the social and behavioural sciences.

The Importance of Measuring Variables and Concepts in the Social and Behavioural Sciences

The practice of adopting measures for variables strengthens several areas of the research process. First, it focuses data collection. Most variables are vague and might be measured by a large number of empirical phenomena. In quantitative research, marital satisfaction might be measured by frequency of sexual activity each month, average amount of time spent together, number of incidents of infidelity, and so on. In qualitative research, marital satisfaction would be defined by each participant. When asked about marital satisfaction, researchers would likely be given stories and personal examples rather than numbers such as frequency of sexual activity in a given week. Given the confusion that can occur as a result of having so many choices, researchers need to clarify variable and concept measures for their own benefit. Researchers must limit their choices and focus their data collection on those choices. If they do not, they will lack direction in their data collection and have less chance of carrying it out coherently.

Second, when data collection becomes focused, it can also become more streamlined and efficient. Data collection devices such as interview guides for qualitative research and tally sheets for quantitative research can be designed so that the data are collected clearly and easily organized for analysis.

Third, selection of measures allows for disciplined and consistent observation of variables and concepts in different situations and, therefore, disciplined and consistent observation of changes in them. If you apply the same measure of the variable "unemployment," such as the official national unemployment rate, over two consecutive years, you can compare the measurements and ascertain whether "unemployment" has changed. If you take different measures of unemployment for two consecutive years—for example, the official national rate in the first year and an unofficial rate in the second—you cannot compare those measurements to ascertain whether unemployment has changed. In qualitative research, the type of measurement doesn't matter so much. What matters is how the individual participants each perceives unemployment. For some people, working part-time would be considered as unemployment because of their preference for full-time work.

Fourth, variable measurements create a context in which data analysis and findings can be expressed clearly. A report on the findings of a study into unemployment that has no consistent measure for unemployment could read, "Given what they observed in welfare offices, job agencies, and the newspapers, the researchers judged that the level of unemployment has increased significantly over the past two years." This statement gives little indication of how the researchers analyzed the data or how the finding was reached. It is vague because it lacks a rigorous context. This kind of vagueness must be avoided in both qualitative and quantitative research.

Alternatively, the report might say, "The national level of unemployment increased significantly during the period investigated. At the beginning of year 1, the official national unemployment rate was 8.2 per cent. Subsequently, the rate increased by an average of 0.1 per cent every three months for the next two years. By the end of year 3, the official unemployment rate had increased to 9 per cent." These findings are expressed in a context that readers should be able to understand—that is, the context of the official unemployment rate, which is the measure for unemployment. Readers have a clear, rigorous context in which to consider the researchers' analysis and findings.

Measuring Variables and Concepts through Data Collection

Once a measure for a variable has been identified, data collection for the measure can be organized and conducted. The collection of such data is the process of variable "measurement."

Quantitative measurement

Imagine you have decided to research the variable "patriotism" among male and female adults on your street. You decide that the measure of patriotism for each group will be the "percentage of males/females who can sing the national anthem." When you collect data on this measure, you are taking measurements of the variable "patriotism" among males and females. Therefore, such directed data collection is variable measurement. From this point, the term "data collection" will be used to signify "variable measurement." Whether or not singing the national anthem actually measures patriotism is a topic we discuss later in this chapter.

There are three basic data collection techniques that researchers use for measuring variables. The first is observation, when researchers observe what is going on and record what they observe. The second technique is **interviewing**, when researchers ask people questions and record the responses. The third technique is examining records and documents. Each technique provides quantitative data for variables—that is, data that can be counted or measured. They also provide data for qualitative research designs; the information that is collected consists of the words, images, and perceptions of the participant and the researcher.

Qualitative measurement

As described earlier in this chapter, the measurement of variables in quantitative research has two major steps, which occur in the following order:

1. choosing an appropriate measuring instrument;
2. choosing units of measurement.

In the social and behavioural sciences, particularly when qualitative research is conducted, this procedure is less definite. After selecting a variable, social and behavioural scientists often develop their measuring instruments and units while they interact with their subjects or after they have stopped collecting data. This is also a valid form of measurement as it allows the participants to define research concepts using their own terms. Although the appropriate measuring instrument is identified before collecting data, in qualitative research, defining the variable happens after the data has been collected. This allows the researcher and the participants to identify and define the variables using their own words and experiences. To some, this is a more valid representation of behaviours, ideas, and reality than the more artificial process of pre-defining measurements as is done in quantitative research.

The quantitative research version of this process can be seen in the following descriptions of data collection techniques.

Using Observation to Measure Variables and Concepts

To conduct "observation" is simply to "watch what happens." However, all research observation is guided by a research question. Researchers do not just go and have a look at their subjects—they look for something in particular that is stated or alluded to, in their research hypothesis or objective in quantitative research, while in qualitative research, they are guided by the research question and nothing more. More important, what the researcher is looking for is best determined before the observation commences. Let's examine the requirements of a proper observational study for which the measure of the variable has been decided before data collection commences.

First of all, decide what to observe and state what it is. This is necessary because in practice, we all tend to get distracted by things that have some personal interest. The following experiment should demonstrate this tendency.

Take a Look

This qualitative exercise is best done with a group. It can be fun for three or more people. Go with the group to a coffee shop, a classroom, a playground, a street, an intersection, a football game—almost any place will do. Let everyone look at the scene around them for two minutes. This should be done quietly, with no sharing of views. Then ask everyone to write down everything they observed. After each person has finished writing, share your observations. Then ask the following questions:

- What did you find?
- Was there much similarity in what was seen?
- Were there many differences in what was seen?

The results of your exercise will probably show that different observers focused their attention on different things. If observation is not directed by the hypothesis or research objective, then we are likely to become distracted and gather irrelevant data. Therefore, we need to discipline ourselves—and any other researchers we are working with—to observe only those things that are relevant to the hypothesis. We do this by identifying the focus of our observations before we begin observing.

Next is an example of an observational study in which the observation is directed by the research hypothesis. You are assigned the task of studying the behaviour of car drivers in September during the first days at school. As a good researcher, you have decided to focus on the concept of "illegal driver behaviour" to keep the study manageable. Further, you have decided to study this concept at a busy city intersection for the four weeks leading up to the first day of school. Your research objective is clearly stated as follows:

> To observe illegal driver behaviour at one city intersection over a four-week period.

You have decided to use "traffic light infringements" as the measurable variable to indicate changes in illegal driver behaviour. Hence, the operationalized restatement of your research objective would be:

> To observe traffic light infringements at one city intersection over a four-week period.

You would not just occasionally look at the traffic and guess whether more or fewer drivers were running the red light. Rather, you would observe the intersection at specified times and ask, "How many motorists are driving through red lights?" The measure of your variable would be "the number of motorists who drive through red lights at specified times."

You might observe the intersection each Thursday during August (assume that 1 September is a Thursday). Each observation session takes place during the peak traffic period, 4 p.m. to 7 p.m. You could record the data for each observation session on a data collection sheet such as that shown in Figure 6.2.

Illegal driver behaviour—data collection sheet
Date: 1 August   Time: 4 p.m.–7 p.m.
Traffic light infringements (place a check mark for each observation):
✓ ✓ ✓ ✓ ✓ ✓ ✓ ✓ ✓ ✓
Daily total: 10

Figure 6.2 • **A data collection sheet**

Next, you would place the totals for each observation session on a data summarization form, which might look like Table 6.3.

Table 6.3 • **A data summarization form**

Weekly Observation	Date	Total Number of Cars Going through Intersection	Total Traffic Light Infringements
1	1 August	694	10
2	8 August	728	16
3	15 August	746	22
4	22 August	801	30

This summarization form provides a systematic record of observations. It shows a steady increase in traffic light infringements from week to week, which might support the hypothesis that drivers become increasingly reckless during the first week of August. From the table, you can construct graphs, charts, tables, or other presentations of your data.

If you studied more than one intersection, you would have a separate summarization form for each. You would also keep a different set of weekly tally sheets for each intersection. It would be essential to record data separately for each intersection in order to make comparisons later.

From the above example, you can see that to prepare for data collection, you need to do the following:

1. Select concepts.
2. Select variables.
3. Select a means for measuring those variables.
4. Design a means for recording the measurements you will make.

If all this is done before you begin to collect data, then data collection and analysis will proceed more smoothly and easily. Failing to measure and record your data properly will jeopardize the rest of the research process. Think back over the preceding example. Ask yourself the following questions:

- What concept was studied?
- What variable was selected?
- How was the variable measured?
- In what unit of measurement was variation in the variable reported?
- What data-recording devices were developed?

The concept was "illegal driver behaviour."
The variable was "traffic light infringements."
The variable was measured by observing traffic at a given intersection, at a given time, and by noting the total number of drivers who had driven through the intersection when the red light was showing.
The unit of measurement was "traffic light infringements."
Two recording devices were developed. The first was a data collection sheet, on which daily traffic light infringements were recorded and later summed. The second was a data summarization sheet, on which the total observed infringements at every observation session were recorded so that comparisons for each week could be made.

The research process has a set of steps. The first two steps—defining concepts and selecting variables—must be done in the order shown in Figure 6.1. However, in the social and behavioural sciences, the fourth step of the process— devising units of measurement—often occurs while data is being collected. This is demonstrated in the next example.

You may hear teachers make the following statement about the students at their school:

Twelve-year-olds behave better in the classroom than ten-year-olds.

You decide to research this claim. The concepts of the hypothesis are "age" (independent) and "classroom behaviour" (dependent). The independent variable can remain as "age." The dependent variable can be "disruptive behaviour." "Age" is relatively easy to measure (use date of birth); our problem will be to find measures for "disruptive behaviour."

This is a difficult variable to measure, because there are many types of disruptive behaviour, which occur spontaneously, and we cannot know for certain which ones will occur when we conduct our observation. Therefore, deciding on a single measure before entering the class could result in a waste of time.

A possible approach would be to devise a checklist of disruptive behaviours before observing the class. The total occurrences of all such behaviours would be the measure for this variable. Data could be collected separately for each group. Each time any such behaviour is observed in a class, we would place a check mark after the behaviour in the appropriate column, "12-year-old" or "10-year-old." If 10-year-olds exhibited more disruptive behaviour than 12-year-olds, the hypothesis would be supported by the data collected. Our completed observation checklist might look like that shown in Figure 6.3.

The data, which are now organized to clearly represent measurements of the variables, indicate that in this particular class, our measurement for disruptive behaviour was greater for 10-year-olds than for 12-year olds. The hypothesis that "twelve-year-olds behave better in the classroom than ten-year-olds" is supported by measurements of the variables.

As can be seen from Figure 6.3, an observation checklist focuses observation of the indicators of change in the variable and enables the researcher to record these observations as data, rendering them "countable."

The results make it possible to move from an impression to facts when describing observations. Instead of saying, "It was my impression that the 10-year-olds were more disruptive in class than 12-year-olds," you would be able to say, "The 10-year-olds were observed to engage in a greater number of disruptive acts than the 12-year-olds." To recap: observation is the most basic data collection technique available to researchers. The first difference between casual observation and scientific observation is that scientific observation is guided by a clearly stated question. The second difference is that researchers systematically measure and record their observations in ways that make the phenomenon being studied countable. Instead of impressions, researchers record numerical data:

Not: I think that drivers are breaking the rules more often during the first week of September.
But: In observations conducted at a certain intersection between 4 p.m. and 7 p.m. on each Thursday of August leading up to September 1,

Class: 10A	Date: 13/4/2016	
Observer:	Reece Ercher	
School:	Canadian High	
Teacher:	T. Cher	
Subject:	Social Etiquette	

Behaviour	12-year-old	10-year-old
1 Pokes neighbour	1	0
2 Talks out of turn	1	3
3 Whispers	0	6
4 Interrupts	5	0
5 Gets up from desk	2	3
6 Dozes	1	0
7 Throws something	2	2
8 Teases	1	3
9 etc.	etc.	etc.
10 etc.	etc.	etc.
Total disruptive behaviour in this classroom	24	32

Figure 6.3 • **An observation checklist for classroom behaviour**

the number of motorists who drove through red light signals increased from 10 to 30.

Not: It is my impression that 12-year-olds are better behaved in the classroom.
But: In one-hour observations conducted in each of six classrooms at such-and-such school, 10-year-olds were found to exhibit an average of 32 disruptive acts per hour while 12-year-olds exhibited 24 such acts.

Thus, one way of measuring a variable is by systematic observation, which is a process that occurs in both quantitative and qualitative research.

Some further examples of research using systematic observation to measure a variable may help to develop your skills in observation. Suppose you were interested in the area of racism in the workforce. Your background reading in this area has indicated that the opinions of racialized minorities are frequently given less weight, ignored, or ridiculed by non-racialized individuals. Moreover, you suspect that this occurs frequently in discussions involving financial decisions in the workplace. You decide to observe a group of co-workers interacting, using a qualitative technique, in order to test the following hypothesis:

> The evaluation of contributions to a conversation within a workplace will be affected by the ethnicity of the contributor.

This can be diagrammed:

Ethnicity is a **categorical variable** (also known as a nominal variable). A person is identified by their membership in one or more ethnic groups. We allow the participant to self-select/self-identify the ethnic groups to which they belong. The dependent variable poses a greater challenge. But you, the researcher, have decided to focus on the evaluation of opinions expressed in a workplace context. You will explore the variable by asking the following questions while observing a conversation between co-workers:

- Is the opinion ignored?
- Is the opinion discussed further?
- Is the opinion ridiculed or scorned?
- Is the opinion discounted?
- Is the person expressing the opinion interrupted?
- Is the person expressing the opinion ignored?

This is a list of indicators of a negative evaluation. You will measure each during the workplace conversation.

How can you conduct the study? Assume that you have received a workplace's permission to record its meeting conversation (we discuss ethical considerations in Chapter 9).

The human resources department at Acme Healthcare Services consists of four people: John, Helen, Ali, and Omar. Once you have the tape of their conversation, you and perhaps others can observe what was going on and fill out an observation checklist (such as Figure 6.4) for each person in the conversation.

The question is "What happens to each worker's contribution to the conversation?" On the checklist, note where on the tape the contribution began (using the counter on the tape recorder). Note the speaker. Then note what happened to the opinion.

By using a tape recording, you can go back over the event and check it. You can also have other people observe the event and compare assessments.

Person: Ali									
Type of conversation: Meeting					Fate of opinion				
	Location on tape	Opinion	Rejected	Ridiculed	Ignored	Interrupted	Discussed	Praised	Adopted
1	137	re: fiscal year end	✓						
2	236	re: new budget model		✓					
3	etc.	etc.							

Figure 6.4 • **An observation checklist for analyzing a conversation**

For example, let us assume that you recorded a conversation that took place during a meeting.

Part of the conversation might have gone as follows:

> **Ali:** (Trying to get a word in) I've got a problem.
> **John:** You always have problems. (He continues speaking about the new budget model.)

In this instance, Ali's comment was ignored. The conversation continues:

> **Ali:** Look, I've got to talk to you about . . .
> **Omar:** Be quiet and let John finish.

Here, Ali is interrupted and stopped by Omar. If this pattern continued throughout the conversation, there would be some evidence to suggest that some members of the human resources group did not take Ali seriously.

Once you have completed the checklist for each person in the conversation, you can compare the fate of each worker's contributions. You can compare managers with other workers and racialized workers to non-racialized workers. By comparing the number of negative fates (being ignored, discounted, ridiculed, or interrupted) to the number of positive fates (discussed further, praised, adopted, or taken seriously), you can assess differences in the variable "evaluation of contributions to a conversation."

Thus, one way to measure a variable is by systematic observation. The following questions should be answered in order to ensure that the proposed observation will yield useful results.

A Checklist for Research Involving Observation in Quantitative Research

1. Have you clarified and narrowed your hypothesis or research objective? What are the key concepts?
2. What variables are to be studied?
3. How is each variable to be measured?
4. Have you devised an observation checklist or some other means of systematically recording your observations?
5. Have you practised using your checklist?
6. In what units will the results be reported?

If you can answer these questions, you are probably ready to conduct your observations. You are not ready until you can answer all six questions.

Using Interview Guides and Questionnaires to Measure Variables and Concepts

The second common data-gathering technique involves asking people questions—that is, interviewing. In an interview, the researcher asks the respondent (the person being questioned) questions in a face-to-face situation or on the telephone using a **questionnaire**. A questionnaire is also used when the respondent reads and answers the questions on his or her own. Questionnaires measure variables by gathering answers to questions. In qualitative research, an **interview guide** (also known as an interview schedule) is used. An interview guide contains a list of questions, but unlike a questionnaire, the questions do not have to be asked in the order provided and new questions can be asked based on the outcome of the conversation between the researcher and participant.

Interview guides and questionnaires must collect data that are measurements of variables. This is extremely important. Each question must be relevant to one of the variables being studied. In other words, these techniques are not simply "fishing expeditions" or chats in which all sorts of interesting questions are asked.

There are two practical issues concerning the relevance of interview questions. First, remember that you are selecting questions for the purpose of measuring variables, not to satisfy simple curiosity. Resist the temptation to include a question just to satisfy your curiosity. Such questions do not generate useful data and often confuse or annoy respondents. More importantly, from an ethical standpoint, we should only ask questions that are relevant to addressing our research question and hypotheses. Anything more is intrusive, unlikely to yield important information anyway, and likely to be an unreasonable waste of a participant's valuable time.

The second issue concerns your planning and preparation. Never attempt to compensate for inadequate preparation by including questions that have only potential relevance to your variables. You must be honest with yourself about this. Before including a question, always ask yourself, "What do I plan to do with the data collected with this question? Which variable am I measuring?" If you cannot give a satisfactory answer, then your preparation is inadequate, and even if you get reliable data, you will have no framework for data analysis. You will not be able to articulate *what* you have measured, and your analysis will be very weak. If you realize that your preparation is inadequate, repeat the steps of the research process, and ask yourself the above questions again.

When consideration is given to what must be asked to measure the variables in a study, the choice of questions becomes straightforward, and the number of questions can be kept within an acceptable limit. It is hardly necessary to say that a short questionnaire is easier to answer and analyze than a long one. Identify which questions must be asked in order to measure a variable adequately, and discard the rest.

It is important to realize that most hypotheses and research objectives can be researched using more than one data-gathering technique. For example, the observational study of driver behaviour discussed earlier could have been done using interview techniques. The same data-recording form would be used, but each week the interviewer would visit or telephone the relevant police station and ask, "How many traffic light infringements were recorded by the cameras this week at 'X' intersection?"

Take another example. Remember this hypothesis?

More study leads to greater academic performance.

One of the operational forms of this hypothesis developed in Chapter 5 was

Increased studying leads to more satisfactory exam results.

This hypothesis was diagrammed as follows:

You have been assigned to do some research related to this hypothesis. How are you going to measure the variables? The problem is straightforward in this case. You can count hours of study easily and examination results can be recorded. For each student involved, you need to have a record of only two things—the number of hours students spent studying and their examination marks.

Assume that your history tutorial group is to have a one-hour examination in a month's time. You could ask each student to keep a record of the time spent studying history. Then get each student's examination mark. One way of doing this would be to give each student a mini-questionnaire such as the one in Figure 6.5.

This questionnaire measures the variable "hours spent studying" by asking each student to keep a record. It assumes that students will be honest in reporting both the time spent studying and marks. You could check with the tutor to

Student name (or identification number*): 2155260
I would be most grateful if you could help me with my research project.
It will not take much time.

We are to have an examination on 8 May. During the month between now
and then, please keep an account of the time you spend studying.

	hrs	mins			hrs	mins
April				April		
8	1	10		24		
9	1	10		25		
10	etc.			26		
11				27		
12				28		
13				29		
14				30		
15				May		
16				1		
17				2		
18				3		
19				4		
20				5		
21				6		
22				7		
23						

Total time spent studying: 45 hrs 30 mins
After the examination place your result in this blank.
Examination result: <u>49%</u>
Return the questionnaire to me.
Thank you.
Harry Doolittle
History 101
Canadian University

*Researchers sometimes assign numbers to people or to groups to preserve anonymity or
to organize their data when names are not important.

Figure 6.5 • A questionnaire on time spent studying

ensure that the marks were honestly reported. One problem with using questionnaires is that you depend on the honesty of the respondents.

Once you have collected all the questionnaires, create a form to summarize
your data. In this case, you have data on two variables, "time spent studying"
and "examination result," for each student. Using a form like the one in Table 6.4
may be useful to summarize and organize your data. It will be particularly helpful when it is time to analyze your data. The data summarization form preserves
all the data required by this study for later analysis.

Table 6.4 • **A suggested data summarization form**

Student Name or Number	Hours Spent Studying	Examination Result (%)
2155	45.5	49
2156	47.5	51
2157	48	53
etc.	etc.	etc.

Here are some helpful hints for writing questionnaires that ask the respondent questions of fact rather than questions about opinions or attitudes:

1. Clarify exactly what it is you want to know. It is also important to ask yourself why you are asking the question. How does this question relate to your hypothesis and your variables?
2. Be direct and simple when asking questions. For example, if you wish to ask some people about the number of vacations they have taken in the past two years, you could design your question in this very indirect and complex way:

   In the past 24 months, on how many occasions have you taken a leave of absence from your usual activities in your home and your place of work to take up temporary residence in another locality for the purposes of recreational activities, relief of stress, and a conscious perception of a change in environment?

   This question is very comprehensive, but the basic theme of its inquiry is not directly stated or easy to understand. A simple, direct question would be much more likely to get a clear answer. For example:

   In the past two years, how many times have you taken a vacation away from your home and paid job?

3. In most research, some questions are asked in order to obtain background information. They are often referred to as "demographic" questions. These questions request information about things such as the respondent's age, sex, religion, marital status, education, income, and number of children. Only ask demographic questions that are directly related to your project.
4. Make sure that each question is clear and elicits a simple response of fact and not one of evaluation as well. Rather than asking a mother how she feels about the amount of television her child watches, a question such as "How many hours did your child spend watching television last night?" will provide a clear and simple factual answer.
5. Address questions to the right person. If you wish to know how many hours workers spend doing their job in their workplace, do not ask the employer or co-workers, who might not know. Ask the worker—the person you are researching.

6. If you are asking for a response about a quantity of something, discourage the respondent from giving vague, general answers such as "often," "a great deal," or "quite a lot." Give a clear indication that the response should be in terms of your choice of variable measurement. For example:

   How much time per week do you spend watching television?

   (in hours) _____

   How often do you watch the news? (Circle your answer.)

   Once a day   Three times per week   Once per week   Never

7. Be sure that respondents are willing to answer your questions. Questions that are deeply personal, are offensively worded, or ask respondents to give secrets or unpleasant information are not likely to be answered. For example, respondents are often uncomfortable about revealing their income. Upwards of 30 per cent of all participants on surveys do not answer this question anyway.

8. Avoid informal terms, informal titles, and abbreviations. The question "Who would you vote for at the next election: the CPC or the Liberal party?" contains a set of initials, "CPC," and an informal title, "the Liberal party." Don't assume that respondents are familiar with such expressions. Formal terms, formal titles, and unabbreviated names are more likely to be familiar to respondents.

9. Avoid asking questions that raise more than one issue. Take the question "Should there be an increase in income tax, and if so, should the increase in tax revenue be spent on arts projects?" This question raises two issues: "Should there be an increase in income tax?" and "Should an increase in revenue be spent on arts projects?" If you wish to research two issues, then ask two separate questions: you will collect clearer information about respondents' positions on each issue.

10. Try not to use colourful or emotional language in writing questions. Here is an example:

    Do you agree that white sugar is "white death"? Yes/No

    This is an emotionally written question and should be stated in a more balanced way that does not attempt to motivate a "No" response. For example:

    Sugar is bad for health. Do you agree or disagree?

11. Do not word questions in such a way that the respondent is placed in an impossible situation—for example, "Have you stopped beating your wife?" or "When did you stop cheating on your exams?"

12. Examine your questions for assumptions that may be wrong. If you asked a group of schoolchildren "What does your father do for a living?" you would be making the assumption that all children in the group know a person whom they think of as their father. Of course, many children grow up without knowing such a person, some may have fathers who are currently unemployed or too ill to work, and others have experienced the death of their father. For them, the question would be inappropriate or hurtful.

13. It is always a good idea to test your questionnaire or interview guide. Conduct a trial with people who are not in your sample but are like the people you plan to study. If respondents give you the wrong information or cannot answer or understand your questions, then your questions and interviewing method need refining. Ask for their comments on the relevance and coherence of each question. This will help to ensure that your questionnaire gives you the information you want. When you do the real survey, the number of questionnaires containing useless responses will be reduced.

Attitudes

The questions examined to this point have been designed to gather facts from the respondent. "How much does your baby weigh today?" "How long have you studied?" "What was your result on the history examination?" Questionnaires and interviews are often also used to assess the respondent's attitudes, values, beliefs, or opinions. The construction of a questionnaire to measure opinions, attitudes, beliefs, and values is much more complex than simply asking questions of fact. Consider the following hypothesis:

> Students who have attended private schools are more sexist in their attitudes than students who have attended public schools.

The concepts involved in this hypothesis are

- social development environment of school; and
- sexism.

Note that the first concept emphasizes the social development aspect of the schooling situation. Students experience social development "only among those who are enrolled in private schools" or "among those enrolled in public schools." This is what the researchers were thinking about when they constructed the hypothesis. The concept does not emphasize the enrolment policy of the school attended, which is the most obvious essential difference between "public" and "private" schools. The essential difference considered by the researchers was "social environment." The variables are

- independent variable—school social environment (public versus private school);
- dependent variable—sexist attitudes.

The independent variable is a categorical variable and easy to measure. Respondents' school social environment is either private or public and this information is easy to access online. Those who have experienced both contexts can either be put into a third category (mixed schooling background) or eliminated from the study.

One of the first questions to be included in an interview guide or a questionnaire designed to measure this variable would be as follows:

Have the schools you have attended from the time you began school until now been (check one)

___ a.   private?
___ b.   public?
___ c.   both (private and public)?

Now comes the more difficult part. How do you propose to measure the dependent variable—sexist attitudes? This is a very complex variable. The abstract concept "sexism" refers to the belief that one sex is in some way inferior or superior to the other. You could not measure this variable by asking the direct, simple question "Are you sexist?" This approach would only measure the respondent's self-perception. What is required is a series of questions or statements (called **scales**) designed to evoke reactions from the respondents that, taken together, provide an indication of the respondents' sexist attitudes. While there are other kinds of scales, the attitude scale is one of the easiest to construct and analyze.

In this case, the respondent is presented with a series of short statements and is asked to agree or disagree with each statement. The questionnaire shown in Figure 6.6 is an example.

Why is this called an attitude scale? It is a device to measure variation in an attitude. Its values range between two points, and all respondents can be placed on that scale according to their responses to the questionnaire. It is also called a **Likert scale**, after the person who invented it. In a Likert scale, the respondent is asked to indicate agreement or disagreement with a series of short statements on a given (usually five-point) range of responses.

How does a Likert scale work? The responses are turned into a numerical scale by assigning numerical values to each response and summing up the results. The scale can be made to run from a low number (indicating a low degree of sexism) to a high number (indicating a high degree of sexism) by assigning low numerical values to those responses indicating non-sexist responses and high values to sexist responses. In Figure 6.6, agreement with statements **a**, **b**, **d**, and **e** indicates a sexist attitude; so does disagreement with **c**. The numerical values assigned to each response in this case would be

For **a, b, d, e**: SA = 5, A = 4, U = 3, D = 2, SD = 1

For **c**: SA = 1, A = 2, U = 3, D = 4, SD = 5

The highest numerical value on this scale would be 25. To get 25, a respondent would have to indicate strong agreement with items **a, b, d**, and **e** and

Name/identification number: _____

Date: _____

1 Have the schools you have attended since you began
   school been (check one):

   _____ a private?

   _____ b public?

   _____ c both (private and public schools)?

2 Please indicate your agreement or disagreement with the
   following statements by circling the response that most
   closely coincides with your own.

   SA = Strongly Agree; A = Agree; U = Uncertain;
   D = Disagree; SD = Strongly Disagree

   a A woman would never make
      a good judge.   SA A U D SD

   b Women are not as good at
      sports as men.   SA A U D SD

   c Women should be encouraged
      to seek leadership positions.   SA A U D SD

   d Men should not have to wash
      dishes.   SA A U D SD

   e Men should be left to make
      money decisions.   SA A U D SD

                                            Total

Do not write
in this area
1

2

a

b

c

d

e

Figure 6.6 • A questionnaire designed to test for sexist attitudes among those attending private and public schools.

strong disagreement with item **c**. If this scale accurately measures sexist attitudes, such a person would be sexist indeed. The lowest score on this scale would be 5. To get a score of 5, a respondent would have to indicate strong disagreement with items **a**, **b**, **d**, and **e** and strong agreement with item **c**. Respondents who failed to answer all the items would have to be eliminated from the analysis. By adding the numerical equivalents to each response, the respondent's total score can be calculated. Each respondent will have a score between 5 and 25.

If you were satisfied that responses to the statements you used gave an adequate indication of whether a person held sexist attitudes, this scale would be all you would need to test the hypothesis above. You now have a measure for each variable. The measure for the dependent variable is an attitude scale. The measure for the independent variable is provided by a single question related to the respondent's schooling. If you were to use a data summarization sheet, it might look like the one in Table 6.5.

Name or Identification Number	Type of Social Situation in School	Score on Sexism Scale
David	Private	.20
Johnny	Public	10
etc.	etc.	etc.

Table 6.5 • A data summarization sheet for a study of sexist attitudes

Remember to ask only questions that are expected to collect data that measure variables. It may be intriguing to ask other questions, but they are not relevant to your study. For example, it may have occurred to you that other questions could be included in a study on sexism. You might have wanted to know such things as

- Does the respondent's mother work?
- Has the respondent any sisters?
- What does the respondent's religion say about sexism?
- Have all the respondent's teachers been men or women?

While these are useful questions in themselves, because of the limitations of time and energy, the need to focus the study, and the intrusiveness of some of these items, the sole independent variable was the type of educational context. Questions dealing with other issues were not raised. The fact that you considered these factors potentially relevant but were not able to include them in your study should be noted in the limitations to your study.

Scales like the one above can be developed for nearly everything. Some basic rules should be followed in designing attitude scales. The following suggestions state an ideal approach and include compromises that are acceptable for student projects, which must be kept manageable so that skills can be learned:

1. The usual procedure is to begin with hundreds of items and, through testing and critical feedback, to narrow the number to between 20 and 50. Student projects should have no more than 15 items.
2. Each item should clearly state one issue. Here are some examples of what not to do. The following items have more than one key element:
   - Ten-year-olds are smarter and better behaved than eight-year-olds.
   - Ten-year-olds should not do the dishes, and eight-year-olds should not do car maintenance.
   - Ten-year-olds are better readers, but eight-year-olds have better imaginations.

   It would be much better if each item were split:
   - Ten-year-olds are smarter than eight-year-olds.
   - Ten-year-olds are better behaved than eight-year-olds.
   - Ten-year-olds are better at washing dishes.
   - Eight-year-olds cannot do car maintenance.

- Ten-year-olds are better readers than eight-year-olds.
- Eight-year-olds have better imaginations than ten-year-olds.

3. For a group of items to constitute a scale, each item must be related to a single theme. Each item should pick up a different aspect of the theme. For example, the above items all relate to the theme of the respective abilities of ten-year-olds and eight-year-olds. It would add a totally different dimension to the scale if items on respective social roles were included.

4. The range of response categories must be designed very carefully. They must be in one dimension (e.g., "agreement") and provide responses across the whole range of the dimension. Although research is done using a wide variety of response categories, several conventions have emerged. The five-point Likert-type response category is the most frequently used. These response categories are strongly agree, agree, undecided, disagree, and strongly disagree.

5. The more specific the response categories, the more accurate and precise the information gathered will be. For example:

Canada should support the creation of more nuclear power plants.
SA   A   U   D   SD

How often do you go to church?
Never   Yearly   Monthly   Weekly   Daily

How long did you study for this quiz?
Two hours   One hour   Half-hour   Quarter-hour   Not at all

Next are examples of unspecific response categories. These are examples of what not to do.

Canada should support the building of additional nuclear power plants.
Agree   Maybe   Perhaps   Not sure   Possibly not

Immigrants should be allowed to practise their cultures.
In principle   Sometimes   Only on Sundays   As long as no one
is offended

Here is a method for constructing a list of items. First, select and list a large number of items arbitrarily. Include any items that you believe to be even partially relevant to your variables. Then, begin sifting through the list, eliminating or rewriting items and retaining those that you believe to be relevant. Do this task with friends or other students. Also, give the whole list to a group of people similar to those for whom the questionnaire or interview is being designed. Talk to them afterwards about what you are trying to measure. They may have useful suggestions.

Try the following exercise to gain more experience in constructing a scale to measure an attitude. Suppose that you have been asked to do a study related to the creation of additional nuclear power plants. Your dependent variable is "attitude towards nuclear power plants." Assignment: construct a five-item scale measuring attitudes towards additional nuclear power plants. Remember that you must not only write the items but also decide what attitude dimensions to measure and the range of responses to offer. Then you will be able to specify the highest and lowest possible scores. Now ask yourself the following questions:

1. How did I measure my dependent variable? How did I measure attitude towards the building of nuclear power plants? List the items.
2. What range of responses do I want to offer?
    a. Simple agree/disagree or a broader range?
    b. Will I include a neutral position, or will I force the respondent to make a choice?
3. Should the statements be collectively designed so that "agreement" responses indicate an anti–nuclear power plant attitude or a pro–nuclear power plant attitude? Alternatively, should the statements be collectively designed so that agreement indicates an anti–nuclear power plant attitude for some and a pro–nuclear power plant attitude for others? Compare the following examples:

    a. There is no need for Canada to invest in new nuclear power plants.
        SA   A   U   D   SD

    b. Canadians should not mine uranium.
        SA   A   U   D   SD

    c. Nuclear-powered electricity should be used as an alternative to burning coal.
        SA   A   U   D   SD

    d. Development of nuclear power plants is a good public investment.
        SA   A   U   D   SD

    SA = Strongly Agree   D = Disagree
    A = Agree   SD = Strongly Disagree
    U = Undecided

    Agreement with **a** and **b** would be taken to indicate an "anti–nuclear power plant" response. However, agreement with **c** and **d** would indicate a pro–nuclear power plant response. It is usually better to vary the response pattern in this way. This prevents people from getting into the habit of checking the same column and helps to keep them awake and thinking.
4. What is the highest possible score on the scale constructed from the items you listed for question 1? What is the lowest? This will depend

on the number of items you included and the number of response categories you used. If you had five items and five response categories (SA/A/U/D/SD), then the highest possible score would be 25, and the lowest would be 5.

Here is how the highest and lowest possible scores are calculated for the scale formed by responses to the four items relating to nuclear power plant creation listed in question 3.

Say that you wanted your scale values to run from high (indicating strong pro–nuclear power plant attitudes) to low (indicating low pro–nuclear power plant attitudes). In this case, the numerical values assigned to each response would be as follows:

For **a** and **b**

SA	A	U	D	SD
1	2	3	4	5

For **c** and **d**

SA	A	U	D	SD
5	4	3	2	1

The reason for this is that agreement with **a** and **b** indicates an anti–nuclear power plant position. When agreement indicates the reverse position (pro–nuclear power plant, as in **c** and **d**), the numerical values assigned to the response categories are reversed. In this case, the highest possible score would be given to the person who made which responses? What is the highest possible score? What is the lowest?

A scale is a set of values among which respondents can be positioned on the basis of their response to items on a questionnaire or an interview guide. A scale is a device for measuring variation in a person's commitment to an attitude or the strength with which an attitude is held. Although there are many complicated issues in the measurement of attitudes, values, and beliefs, you should now be familiar with the basic logic.

There is one more form of questionnaire to be considered. This involves ranking options. Ranking is often used in research into values and preferences. Canadian voters are asked to rank candidates. Respondents can be asked to rank options, candidates, preferences, commodities, or values. Ranking forces respondents to express the relative strength of their attitude to all the options. It is important that all the options be of the same kind. Here is an example:

Rank the following values from highest (1) to lowest (7) in terms of their importance to you:

_____ loyalty	_____ independence
_____ excitement	_____ equality
_____ peace	_____ creativity
_____ security	

Here is another example:

> Rank the following qualities from most important (1) to least import-
> ant (8) in terms of how you would assess a potential marriage partner:
>
> _____ appearance   _____ sensitivity
> _____ honesty   _____ ability to earn money
> _____ integrity   _____ religiosity
> _____ sense of humour   _____ flexibility

Respondents, or groups of respondents, can be compared in terms of the way they ranked options. For example, you might find that a group of teenagers on average ranked sensitivity higher than appearance, while a group of adults on average ranked sense of humour above flexibility. Ranking options provides another way of measuring respondents' values and preferences.

The questionnaire and the interview guide are data-gathering techniques by which a researcher can measure the variables being studied. Questions are asked in order to gain information. This information can be factual: "How did you vote?" "How old are you?" "How much does your baby weigh?" Or questions may be asked in order to determine respondents' attitudes, beliefs, or values: "Would you support Canada becoming a republic?" "Do you believe in heaven?" "What is the most important thing in a relationship?"

Examining Records and Publications to Measure Variables and Concepts

The third common data-gathering technique is to measure variables by using the information kept in records or official reports of organizations, government agencies, or persons. Possibly the most familiar example of this kind of data is the Census of Canada. Government departments keep records of marriages, divorces, deaths, and financial transactions. Organizations keep records. Hospitals have records of admissions, discharges, and types of surgery performed. Some churches retain documents about members, marriages, baptisms, and amounts of money received and paid. Schools archive information about student numbers, student–teacher ratios, and subjects taught.

The basic problem with using records to gather data is gaining access. Some census material is available from Statistics Canada and many libraries and on the internet. The yearbooks or annual reports of many organizations often give information on various aspects of the organization. However, sometimes researchers do not know the location or nature of records—whether they are computer files, bound annual reports, or uncollated documents in filing cabinets. There are often occasions when a researcher does not know whether records are available or even exist. Other times, more detailed information does exist, such as with the master data files of the Canadian census—but this database is not accessible without obtaining permission from the government first. Finding records and gaining permission to access them can take a great deal of time.

The second problem is that the records often do not contain the exact information you want. The data may be for the province of Alberta when you are interested in the city of Edmonton. Or they may be for the city of Toronto, and you want only the records for the Jane and Finch neighbourhood. Information may have been collected in one way in 1996, in another in 2000, and in yet another in 2006, making comparison difficult.

If you are interested in such information as trends in divorce, birthrate, population growth, the proportion of people of a certain age in the population, average age at first marriage, average age at divorce, the number of children affected by divorce in a given year, the incidence of teenage pregnancy, or the percentage of weddings performed by civil celebrants, you can find answers in documents available from Statistics Canada or in a provincial website.

If you attend a post-secondary institution, these kinds of documents will be available to you in or through your library or on the internet, or you can make direct inquiries to Statistics Canada, which has a website and publishes census data on the internet and in reports.

Content Analysis

Content analysis is a different way to examine records, documents, and publications. It is very like an observation study. In a content analysis, a checklist is developed to count how frequently certain ideas, words, phrases, images, or scenes appear. However, in a content analysis, the thing being analyzed is a text, a film, or a radio or television program.

Recently, some of our students conducted a study of the perception of the aged in our society. This involved the researchers watching a night's television to observe the roles played by the elderly in television commercials. Another approach required that the researchers deduce the needs of the elderly on the basis of advertisements aimed at them.

The procedure for a content analysis of a television or radio program follows the same lines as an observation study. Recording the program allows the researcher to check the material several times for accuracy and make a more accurate analysis. It provides an opportunity for several people to do a content analysis of the same material, and it helps them to examine the material to see what things can be observed and counted. The steps for preparing a quantitative content analysis of television or radio material are as follows:

1. Clarify and narrow your hypothesis or research objective. What are the concepts involved?
2. Identify variables related to the concepts under study. This may involve watching some television programs or listening to radio programs to become familiar with what there is to be observed.
3. Devise a way to measure the variables. Develop a checklist to count how often the things you have selected to observe appear—for example, the number of advertisements featuring the elderly or the number of advertisements in which women play roles of authority.

4. Decide what programs to examine. Decide whether your **unit of analysis** is a time period (e.g., two hours of Wednesday-night prime-time television) or a specific program, or a number of advertisements over a period of time (e.g., the first 10 advertisements screened after 6 p.m. on a particular cable channel on Friday nights).
5. Devise a data summarization sheet.
6. Collect your data by doing the observations you propose.
7. Summarize the results on the data summarization form.

The Content Analysis of Published Material

Published material is a storehouse of material for content analysis. Magazines, website articles, periodicals, books, novels, and textbooks—all can be subjected to content analysis. The logic of research using content analysis of published material is the same as the logic of other kinds of research. The first step is to clarify your hypothesis or research objective. Once the concepts under study have been identified, variables that are related to the concepts can be selected. Then the problem of how to measure and record variation in the variables can be tackled. Once measurement problems are settled, the units of measure in which to report findings can be decided upon. Remember this flow?

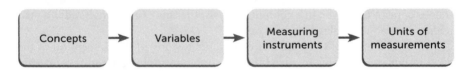

This same flow of issues occurs in designing research using the content analysis of written material. Let us assume that you are interested in the area of sex-role stereotyping. You are interested in the origin of sex-role stereotypes—where do they come from? One possible source would be children's books. This might lead you to ask whether there has been a change in the amount of sex-role stereotyping in children's books. How could you measure change in the amount of sex-role stereotyping over a number of years?

One possible way would be to examine the reading material used to teach reading to Grade 1 students. What are Grade 1 children reading today compared with 20 years ago? To do this, you need access to the material used 20 years ago and the material used now. Next, you need to develop a set of indicators of role stereotyping. What roles do girls and boys play? What roles do men and women play? What activities characterize each sex? Do the illustrations promote sex-role stereotyping? Once you have begun to identify countable features, you can devise a checklist on sex-role stereotyping in Grade 1 books.

Or you might devise a set of questions like the ones in Figure 6.7.

In this way, a scale of sex-role stereotyping in literature can be developed. By applying it to literature from different times, changes can be observed and systematic comparisons made.

	Check the appropriate column				
	Always	**In over half the stories**	**Half and half**	**In less than half the stories**	**Never**
1 Are boys shown to dominate girls?					
2 Are girls shown to win against boys?					
3 Is unisex clothing used?					
4 Are women shown in traditionally male roles (e.g., a female physician or a female priest)?					
5 Does a male ask a female for help or directions or information?					
6 Are females shown to be helpless?					

Figure 6.7 • **A content analysis questionnaire**

Here is an example of research using content analysis of published material. Since the Second World War, an increasing proportion of Canadian married women have been employed. Has this movement into paid work outside the home had an impact on the publications directed at women? The hypothesis could be this:

As the proportion of women who are employed outside the home increases, there will be an increase in the attention paid to working women in the publications aimed at women.

This can be diagrammed as follows:

Since we know that there has been an increase in the proportion of married women who are employed, we only need to find variables to provide an indication of change in the dependent concept—change in content of material published for women. Several approaches are possible.

First, the number of magazines published for women may have changed between 1945 and the present. Are there more or fewer now? Are some of the new ones directed mainly at employed married women? You might gain help from your library on the number and kind of women's magazines that have come and gone since 1945.

A second approach would be to select one title that has been published continuously through this time. For example, *Chatelaine* and *Vogue* have been published continuously since 1945. It would be interesting to see whether the number of articles that appeal to working women, or that address the problems faced by working women, has changed. Here you must decide what to count. Do you count articles or the number of pages? Do you examine just one issue or an entire year of issues? It would be better to select more than one issue in each year in case the issue you chose for a given year is atypical. The results would be reported as the number of articles or pages per year appealing to working women.

A third approach would be to see whether the magazine's attitude to the idea of married women working has changed. It is possible that over the years *Chatelaine* has devoted roughly the same number of articles or pages or proportion of space to the subject of employed married women but that its attitude has shifted from disapproval to approval. This would require not only counting articles or pages devoted to the subject but deciding whether each was favourable, unfavourable, or neutral. Your record of research might look like Figure 6.8.

Magazine: _____   Issue: _____

Year: _____   Total no. of pages: _____

Total no. of articles: _____

Title of Article	Number of Pages	Orientation Expressed
Total no. of articles	**Total no. of pages**	

Figure 6.8 • **A record sheet for a content analysis of articles dealing with employed married women**

Let us say that 12 issues for each of the years 1945 and 2018 were read. There would be 24 record sheets, one for each issue. The analysis would be by year.

The classification of the content of the articles as favourable, unfavourable, or neutral would proceed on similar lines. Additional categories might need to be introduced after all the material has been read.

Content analysis can be fun. Popular music, movies, websites, social media, and magazines are interesting and valid items to analyze.

Before you begin content analysis, refer to the following checklist:

1. Clarify the hypothesis. What concepts are involved?
2. What variables can be used to indicate changes in or differences between the concepts?
3. How can this variable be measured using content analysis? What is to be counted—pages, words, articles, pictures, or something else? Devise a record sheet for recording your data.
4. In what units are the results to be reported—pages per issue, words per year, articles per issue, or something else? Devise a data summary sheet for reporting your data (for example, Table 6.6).

Table 6.6 • **A data summarization sheet for content analysis**

	1945	2018
Total pages		
Number of pages devoted to employed married women		
Proportion of total pages devoted to employed married women		
Total number of articles		
Number of articles devoted to employed married women		
Proportion of articles devoted to employed married women		

Validity

At the end of Chapter 5, the problem of validity was discussed. This is concerned with how accurately a variable fits a concept. For example, is "absence of disease" a valid indicator of health? Is a history test a valid way to test a student's grasp of historical material? Most variables can be questioned in one way or another.

The problem of validity is most acute in the construction of questionnaires or interview guides to "measure" a person's attitudes, beliefs, or values. For example, it is necessary to ask whether the items used to measure variation in a person's attitudes to the building of additional nuclear power plants, developed earlier in this chapter, are valid. On reflection, one of the items does not deal with nuclear power plants but with the mining of uranium. It is quite possible for someone who is very much against nuclear power plants to favour the peaceful use of nuclear material in other ways, such as medical diagnostics. This item does not focus clearly on the variable to be measured. Therefore, it lacks validity. Similarly, earlier in the chapter, we suggested that the percentage of people who are able to sing the national anthem would be one way to measure patriotism. Is this a valid measure of patriotism?

It is important to be aware of the problems of validity. In professional research, a great deal of time and effort is spent ensuring validity. As a student, there are things that you can do, too. In addition to being very careful in your construction of measuring devices, record sheets, questionnaires, and checklists, you can ask your friends and your professor to comment on your measures. This may help to increase the measures' validity. Moreover, you can pre-test scales using individuals known to exhibit extremes of the dimensions you are trying to measure. For example, what would it mean for the validity of your scale if someone whom you knew to be very sexist got a low score on a sexism scale that you had devised? Clearly, you would have to rework your scale! It is very important to pre-test your research instrument to ensure that it is working properly before actually doing your research.

Validity, in both qualitative and quantitative research, is very important. Although data are collected differently and the way we define and identify variables in each method varies, we are still concerned that the variables accurately measure the concepts we are interested in.

Reliability

The question of **reliability** is different from the question of validity. When someone asks whether a measure is reliable, they are asking whether different researchers using the same measuring device would get the same results when measuring the same event. For example, will a group of 10 students who weigh the same baby, one after another, record the same weight? Is a baby-weighing scale reliable? This may depend on how difficult it is to hold the baby still, which is relevant to the reliability of a weighing scale. The basic question is whether the measurement device employed provides the same results when the test is repeated. This is called test-retest reliability.

The reliability of observation techniques is often questioned. Will a group of observers report the same observations? This is also a problem in content analysis. Will several people agree that article X dealt with a topic related to the needs of working married women? Will they agree that it recognizes the right of married women to work? The more agreement there is in coding observations on content analysis, the more reliable the instrument is.

A feature of recorded or published materials that facilitates the testing of their reliability is that others can review the exact material. When there are differences, it is possible to sort them out with those who are evaluating the material. Was the daughter's comment ignored, or was it ridiculed? If you are unsure, you can go back to that section of the tape and check. The challenge to the reliability of a measure is that different researchers using the same measure may record different results.

Questions of reliability refer to problems in the accuracy of the measuring device. Questions of validity refer to the appropriateness of the measuring device. It is important for you to be aware of both these problems. It is appropriate to include questions about validity and reliability in any discussion of the limitations of your research.

In quantitative research, reliability is very important. We want to be able to ensure that if another researcher asked the same question of the same people, we would get the same answers. Alternatively, we want to be able to amass a quantity of results across different populations but still get the same results. For example, when I ask Canadians what their ethnic origin is, I want them to understand that we are asking about their cultural heritage. If we ask the same question of Americans, we hope that the participants understand the question in the same way. In qualitative research, however, reliability is not as important. Yes, qualitative researchers can and do have reliable research, but they are not concerned with whether or not another researcher can exactly replicate the results. This is because qualitative research is concerned with understanding phenomena in a small scale, not necessarily generalizing the results to a larger population. Qualitative researchers understand that personal experience is unique and not necessarily shared by larger groups of people, an issue we discuss in the next chapter.

In Focus

Process of Qualitative Research

Variable measurement in qualitative research takes a very different approach. The purpose of qualitative research is to provide an inductive view of society. Using the inductive approach, qualitative researchers do not want existing theories to prejudice their observations. Instead, they prefer that their research participants give their unbiased views of the topic. In this way, the researcher can obtain more authentic observations and analysis without being biased by previous findings and prescriptive theories. Because of this approach, data collection and identification of variables become a "self-feeding" process rather than the linear, step-by-step process that quantitative researchers prefer. This means that data collection occurs, after which data analysis and identification of variables are conducted; these steps are then followed by more data collection and more interpretation until the research question is saturated (i.e., no new data or variables or interpretations can be made by collecting additional data).

Continued

The following is a visual interpretation of the research process:

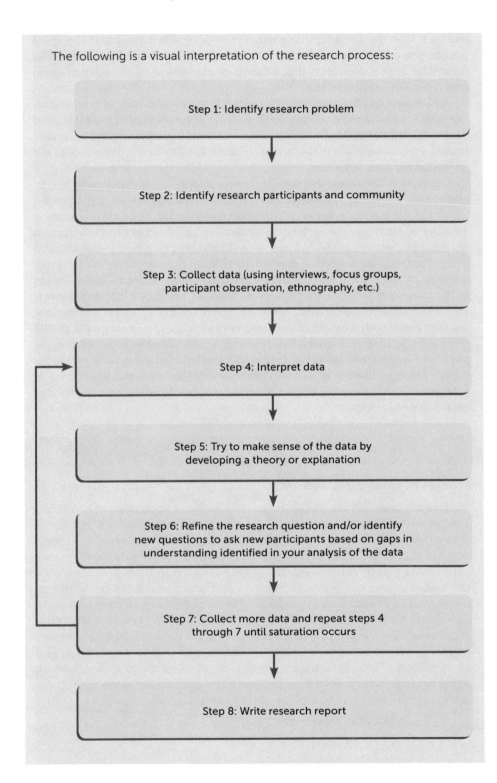

Step 1: Identify research problem

Step 2: Identify research participants and community

Step 3: Collect data (using interviews, focus groups, participant observation, ethnography, etc.)

Step 4: Interpret data

Step 5: Try to make sense of the data by developing a theory or explanation

Step 6: Refine the research question and/or identify new questions to ask new participants based on gaps in understanding identified in your analysis of the data

Step 7: Collect more data and repeat steps 4 through 7 until saturation occurs

Step 8: Write research report

As you can see by this diagram, data collection, identification, and definition of variables and data analysis are all intertwined in a feedback loop. The identification of variables is dependent on individuals who are interviewed, observed, or studied. Definition of the concepts is determined by the research participants. These definitions are continually refined by the researcher as she talks to more people (or observes different situations). Once new variables stop arising from the research and once definitions of variables begin to crystallize, the researcher may be confident that there is some "agreement" being reached and it is time to stop collecting data and move on to writing the research report.

Summary

Once you have clarified your hypothesis and selected variables for study, the issue of measurement must be considered. Three basic techniques for measuring variables quantitatively have been discussed: observation techniques, questionnaires or interview guides, and content analysis. The importance of developing systematic data-recording forms and data summarization forms has been emphasized. The fact that you collect data to measure variables in a hypothesis is the major emphasis of this chapter. Data are gathered to measure variables you have clarified beforehand.

In qualitative methods, variable measurement is approached differently. This type of research uses different data—words, images, and subjective observations—to give voice to the research participants. As a result, variable measurement comes after the data have been collected and is part of the analytical process.

Key Terms

Categorical variable 98
Content analysis 113
Interviewing 92
Interview guide 100
Likert scale 106
Measuring instrument 88

Questionnaire 100
Reliability 118
Scale 106
Unit of analysis 114
Units of measure 88

Questions for Review

1. What are the basic steps in preparing to do research involving observation as a data-gathering technique? How might they differ between qualitative and quantitative researchers?
2. What is the purpose of a checklist for observation?

3. What is the purpose of a data summarization sheet?

4. What are the basic steps in preparing research involving the use of a questionnaire or an interview guide?

5. What is the difference between an interview guide and a questionnaire?

6. How do you determine the highest and lowest possible scores on a scale framed by responses to items designed to measure a respondent's attitudes, values, or beliefs?

7. What does it mean to reverse the polarity of response for an item? What impact does this have on the way the responses are scored for scale construction?

8. What are the steps involved in preparing to do research involving the use of content analysis?

9. What is the problem of validity?

10. What is the problem of reliability?

11. Earlier in the chapter, we indicated frequency of sexual activity each month, average amount of time spent together, and number of incidents of infidelity as indicators of marital satisfaction. Are these valid measures of this concept? If so, why? If not, why not?

12. Explain how reliability is understood by quantitative and qualitative researchers. Are their understandings the same or different?

13. Is validity a concern for qualitative researchers?

14. What are six tips for creating questions in qualitative research?

15. In what aspects is asking a question different for qualitative versus quantitative research?

16. Where are some places you can find information on unemployment rate and average income among Canadians?

Suggestions for Further Reading

Chambliss, D. F., & Schutt, R. K. (2010). *Making sense of the social world: Methods of investigation* (3rd ed.). Los Angeles: Pine Forge.

Dillman, D. A., Smyth, F. J. D., & Christian, L. M. (2014). *Internet, phone, mail and mixed-mode surveys: The tailored design* (4th ed.). Hoboken, NJ: John Wiley.

Mason, J. (2017). *Qualitative researching* (3rd ed.). Thousand Oaks, CA: Sage Press.

Roberts, L. W., Kampen, K., & Peter, T. (2009). *The methods coach: Learning through practice.* Don Mills, ON: Oxford University Press.

Suggested Web Resources

Chumney, F. (2016, October 8). *Types of reliability* [Video file]. Retrieved April 11, 2018 from www.youtube.com/watch?v=p2YtZn2xc-k

Fernandez, K. (2014, September 26). *Survey design essentials: 7 tips for good survey questions* [Video file]. Retrieved April 11, 2018 from www.youtube.com/watch?v=Iq_fhTuY1hw

7   Selecting a Research Design

Qualitative or Quantitative? Which Approach Should You Use?

Even the most accomplished researcher must decide which method to use. Good researchers will use the approach that best fits the research question. Some research questions are best answered by gathering rich, deep, descriptive data from a small number of participants. Other research questions are more amenable to more large-scale, numerical data gathered from a larger number of participants. The first step for students is to decide what kind of data are needed to answer the research question. This chapter provides researchers with the basic information necessary to make that decision by providing an overview of selected modes of data collection. We have tried to differentiate qualitative from quantitative research in earlier chapters. Here this distinction is made clearer as we discuss the many ways to collect data. Some of the most popular methods are described here.

Qualitative research is intended to gather a great deal of information on a small number of individuals or groups with specific characteristics. Research questions that are best answered using qualitative research are based on previous observations and research on a particular phenomenon but require deeper exploration of the issue. Suppose that you have been assigned a research project to understand why international students decide to remain in Canada after they graduate from university. We know that many international students return home after they graduate, but others wish to stay in Canada. We already know how many stay in the country, since we can gather these figures from the federal government department Immigration, Refugees and Citizenship Canada, but we know very little about their decision-making processes. We do not have a hypothesis, since the existing research does not deal with the motives of international students for remaining in Canada. We do, however, have some hunches, based on our knowledge of the decision-making processes made by other immigrants coming to Canada. Many students wish to stay because they feel they have better job prospects or may have a better standard of living in Canada. Others may marry a Canadian or have children enrolled in school here. Still others may have experienced changes in their family of origin, or the political situation in their home country may have changed since they arrived in Canada. As researchers, we want to figure out why they stay, but we do not want to prejudice their ideas by asking them a series of directed questions as we would in a quantitative study. This is an example of a research project that would be amenable to a qualitative data collection strategy.

CASE STUDY

An Overview of Qualitative Research Methodologies

Because qualitative research is not linear and does not want to prejudge the observations and results in its conclusions, the methodologies used by these researchers are multiple, complex, and very interesting! Since the purpose of qualitative research is to obtain an authentic representation of the problem through the eyes of participants, we must use multiple ways of collecting data. Researchers in recent decades have created an array of different ways to collect qualitative data from photovoice exercises (giving participants cameras and having them take pictures that are visual representations of their daily lives), to urban mapping exercises (giving participants maps of their neighbourhood, showing available transportation, to identify places where they feel included and excluded), to cultural collages (where participants fasten objects, photos, and drawings to a poster board to represent their thoughts on a particular topic). The following are some of the more "traditional" methodologies used by qualitative researchers to collect their data. What all these methods have in common is that researchers avoid the "artificiality" of standardized tests and subject controls found in surveys and natural experiments.

Focus groups: a type of qualitative group interview. See the case study in Chapter 4 for definition and example.

Participant observation: a method of collecting data where the researcher immerses herself in the lives of the individuals, group, or situation she is studying. The researcher attempts to understand the situation or context from the view of the participants for a more authentic, experiential view of the problem. As a result, the researcher gains "insider" knowledge of the social context and develops personal relationships with her research participants. Trust between the researcher and the participant contributes significantly to a better understanding of the situation.

Unstructured interviews: the researcher interviews participants but does not have a list of questions. The interviewer introduces the research problem and allows the participant to speak about the issue freely. This reduces researcher interference (or bias), especially by avoiding asking direct questions that may influence the types of answers given by the respondent. These interviews take a conversational tone and may identify new aspects of the problem that the researcher had not previously considered. In this way, the researcher may identify new areas of research and develop new theoretical perspectives given the deep, detailed, and unbiased information provided by participants.

Autoethnography: a methodology where the researcher uses him or herself as the source of data collection. Like an autobiography, in the autoethnographic method, the researcher reflects on their life history and how it has been shaped by their experiences and the outside world.

Art-based research: a non-traditional/non-invasive data-gathering procedure to understand various aspects of human life that can be difficult to for some individuals to vocalize. Sometimes, this method is used in a professional setting when retelling and remembering past events can be too traumatic to discuss using words. Poetry, for example, has been used in management research to rethink organizational structures in businesses. It has also been used when interviewing young children who have experienced war or witnessed traumatic events. Art-based research has been successfully used with students, persons who are unable to verbally communicate, refugees, soldiers, PTSD sufferers, and victims of war and torture.

What are the characteristics of qualitative research? For one thing, the research question is larger, more complex, and more explanatory in nature than questions used in quantitative research (see later in this chapter). It may have the word "why" or "how" in it. It is not intended to test relationships among a small number of independent variables. Instead, it is supposed to contextualize a situation or tell a story about the topic. The idea is to provide a holistic account of a phenomenon or social problem.

An example of a topic for qualitative studies is described here. The suicides of Amanda Todd and Rehtaeh Parsons are two high profile examples of teen suicides in Canada. Both committed suicide after months of cyberbullying by classmates and friends. Sadly, their deaths, while tragic, are not unique. Bullying and specifically cyberbullying is on the rise in North America. Research has also found that LGBTTQ (an acronym for lesbian, gay, bisexual, transgender, Two Spirit, and queer/questioning) youth are far more likely to be bullied and commit suicide than straight youth. Suicide is the second leading cause of deaths of adolescents in Canada (Statistics Canada, 2018). Clearly, bullying and suicide are both a public health and a social problem. We know a lot about the rates of teen suicide and we even know some of the factors that increase the risk of committing suicide. What we don't know is how schools are structured and how they might contribute to this problem. Tracey Peter and her colleagues have investigated this phenomenon and find that "students who attend hostile schools are more likely to experience depression, which in turn leads to a greater likelihood of suicidal behaviour (Peter, Taylor, & Campbell, 2016, p. 195). They interviewed LGBTQ and straight youth about their perceptions of their school environment and how bullying was dealt with. Analyzing their interview results, they found that LGBTQ youth were not "attached" to schools because they didn't feel that they belonged there. This feeling was compounded by a sense that the teachers did not use respectful language when discussing sexual issues and tended to assume everyone was straight. They felt unsafe at school, and when they were bullied their impression was that the teachers did not take their complaints as seriously as they did with straight students. In this research, Peter and her colleagues were able to gather data that could not be collected in a survey. This experiential data gives researchers a view of the everyday experiences of bullied LGBTQ youth. Their observations, feelings, experiences, and perceptions of how others reacted to these situations are difficult to gather using other data collection means. The experiences their participants shared provide researchers, policy-makers, educators, and health-care professionals some idea of the situations where bullying occurs and how bullying is directed at LGBTQ youth.

In contrast to the rich detail provided by qualitative research, quantitative research is used to test relationships between two variables. This relationship is formulated by devising a hypothesis. A hypothesis states that a relationship exists between two or more concepts. In a research project, the hypothesis is the reference point on which researchers focus their activity. The role of a research objective is the same. Researchers should keep a statement of their hypothesis or research objective visible as a constant reminder of their specific task.

How does the hypothesis guide the research? The hypothesis claims that there is a relationship between concepts X and Y. Research is undertaken to determine whether there is evidence to support this claim. In order to carry out the research, two general tasks must be done. First, the concepts in the hypothesis must be defined in such a way that they can be measured. In Chapters 5 and 6, we learned how to select and measure variables that relate to concepts. However, research requires more than measuring the concepts in a hypothesis.

The second task is to find evidence that the relationship stated in the hypothesis actually exists. Measuring X and Y is one thing. Finding evidence that X and Y are related is another. While the issues concerning measurement of concepts are narrowed by the operational definitions, the existence of a relationship between X and Y is assessed by the research design.

Let us look at the diagram of a hypothesis again:

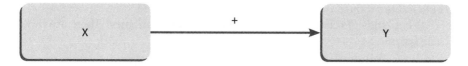

This hypothesis states that a change in X will produce a change in Y and that the nature of the relationship between X and Y is such that an increase in X will produce an increase in Y. One of the hypotheses we have been using as an example states the following:

More study leads to increased academic performance.

The conceptual form of this hypothesis was diagrammed:

A number of variables for each of the concepts were identified (if you cannot remember how this is done, return to pages 77–79 in Chapter 5). The selected variables were "number of hours spent studying" for the concept "study" and "exam results" for the concept "academic performance." The hypothesis can be restated in its variable form as follows:

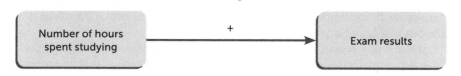

In Chapter 6, we devised measures for each variable. Students were asked to keep a record of the time they spent studying and to state their result for the history exam. The operational definition of the hypothesis—the statement of the hypothesis as a relationship between measures—would be as follows:

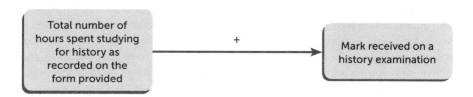

You may be thinking, "Surely that is enough!" But it is not. You do not have a measurement of the relationship between study and academic performance.

How do you know that, generally speaking, it was the amount of study that produced the examination result? How do you know that a change in the independent variable produced a change in the dependent variable?

What kinds of relationships can there be among variables? There are three basic types:

1. The variables are causally related—that is, a change in one variable will produce a change in the other variable.
2. The variables are only associated—that is, they change together, but this happens through no perceived causal relationship and, in the absence of contrary evidence, could be a coincidence.
3. The variables are neither causally related nor associated.

It is relatively easy to determine whether two variables are associated. It is more difficult to determine that X (independent variable) causes Y (dependent variable). To establish that two variables are causally related, it is necessary to show the following:

1. X and Y are associated.
2. Changes in the dependent variable, Y, always occur after changes in the independent variable, X.
3. All other variables that might produce changes in Y are "controlled"— that is, their possible effects on Y are accounted for.

As we shall see, the experimental research design is the only design truly adequate for testing a causal hypothesis. Given that an experimental design is not always possible, practical, or permissible, other designs are used to approximate an experimental design or to provide some information relevant to the test of a causal hypothesis.

Choosing a research design is one of the most important and difficult parts of doing empirical research. For example, you may feel certain that an increase in study will produce an increase in academic performance. But how do you prove that these concepts are related in this way? How do you design your research to answer this question?

How Do You Choose a Research Design?

Research designs should be selected so that the collection strategies provide the data that will best answer the research question. Therefore, one of the first considerations in selecting a research design is to determine "What kind of question is being asked?" Table 7.1 is a summary table of research designs and the questions each asks. Review it from time to time as we go on to describe the various methods.

If the hypothesis you are testing asks, "Does a change in the independent variable produce a change in the dependent variable?," then an experimental design is required. However, an experiment is not always possible. What can be done then? Use one of the other research designs, and mention in the limitations section of your research report that it is not the ideal design. Make sure that you draw only such conclusions as your data and research design permit.

Once you have formulated your hypothesis or articulated the aspects of the problem you are researching, the next step is to decide how you will collect your data. As Table 7.1 indicates, there are five basic types of research design. Each type is appropriate for a different general kind of research question or problem, and the type you select depends on your hypothesis or research objective. In this chapter, we will examine the five types of research design by using each to examine the relationship between study and academic performance. Although one design may be more desirable than another, each can make a contribution to our knowledge about the relationship.

Table 7.1 • The five basic types of research design

	Type of Design			Question Asked
1	Simple case study			
		Ⓐ		What is happening?
2	Longitudinal study			
		Ⓐ	Ⓐ	Has there been a change in A?
		Time 1	Time 2	
3	Comparison study			
		Ⓐ		Are A and B different?
		Ⓑ		
4	Longitudinal comparison study			
		Ⓐ	Ⓐ	Are A and B different through time?
		Ⓑ	Ⓑ	
		Time 1	Time 2	
5	Experiment			Is the difference between A and B due to a change (↓) in the independent variable?
	Experimental group	Ⓐ	↓Ⓐ	
	Control group	Ⓑ	Ⓑ	
		Time 1	Time 2	

One way to become familiar with the logic of research design is to understand that each type of research design asks a different kind of question or confronts a different type of research problem. Thus, the five basic types of research design can be grouped according to five different sets of questions:

1. **The case study**
    What is going on?
    Is there a relationship between variables X and Y in entity A? (An entity is a group, social situation, text, or other focus of research.)
2. **The longitudinal study**
    Has there been a change?
    Is the relationship between variables X and Y in entity A the same or different at time 1 and time 2?
3. **The comparison study**
    Is Group A different from Group B?
    Is the relationship between variables X and Y the same in entities A and B?
4. **The longitudinal comparison study**
    Has there been a difference between Group A and Group B over time?
    Has there been a change over time in the relationship between X and Y in entity A compared with entity B?
5. **The experiment**
    In what ways are Groups A and B different?
    Is the difference in Y (dependent variable) between Group A and Group B due to a change in X (the independent variable)?

We will develop each design in detail so that you can see the value and limitations of each.

1. The Case Study

The **case study** can answer the question "What is going on?" The key element of the case study design is that it focuses on a single "case" or "entity," which might be one person, one group, one classroom, one town, or a single nation. The single case or entity is studied for a period of time and the results recorded. The aim of the case study is to find out whether there is a relationship between variables X and Y within the entity.

People who discuss research design have given the term "case study" several meanings. Some limit the use of the term to an exploratory study in which no hypothesis is tested (i.e., this is a qualitative study). For example, you might be interested in the factors a particular group of families considers when planning meals. You simply want to know what is "going on" inside the entity (i.e., the group of families being studied). You are not testing a hypothesis. You are not comparing one group of families with another. The researcher in this case has no preconceived notions about what issues will be revealed in such a study.

Researchers may also carry out exploratory case studies to ascertain relevant variables for further research. Such studies might also be done to formulate hypotheses for later study. An exploratory case study takes a very broad look at the phenomenon being investigated. The purpose is to gather information to build a description of "what is going on." These case studies may be used as a starting point for larger quantitative studies.

Other researchers use case studies to make initial tests of hypotheses. It is often useful to check whether two variables show an association before doing more rigorous testing. The sort of hypothesis that can be tested by a case study could take this form: "There is an association between variables X and Y." Case studies are not usually appropriate for testing causal relationships. This is because case studies usually bring the researcher into environments where several variables are operating and the case study design is not structured to isolate the influence of any individual variable. In this case, the study would be considered quantitative.

CASE STUDY

Vancouver's Insite Project

Since 2003, Vancouver Coastal Health, in conjunction with the BC Ministry of Health Services, has operated Insite, a supervised drug injection facility for drug addicts on Vancouver's Downtown Eastside. It is the first of its kind in North America. Its purpose is to provide a clean, safe, sterile environment for intravenous drug users to inject illegal drugs (Vancouver Coastal Health, 2011). There has been much controversy over its efficacy, however. Proponents of the site argue that providing illegal drug users with sterile needles and safe injection sites decreases the spread of deadly communicable diseases. The site also provides accessible health and counselling services for those wanting to quit. Opponents of the site argue that the services promote illegal drug use and direct a disproportionately high amount of health funding towards a population that doesn't care enough about health to look after themselves. Other opponents suggest that the location of Insite is a magnet for criminal activity.

Researchers are very interested in understanding this debate. A qualitative case study could be used to examine the efficacy of Insite. The Insite facility would be the case identified for the purposes of this study. Perhaps a group of clients could be interviewed and their experiences with illegal drug use, health history, and use of the site investigated further. Physicians, nurses, and other clinicians at the site could participate in focus groups to gain more information about the utility of Insite in this east Vancouver neighbourhood. Perhaps the researchers could interview community residents to get their opinions on the site. All this information could be gathered into a report that highlights the concerns and opinions of each of these constituents as part of the case study process. Students will notice that although many people will participate in the process of data collection, the procedure is still called a "case study" since the researchers are concerned only

Continued

with the information pertaining to the evaluation of the Insite program. Thirty case studies have in fact already been performed on Insite and have been published in prestigious medical journals such as *The Lancet* and *New England Journal of Medicine* (Urban Health Research Initiative—British Columbia Centre for Excellence in HIV/AIDS, 2009). The results have been largely positive. Insite has reduced the spread of HIV/AIDS in this high-risk population and has encouraged more illegal drug users to quit, particularly women and young people. Unfortunately, the political and community debate continues. In April 2011, the existence of Insite was threatened by a case brought forward to the Supreme Court of Canada; this case hoped to overturn a lower BC Provincial Court ruling that found that Insite provided a constitutionally valid public health service (International Drug Policy Consortium, 2011). The Supreme Court subsequently upheld the lower court's findings and has allowed Insite to continue operating. Several other Canadian cities have now created their own safe-injection sites.

Our example concerns the relationship between study and academic performance. What can a case study tell us? It can test for an association between the variables, "hours of study" and "exam marks" within the case being studied. Given the results, we can decide whether a more complicated test for a causal relationship between the variables is likely to show a causal relationship. In this case, the study would involve a quantitative investigation.

A case study designed to discover whether there is any relationship between study and academic performance might take this form: the questionnaire on time spent studying, developed in the last chapter, would be distributed to a specific history class that is the "case" being studied. The measurement is carried out once. The results are assessed once for one class and one examination. The data would then be analyzed. While we will deal with data analysis in detail later, let's say that you discovered that the amount of study time was positively associated with the marks achieved. Your graph might have looked like Figure 7.1.

What would your graph have looked like if you had found that the amount of time spent studying related negatively to the marks achieved? What could you have concluded from this study if you had done it as described and obtained results like those in Figure 7.1? You could conclude that in the group of students examined, there was a positive relationship between amount of study and academic performance as measured by the instrument devised. You could not conclude that greater amounts of study caused higher marks. All you know is that in one case (i.e., the class studied), at one point in time, the hypothesis was supported (by an observed association). This observation is very interesting, but it may well have occurred by chance. Also, you cannot rule out alternative explanations. For example, the students who studied longer might also have sat at the front of the room and paid better attention. What caused the differences in result—study or attention?

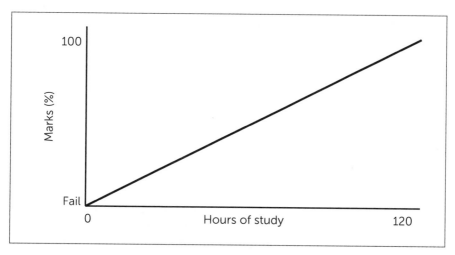

Figure 7.1 • **A sample graph of possible results from a case study**

You might be prompted by your curiosity to test other factors or to compare test results from other groups of students. Knowing what happened in one case may prompt you to try other cases. Or it might persuade you to test whether it really was the amount of time spent studying that produced the results (by repeating your research with an experimental design).

Consider now the following example. You are an occupational health and safety (OH&S) officer at a large worksite. You are concerned that the nutritional status of the company's workers may affect the frequency of injuries on the job. You arrange for a guest speaker to talk to groups of workers during working hours about nutrition. You hope that this will motivate the workers to eat healthier food. You have also decided that you want to evaluate the effectiveness of the speech. How can you do so? What can a case study tell you? A case study can tell you "what is going on"—whether the speech had the desired effect. You have the impression that the speech has not had the desired effect and that workers are continuing to choose less nutritious food. But you have no evidence to support that belief. You can check this impression by doing a case study.

Your research objective for a case study related to the issue of food selection might be

To discover what snack food choices a particular group of workers makes at the company cafeteria.

To measure this concept, variables will have to be selected and a measuring instrument devised. You talk with the manager of the cafeteria. She agrees to let you observe the selections made at the cafeteria. You decide to devise a checklist to record your observation of the food selections made by a particular group of workers—for example, machine operators on A-shift. It might look like the chart in Table 7.2.

Table 7.2 • A checklist for observing the snack choices of machine operators on A-shift

Junk Food	Fruit	Other

In this case study, you would be recording the total choices for the whole shift. The way you gather your data depends on whether you are asking about individual selections or the pattern for the group. Here our interest is the pattern of snack decisions for all machine operators on A-shift. Tables 7.3 and 7.4 present some hypothetical results. What would you conclude from each?

Table 7.3 gives the numbers of selections made in each category. The workers appear to select less nutritious foods, such as potato chips, more often than nutritious items, such as fruit. Table 7.4 presents the same findings as percentages. The use of percentages helps in making comparisons among groups of different size. It is also a very common way of showing the pattern of a variable for a group within a case study.

Table 7.3 • A table of hypothetical results from a case study of the snacks selected by machine operators on A-shift

	Junk Food	Fruit	Other	Total
Number of selections	24	3	3	30

Table 7.4 • Percentage of snacks selected by a class of machine operators on A-shift

	Junk Food	Fruit	Other
Percentage of selections	80%	10%	10%

In a case study, you could collect data showing the distribution of worker food selections at the cafeteria. What proportion of the selections were nutritious foods, such as fruit, or non-nutritious foods, such as junk food? There would be little point in pursuing a major study if in this simple case study you discovered that, contrary to your impression, most workers selected fruit for their snacks.

The case study is the basic building block of research design. In a case study, a variable or set of variables is measured for one entity at one point in time. The other research designs involve the study of more than one entity or compare studies of the same entity at different points in time. In a sense, all other research designs facilitate hypothesis testing by comparing additional case studies designed to isolate the influences on the variables under study.

2. The Longitudinal Study

The **longitudinal research design** involves two or more case studies of the same entity with some time elapsing between the studies. The basic question posed by a longitudinal study is "Has there been any change over a period of time?"

The longitudinal research design tests for an association between two variables in the same entity at different points in time. It asks, "Has there been any change in the level of association between the variables over a period of time in entity A?" The answer is "yes" or "no." If the answer is "yes," the research design should also indicate the nature or size of the change. Given that longitudinal studies are really comparisons of case studies, they cannot identify and isolate the causes of changes in associations. The longitudinal design can be diagrammed as in Figure 7.2:

Figure 7.2 • A diagram of a longitudinal study involving two measures of one group, entity, or individual A, at more than one point in time

To do a longitudinal study, you

1. select variables relevant to the concepts under study;
2. devise a way of measuring those variables;
3. develop a data-recording device;
4. measure the same variables in the same way in one group (or for one person) at two or more times.

Longitudinal research designs are often employed in analyses of national data. You may hypothesize that the increase in the numbers of women delaying childbirth has led to an increase in the number of low–birth weight infants. A possible way of investigating this would be to analyze national statistics as measures for the variables "female infant birth weights" and "male infant birth weights" at a number of points in time.

Table 7.5 compares the relationship at seven points in time from 2009 to 2013. As can be seen, the two variables are associated because measures (national statistics) for both variables have risen throughout the period under study. Therefore, the hypothesis is supported by the research.

Table 7.5 • Incidence of low birth weight by sex of infant, 2009–2013, Canada

	Female Infants (Rates per 1000 Births)	Male Infants (Rates per 1000 Births)	Total Infants (Rates per 1000 Births)
2009	6.1	5.7	6.5
2010	6.2	5.7	6.7
2011	6.1	5.7	6.5
2012	6.1	5.7	6.6
2013	6.3	5.9	6.7

Source: Statistics Canada. (2013). *Canadian Vital Statistics: Birth Data*. Table 102-4005. Ottawa: Statistics Canada. Retrieved July 29, 2017 from www5.statcan.gc.ca/cansim/a26?lang=eng&retrLang=eng&id=1024005&pattern=&csid=

You could also do a longitudinal study of the population growth rate of your neighbourhood and its relationship to the number of people actively participating in a religion in your neighbourhood for the past 10 years. Think of a longitudinal study you could do using the position of your favourite hockey team at the end of each of the past 10 seasons as a dependent variable.

Another common form of the longitudinal study is the "before and after" study. Some professors give "before and after" tests to see whether their lessons have had any effect on their students' knowledge. Studies of the impact of diet on physical characteristics frequently use a "before and after" longitudinal research design: "He weighed 96 kilograms before following our strict diet and exercise regime, and three months later he weighed 80 kilograms."

Taking our example of the relationship between study and academic performance, we can ask, "What additional information would a longitudinal study provide?" In the section on the case study, we suggested that the result of the research was that the amount of time spent studying and the mark on a history test were positively related. The more time a student spent studying, the better that student's mark was. One possible longitudinal study would be to repeat the same case study for the next history test to see whether the relationship continued to hold. This would help us to find out whether the result in the first study had been a fluke. If the result occurred again, our confidence in the finding and in the worth of the hypothesis would increase.

The study of workers' snack selections at the cafeteria lends itself to a "before and after"–style longitudinal research design. Let us assume that when the OH&S officer conducted the case study, it was discovered that 70 per cent of the workers' choices were for junk food and only 10 per cent were for nutritious foods such as fruit. The OH&S officer decided to invite a guest speaker to speak to the machine operators on A-shift about nutrition. After this had taken place, the initial research would be repeated to see whether there were changes in workers' food selections.

What could the OH&S officer conclude if the results looked like those in Table 7.6? Would it be valid to conclude that the talk was a success? Could the OH&S officer conclude that as a result of the talk there had been a shift in workers' snack selections towards more nutritious food?

Table 7.6 • Hypothetical results of a longitudinal study of workers' snack selections

	Before (%)	After (%)
Junk food	70	50
Fruit	10	30
Other	20	20

The only valid conclusion is that workers were selecting more nutritious food—that is, more fruit. Although it is likely that the speech had some impact, only an experimental design (see later in this chapter) could test whether the speech had produced the results.

There may have been other factors that caused the change in food selections, quite unrelated to the speech. For example, the stock at the cafeteria might have changed. The price of junk food might have gone up. Neither the simple case study nor the longitudinal study can control the influence of these other factors.

3. The Comparison Study

In a **comparison study**, the research question is "Is the relationship between variables X and Y the same as between entities A and B?" A comparison study compares case studies of the relationships between the same variables done for different entities at the same point in time. The comparison study can be diagrammed as in Figure 7.3.

A great deal of research is of the comparative type. Basic examples are "Is the relationship between 'contraception availability' and 'youth pregnancy' the same in Halifax and St John's?"; "Is the relationship between 'health' and 'sports achievement' the same for both the local girls' and boys' soccer teams?"; and "Is the relationship between 'family type' (one parent/two parents) and 'academic achievement' the same for students at Vincent Massey Collegiate and Yorkton Regional High School?"

Comparison studies are undertaken for two main reasons:

1. To investigate a relationship further by testing it within different types of entities. This practice might be called "doing the same test

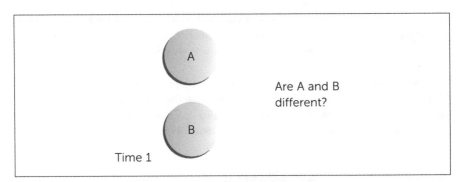

Figure 7.3 • **A diagram of a comparison study**

under different conditions." Car tires are tested under different conditions, such as dry roads, wet roads, icy roads, snow-covered roads, paved roads, gravel roads, and so on. A social relationship hypothesis can be tested under the same principle, with tests conducted for the same point in time or time period for different social entities. If we hypothesize that there is a relationship between "health" and "sports achievement," we may wish to test this relationship under different "sex conditions" to see whether the relationship is affected by the variable "sex." A possible way to do this would be to test the relationship in similar entities of different sex composition, such as the local girls' and boys' soccer teams.

2. To investigate a relationship further by testing it within similar types of entities. This practice might be called "doing the same test under similar conditions," in which the tests are conducted for the same point in or period of time. Such studies are done to test the reliability of research and to examine the effects of outside variables. If we accept that Halifax and St John's are similar cities, we could use them to study the relationship between "contraception availability" and "youth pregnancy." If our research demonstrates a relationship between the variables in both places, then the reliability of the research is supported. However, if our research shows a relationship in St John's but not in Halifax, then our research method could be unreliable and in need of re-evaluation. There may also be an unconsidered but critical difference between the two cities that is affecting the relationship— that is, there could be a third variable in the relationship. If we strongly suspect this, then further research needs to be carried out to identify the mystery third variable.

Let's explore this last point with an example. Suppose you postulate a relationship between the variables "English proficiency" and "unemployment"—that is, groups with lower English proficiency experience higher levels of unemployment.

You decide to compare this relationship in Richmond and Surrey, both located in British Columbia near Vancouver.

Suppose your research yields different results for the cities. In Surrey, the results support your hypothesis because you find that adults with low English proficiency do experience high unemployment. On the other hand, the research carried out in Richmond does not support your hypothesis. In Richmond, adults with low English proficiency have a rate of unemployment that is unexpectedly low. Therefore, the hypothesis that English proficiency is related to employment would not be supported for both cities. Consequently, the simple theory would need to be refined or challenged. This refinement would usually begin with the question, "What are the differences between Richmond and Surrey that change the relationship between English proficiency and employment?"

Further research could confront this question by pursuing the research objective "To observe patterns of employment acquisition" in Richmond. It might be observed that the language spoken most frequently by adults in Richmond is Mandarin. As a result, many local employers (given that they do business with local residents) tend to hire people proficient in Mandarin rather than English.

A more complete view of the relationship between English proficiency and unemployment begins to emerge. It has been shown that the significance of the relationship between English proficiency and unemployment is inconsistent between the two cities. Further research has found a possible factor in this inconsistency—that is, the prevalence of languages other than English among local residents. In fact, the independent variable can be modified to "local language proficiency," developing our hypothesis for further testing.

To do a comparison study, you do the following:

1. Select variables relevant to the concepts under study.
2. Devise a way of measuring those variables.
3. Develop a data-recording device.
4. Measure the same variables in the same way in two or more entities at the same time (or at practically the same time).

Such a study will enable you to determine whether there is any difference between the two groups.

For example, the OH&S officer concerned about workers' snack selections in the cafeteria might have been interested in finding out whether there was any difference between machine operators on A-shift and those on other shifts. To make this comparison, the OH&S officer would have to observe and record the selections made by two groups of workers. It would be best if they could be observed at the same time (in this case, on their respective meal breaks on the same night). The data-recording form might look like that shown in Table 7.7.

Table 7.7 • **A data-recording form for a comparison study of snack selections made by two groups of machine operators**

	Group A	Group B
Junk food		
Fruit		
Other		

Let us say that Group A is composed of the workers on A-shift and Group B, the workers on other shifts. What could the OH&S officer conclude if the results looked like those in Table 7.8? She could conclude that of the workers observed, workers on A-shift on average selected less junk food and more fruit than workers on other shifts did. The OH&S officer might think that this difference was due to the nutrition education talk given to the workers on A-shift. However, there is no way of telling that from the preceding study. The study simply asks the question "Are these two groups of workers different?" From the results in Table 7.8, the answer would be "yes."

Table 7.8 • **Hypothetical results of a comparison study of workers' snack selections**

	Machine Operators on A-shift (%)	Machine Operators on Other Shifts (%)
Junk food	60	70
Fruit	30	20
Other	10	10

Information regarding the relationship between study and academic performance can be provided by a comparison study (see Table 7.9).

Table 7.9 • **A data-recording form for a comparison study of the relationship between amount of study and marks by each class member in the separate subjects of history and math**

History Class			Math Class		
Student	Study (Hours)	1st Semester Exam Mark (%)	Student	Study (Hours)	1st Semester Exam Mark (%)
Craig	95	90	Elise	53	90
Casey	85	80	Ben	59	80
Emoke	75	70	Kim	29	70
Kathy	65	60	Tina	64	60
Eva	55	50	Narindra	72	50
etc.	etc.	etc.	etc.	etc.	etc.

It may have occurred to you that the relationship between amount of study and mark on the history test held true for history but might not hold true for the math class. You might ask the question "Is the relationship between study and academic performance the same in the math and the history class?" One way to find out would be to compare the results of case studies of this relationship, conducted during the same period, for the math and the history class.

The results of the two classes could be plotted on one graph, as in Figure 7.4.

Figure 7.4 shows a clear and positive relationship between the number of hours spent studying and examination results in history. The same is not true for the math class, where there is no strictly linear association between the variables and more studying does not necessarily produce higher grades. You would conclude that the relationship between the amount of time spent studying and examination results differs between Groups A and B. Therefore, the relationship between study and results is different for Groups A and B, and the hypothesis is supported in the history class but not in the math class. A and B are different.

What would be concluded if the results had been like those in Figure 7.5? Be careful in reading this graph.

Given these results, you would conclude that in both the history and the math class, the amount of time spent studying was positively related to examination results. The conclusion would be that Groups A and B were not different in terms of the relationship between hours of study and marks in history and math.

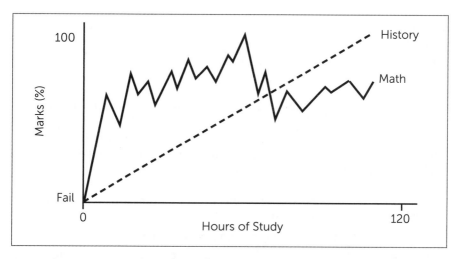

Figure 7.4 • **A sample graph of possible results from a comparison study**

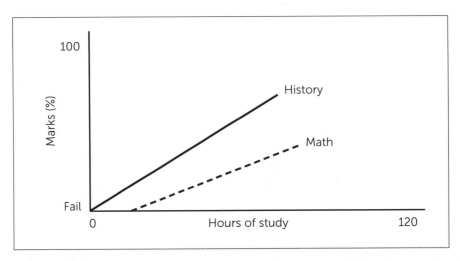

Figure 7.5 • **A sample graph of possible results from a comparison study**

4. The Longitudinal Comparison Study

We noted earlier that the case study was, in a sense, the basic building block of research design. We combined two case studies of the same group at two different times to produce a longitudinal study. Similarly, by combining two case studies, each one of a different group at the same time, we produced a comparison study. When the comparison and the longitudinal types are combined, the **longitudinal comparison research design** is produced. This type of research design asks the question "Have the differences between X and Y in entities A and B changed over time?"

A good example of this type of research would be a study of two groups of babies: one group bottlefed and the other breastfed. Each group would be measured at the same interval—weekly for eight weeks beginning one week after birth. The observation-recording device developed earlier would be used. We will assume that Group A is bottlefed and Group B is breastfed.

This study is longitudinal in that it involves a series of measures of the same variables in the same groups over time. It is also a comparison because it compares two separate groups. How might the data look? You have weight and length measures for each infant at weekly intervals. For the purpose of comparison between the two groups, assume that you report the average weight gain each week. Table 7.10 might be used to present the results:

Table 7.10 • **A table of possible results from a longitudinal comparison study of two groups of babies**

Average Weight Gain per Week (Grams)									
Week	1	2	3	4	5	6	7	8	Total
Group A	13	14	14	15	16	16	15	15	118
Group B	14	15	15	16	16	17	16	16	125

The research into the relationship between amount of study and academic performance can also be done using a longitudinal comparison type of research design. We will retain the comparison between a history class and a math class. We will also use the same data-recording form as before. In our last hypothetical research into this topic, we discovered that there was a difference between math and history in the relationship between time spent studying and examination result. The question that can be asked is "Does this difference persist through time?" By having the two classes keep a record of the time spent studying each subject before two exams a few months apart, we produce a longitudinal comparison. We have two measures for each of the two groups at two different times. A diagram of this research design might look like Figure 7.6.

You may recall that our first comparison study of history and math results looked like Figure 7.7. A longitudinal comparison essentially involves doing a

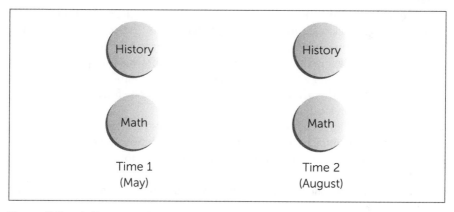

Figure 7.6 • A diagram of a longitudinal comparison study of effect of amount of study on academic performance

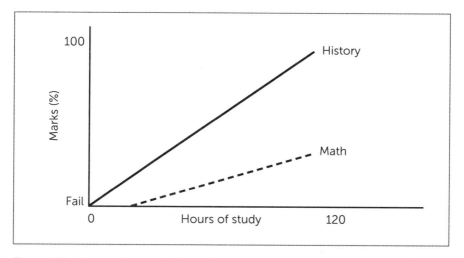

Figure 7.7 • A sample graph of possible results from a longitudinal comparison study (first trial)

second comparison study using the same measures as the first one to see if there has been any change between the two groups.

If the results of the second study are the same as those for the first, the conclusion would be that the difference between the two groups has persisted. On the other hand, the results of the second part of this longitudinal comparison study might look like Figure 7.8.

What conclusions could be drawn from these results? First, the differences between Groups A and B (history and math in this study) have lessened. Second, the pattern for both subjects has changed. Have the students changed their study patterns? Were the examinations different? What has produced the change? That is still unknown. The longitudinal comparison research design can demonstrate changes in differences between groups over time, but it does not provide the tools to test hypotheses about factors that cause changes in differences.

The same problem arises in the case of the OH&S officer who is concerned about workers' snack selections. Let us say that the OH&S officer, after conducting the first comparison study between machine operators on A-shift and other machine operators, decided to put up posters in the cafeteria that promoted fruit as a healthy snack. After a few weeks, she repeats the original comparison study. By being repeated, the original comparison study is transformed into a longitudinal comparison study.

What conclusions could the OH&S officer draw from the results shown in Table 7.11? Both groups have changed. Both groups shifted 20 percentage points in the direction of greater consumption of fruit. What is more significant, though, is that the difference between the two groups has persisted. The machine operators on A-shift are still more likely to select fruit than the machine operators

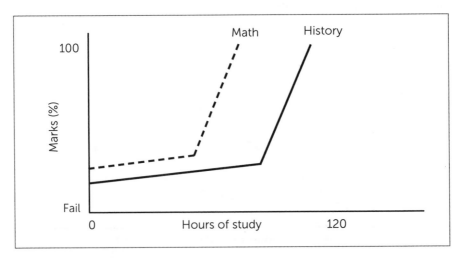

Figure 7.8 • **A sample graph of possible results from a longitudinal comparison study (second trial)**

Table 7.11 • **Hypothetical results of a longitudinal comparison study of workers' snack selections**

	Machine Operators on A-shift (%)		Machine Operators on Other Shifts (%)	
	May	July	May	July
Junk food	60	40	70	50
Fruit	30	50	20	40
Other	10	10	10	10

on other shifts. However, it is impossible to conclude that the posters produced the change. It might have been something else, as suggested before. There might have been a change in the offerings at the cafeteria. There might have been a major television campaign at the same time that promoted potato chips and other junk food. Other factors, not accounted for in this research, might have produced the result.

To use a longitudinal comparison research design you must

1. select variables relevant to the concepts under study;
2. devise a way of measuring those variables;
3. develop a data-recording device;
4. measure the same variables in the same way in two (or more) entities at two (or more) different times.

Such a research design is diagrammed in Figure 7.9. A research design like this can answer the question "Are entities A and B different through time?" It cannot, however, explain differences between variables in time or test hypotheses about the causes of such differences.

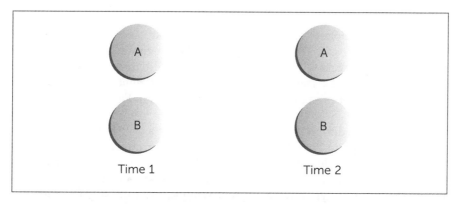

Figure 7.9 • **A diagram of a longitudinal comparison study**

5. The Experiment

If the aim of your research is to determine the effect that a change in one variable has on another, an **experimental design** is required. While the other research designs provide useful information, the experimental design provides the most rigorous test of a hypothesis that specifies that changes in variable X cause changes in variable Y. The fundamental requirement of an experimental design is that the researcher has some control over variation in the independent variable and can control the influence of other variables.

The ideal form of the experimental design can be set out as follows. Take the hypothesis that a talk on nutritious snacks will promote healthier snack selection by workers at the cafeteria. It can be diagrammed in this way:

To test this hypothesis using an experimental design, the researcher must follow this procedure:

1. Select two groups of workers. These two groups must be as alike as possible on any variable that might affect the dependent variable or the relation between the independent variable and the dependent variable (e.g., age, same proportion of males to females).
2. Devise measures for the variables. The dependent variable will be measured by the workers' snack selections observation checklist we developed earlier. The independent variable is whether the worker was present at the talk on nutritious snacks ("yes" or "no").
3. Select one of the two groups of workers to be the control group. The control group will not be given the talk on nutritious snacks; the other group will.
4. The dependent variable will be measured before and after the talk is given to Group A.
5. The principle of experimental design is that since the groups are as alike as possible, except that one has been exposed to the talk on nutritious snacks while the other has not, any difference between the two groups' snack selection behaviour can be attributed to the talk. The diagram of the experimental design is shown in Figure 7.10.

This research design asks the question "Is there a change in the difference between the experimental group and the control group following the manipulation of the independent variable?" Here the manipulation of the independent variable is the talk on nutritious snacks. Tables 7.12 and 7.13 provide two sets of hypothetical results. What would each set of results lead you to conclude?

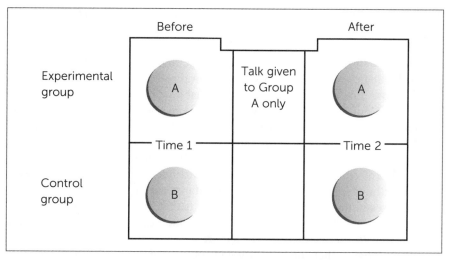

Figure 7.10 • **A diagram of an experimental research design**

Table 7.12 • **Hypothetical results of an experimental study**

| | Workers' Snack Selections at Cafeteria 1 (%) | | | |
| | Before | | After | |
	A (Exp)	B (Control)	A (Exp)	B (Control)
Junk food	A1 70	B1 70	C1 50	D1 70
Fruit	A2 20	B2 20	C2 40	D2 20
Other	A3 10	B3 10	C3 10	D3 10

Table 7.13 • **Hypothetical results of an experimental study**

| | Workers' Snack Selections at Cafeteria 2 (%) | | | |
| | Before | | After | |
	A (Exp)	B (Control)	A (Exp)	B (Control)
Junk food	A1 70	B1 70	C1 60	D1 60
Fruit	A2 20	B2 20	C2 30	D2 30
Other	A3 10	B3 10	C3 10	D3 10

For practice, make additional tables of possible results and interpret them. In the first instance, referring to Figure 7.10, we need to decide why the control group changes but the experimental group stays the same. What would you conclude?

What do you conclude from these tables of data? Did the talk have any impact on workers' snack selections? In Table 7.12, we can say that Group A, the workers exposed to the lecture about nutrition, were more likely to select more healthy options after the lecture. How do we know this? Let's look at cell A1, which is located in the top left corner of the table. It says that before the lecture, 70 people in Group A selected junk food for a snack. After listening to the lecture (the data located in cell C1), only 50 people selected junk food as snacks. Using this logic (A1 – C1) we can conclude that 70 minus 50 (i.e., 20 fewer) people chose junk food after the lecture. What kind of food did these 20 people select? If we look at the second row, "Fruit," we can see that after the experiment, 20 more people selected fruit than before the lecture. How do we know this? In cell A2, we see that only 20 people ate fruit as a snack prior to the lecture. After the lecture, in cell C2, 40 people ate fruit—which is 20 more than the last time. In the control group, there is no change in attitude (we can't know the reason for sure without conducting more in-depth statistical analysis—which is beyond the purposes of this book). What we can say is that it looks like the lecture had an effect because 20 fewer people in the experimental group chose to eat junk food for snacks after listening to the lecture.

Alternatively, what conclusion would you draw if the results were like those in Table 7.13? Both groups changed, but they changed by the same amount (A1 – C1 = B1 – D1). If we look at the first row, the junk food eaters, we see that before the lecture, 70 of those in the control group ate junk food. After being exposed to the lecture, only 60 people selected junk food for a snack. If we compare these observations to the control group, we find the same results. At time 1, 70 people in the control group selected junk food as a snack and at time 2, 60 selected junk food as a snack. If we subtract 70 from 60 as we did above, we also find that the change in behaviour for both groups is 10, meaning that 10 fewer people selected junk food as a snack regardless of whether or not they were in the control group or the experimental group. Thus, we are tempted to believe that the lecture had no effect.

How can an experimental research design test the hypothesis that changes in study cause changes in academic performance? Which is the independent variable? Which is the dependent variable? The operationalized form of this hypothesis has been diagrammed as follows:

To design an experiment, the researcher must be able to manipulate (change) the values of the independent variable. How can the researcher exercise control over the independent variable in this hypothesis? How can hours of study be manipulated?

The researcher selects two history classes that are the same in terms of variables considered critical to academic performance—age, past performance level, standard of teaching, and lack of personal problems. For each class, the researcher distributes a reading and allows students 45 minutes to study it. She then administers a test on the reading. Later in the year, the researcher

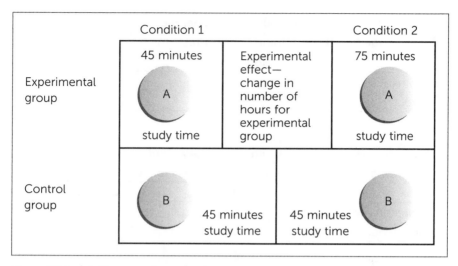

Figure 7.11 • **A diagram of an experimental research design testing a hypothesis on study time and academic performance**

repeats this exercise with a reading of similar difficulty. For one class (the experimental group), she changes the amount of study time to 75 minutes. For the other class (the control group), she does not change the amount of study time. This class receives the same amount of time that was allocated in the original exercise—45 minutes. The researcher collates the results of each test for both classes and compares the results. This research would be diagrammed as shown in Figure 7.11.

The independent variable "time spent in study" is manipulated by the researcher in such a way that any time spent in study should be observable in the form of a change in the dependent variable "test marks." The groups have been selected to be as alike as possible in all other respects. The results will be reported as average scores for each group, since the researcher is interested in group performance rather than individual performance.

Tables 7.14, 7.15, and 7.16 depict possible results of such an experiment. Assume that the possible scores on the test ranged from 0 to 100. How would you interpret the results in Table 7.14? Clearly, the results for the experimental group have improved, and those of the control group have not. The results show that an increase in study has led to improved test results.

Table 7.14 • **Hypothetical results of an experiment**

Average Results on Comprehension Tests for Two Classes 1 (%)		
	Condition 1	**Condition 2**
Experimental group	70	80
Control group	60	70

Table 7.15 • **Hypothetical results of an experiment**

Average Results on Comprehension Tests for Two Classes 2 (%)

	Condition 1	Condition 2
Experimental group	65	78
Control group	60	65

Table 7.16 • **Hypothetical results of an experiment**

Average Results on Comprehension Tests for Two Classes 3 (%)

	Condition 1	Condition 2
Experimental group	65	80
Control group	60	65

The data in Table 7.15 are inconclusive because results for both groups changed in the same direction by the same amount. The experimental group did better than the control group under both conditions, but both groups improved from the first time to the second. It is not possible to conclude that an increase in study time contributed to the increase in results for the experimental group, because the control group increased by a similar amount.

Look at Table 7.16. What would you conclude from these results? They indicate that both groups improved but that the experimental group showed a much greater improvement. A likely conclusion would be that some of the improvement (that exhibited by both groups) was due to increased skill in doing this sort of examination because of the practice both groups received when writing the first test but that the rest of the improvement (that shown only by the experimental group) was due to the increase in study time. Produce other hypothetical results in tables similar to these ones and practise interpreting them.

In summary, an experimental research design is used to determine whether changes in the independent variable actually produce changes in the dependent variable. Does a change in X cause a change in Y? If you are planning to design an experiment, consult the following checklist.

Checklist for Designing an Experiment

1. Are you able to manipulate the independent variable? Are you able to change the independent variable for the experimental group while holding it **constant** for the control group? Many independent variables cannot be manipulated satisfactorily. This may be due to our sense of what is ethical. For example, we do not arbitrarily move babies from one caregiver to another in order to assess the impact of the change.
2. Are you able to select two (or more) groups that are alike in all essential ways, one of which will become the control group and the other the

experimental group (the group that gets the treatment)? Are you able to isolate the two groups so that the experimental group does not communicate with or otherwise affect the control group?

3. Are you able to measure the dependent variable for each group both before and after the change in the independent variable? An experiment requires before and after measures of the dependent variable for both the experimental and the control group.

4. Have you recorded your data and presented your findings in such a way that you can draw conclusions about the effect (or lack of effect) on the independent variable?

If you can answer "yes" to all of these questions, then you have designed an experimental study to test your hypothesis. You must be able to answer "yes" to the first two questions in order to eliminate other possible explanations for the relationship between variables X and Y. By studying two groups that are as alike as possible, you eliminate the effects of outside variables. By manipulating the independent variable, you come as close as possible to demonstrating that changes in variable X cause changes in variable Y.

CASE STUDY

Photovoice

Photovoice has grown in popularity over the past two decades. Participants are given cameras to take photos of their everyday lives. Afterwards, they are asked either to complete a questionnaire for each photo or to meet with a research team to construct a narrative about the photo. This provides visual evidence that enhances the data collected by the survey. These photos and the information collected about them form an important part of the knowledge that researchers gain from underprivileged groups. Photovoice is also known as photoscape, photojournal, participatory photography, or participatory visual methods.

Often, photovoice is used to give voice to the voiceless. It has been used successfully by one of the authors of this book to examine the daily lives of Grade 10 students in Calgary, Winnipeg, and Toronto. In this study (Hébert et al., 2008), we wanted to better understand how youth in Canada see themselves. Of course, we asked them many questions about their lives, but a different kind of data is produced by using photovoice. We gave the Grade 10 students cameras for one week. The instructions were for them to take photos of where they spent their time, where they felt safe and included, and spaces where they felt unsafe and excluded. Students were given a lesson in social science data collection and were taught important concepts such as anonymity and confidentiality, which meant that no photo could have people in it. Naturally, if the space was

Continued

dangerous, we had the student give us the address and we took the photo for them. After the week was up, the research team had the photos developed and returned them to the students. Then we asked them to create a photo album for us with the following instructions: one photo per page and a written description of the space and the answers to some questions we had proposed. The results were spectacular and took the research team by surprise. The students spent significant effort decorating their scrapbooks and spent an enormous amount of time with the researchers and assistants discussing their work. The students in Winnipeg all completed their assignments, and, as part of the research process, they came to visit me at the university where they learned more about social science research. The data we gathered as a result was significantly more detailed, more interesting, and provided a better view of the life of 15- and 16-year-olds in Canada. In addition, the teachers learned a new method and have since incorporated the activity into their history lesson plans. The type of data we collected could not have been gathered by a traditional structured or unstructured interview. Asking people about their spaces without taking them to their spaces means that important details are left out. Having photos of spaces helps the researchers gain more information about the topic as well.

Controlling the Influence of Other Variables

At a number of points in this chapter, we have referred to the possibility that other variables not included in the study might have been responsible for observed changes in the dependent variable. This is one of the greatest fears of a researcher—that their results may be due to something not accounted for in the research design. For example, the improvement in students' exam performance might be due to increased skill in taking such exams and not to the increase in study time. For such reasons, it is important to control the influence of all other variables that might affect the variables under study. We introduced the concept of a control variable in Chapter 5.

How does the researcher control the influence of other variables? First, be aware of the fact that other variables may be influencing the data. As you design a piece of research, it is important to keep a list of other potentially influential variables. You may or may not eventually do anything about them, but it is important to be aware of such variables. All scientific conclusions are tentative, partly because of the impossibility of controlling everything. Thus, the first step is to be aware of the possible influence of other variables.

The second step is to take some of these variables into account when you design your study. You may wish to select people for your study who have the same characteristics so that the effects of outside variables will be the same for all people observed. If you were studying the relationship between age and smoking, you would have to control the effects of variables outside your research hypothesis—for example, sex, social class, type of schooling. Controlling the effects of these variables is a matter of keeping their effects constant for all people being studied—that way, differences in results cannot be caused by differences in the outside variables. For the study on smoking, you would ideally locate a sample of people whose attributes, according to the outside variables, are the same. The people would be of the same sex and social class, and would have attended the same type of school. Then you could be confident that differences in the smoking behaviour of respondents of different ages are not caused by differences in the variables you have controlled or kept constant.

The most important point about controls is to be aware of the possible influence of variables outside your hypothesis. Select groups in such a way as to eliminate the influence of as many outside variables as you can. Note the absence of controls for other outside variables in the limitations section of your report.

Key Terms

Case study   130

Comparison study   137

Constant   150

Experimental design   146

Focus group   124

Longitudinal comparison research design   142

Longitudinal research design   135

Participant observation   124

Unstructured interview   125

Questions for Review

1. What basic question is answered by research design?
2. List the five types of research design. Diagram each design.
3. What question does each design ask?
4. Why is the case study said to be the basic building block of all research design?
5. What is required to be done in a longitudinal study?
6. What is required to be done in a comparison study?
7. What is required to be done in a longitudinal comparison study?
8. What are the key features of an experiment?
9. On what basis does a researcher choose a research design?
10. Why is it important to control for other variables?
11. How does one control for other variables?
12. What is done about variables over which the researcher has no control?
13. Name the problem that occurs when a researcher asks a question on a survey and everyone provides the same answer. Why is this a problem?
14. Compare and contrast the purpose of and data collected for qualitative and quantitative research.

15. Why is it difficult to conduct experiments in social science research?
16. What differentiates participant observation from just watching something?

Sources

Bartlett, D., & Steele, J. B. (2010, December 2). Deadly medicine. *Vanity Fair. Retrieved April 18, 2011 from* www.vanityfair.com/news/2011/01/deadly-medicine-201101?currentPage=3&printable=true#ixzz18NY8yGh9

Hébert, Y., Ahmad Ali, M., Wilkinson, L., & Oriola, T. (2008). New modes of becoming in transcultural glocal spaces: Second generation youth in Calgary, Winnipeg and Toronto. *Canadian Ethnic Studies, 40*(2), 61–88.

International Drug Policy Consortium. (2011). *International coalition to save Vancouver Safe-Injection Site*. Retrieved February 23, 2011 from www.idpc.net/alerts/international-coalition-vancouver-injection-site

Peter, T., Taylor, C., & Campbell, C. (2016). "You can't break . . . when you're already broken": The importance of school climate to suicidality among LGBTQ youth. *Journal of Gay and Lesbian Mental Health, 20*(3), 195–213.

Statistics Canada. (2018, February 23). Death and causes of death, 2015. *The Daily*. Retrieved June 20, 2018 from www150.statcan.gc.ca/n1/daily-quotidien/180223/dq180223c-eng.htm

Urban Health Research Initiative—British Columbia Centre for Excellence in HIV/AIDS. (2009). *Findings from the evaluation of Vancouver's pilot medically supervised safer injection facility: Insite*. Retrieved June 28, 2018 from www.cfenet.ubc.ca/publications/findings-evaluation-vancouvers-pilot-medically-supervised-safer-injection-facility

Vancouver Coastal Health. (2017). *New supervised injection site to be opened in Vancouver*. Retrieved June 20, 2018 from www.vch.ca/about-us/news/new-supervised-injection-service-to-open-in-vancouver

Suggestions for Further Reading

Berg, B. (2001). *Qualitative research methods for the social sciences*. Toronto: Allyn & Bacon.

Bryman, A., Teevan, J. J., & Bell, E. (2009). *Social research methods* (2nd Cdn ed.). Don Mills, ON: Oxford University Press.

Hesse-Biber, S. N., & Leavy, P. (Eds.). (2004). *Approaches to qualitative research: A reader on theory and practice*. New York: Oxford University Press.

Palys, T., & Acheson, C. (2014). *Research decisions: Quantitative and qualitative perspectives* (5th ed.). Toronto: Thomson Nelson.

May, T. 2001. *Social research: Issues, methods and process*. Philadelphia: Open University Press.

Wall, S. (2006). An autoethnography on learning about autoethnography. *International Journal of Qualitative Methods, 5*(2), 1–12. Retrieved from https://sites.ualberta.ca/~iiqm/back-issues/5_2/PDF/wall.pdf

Suggested Web Resources

Patten, M. Q. (2015, January 23). *Introduction to research design* [Video file]. Retrieved April 11, 2018 from www.youtube.com/watch?v=GYywR7SA03E

Photovoice. (2018). *Photovoice manual*. Retrieved April 11, 2018 from http://photovoice.ca/

Wang, C., & Burris, M.A. (1997). Photovoice: Concept, methodology and use for participatory needs assessment. *Health Education and Behaviour, 24*(3), 369–87. Retrieved April 11, 2018 from http://journals.sagepub.com/doi/abs/10.1177/109019819702400309

8

Selecting a Sample and Participants

To whom are you going to administer your questionnaire? Which history class will be the subject of your experiments? Which babies will be weighed and measured? Since it is impossible to weigh all babies, administer questionnaires to everyone, or experiment on all history classes, researchers study a "sample" of their subject populations. Indeed, it is often more desirable to study a sample than to try to study the whole population. A carefully drawn sample not only makes the task possible, it often produces more accurate results.

In everyday life, we commonly use sampling to make judgments about facts and issues. If we want to check the seasoning of soup, we stir it, take a sample, and judge the seasoning level of the broth by tasting that sample. If we are buying a new car, we decide how the car can usually be expected to perform by taking it on a test drive. We make many judgments based on samples.

Care is taken to make sure the sample is an accurate reflection of the whole from which it is taken. In the case of soup, we stir so as to make sure the ingredients are as evenly distributed as possible, then we take a sample, taste it, and draw a conclusion about it—that is, we generalize the findings of our study to the whole pot of soup. If we have heard that the car we are thinking of buying drives well on city roads but not on country roads, we would sample its performance on both types of road for an idea of how it handles in general.

Sampling is an important feature of all quantitative and qualitative research. Part of the whole is studied, and the results are taken to be an accurate reflection of the whole.

The most important point to remember about sampling is this:

The manner in which the sample is drawn determines to what extent we can generalize from the findings.

Only if the **sample** studied can be shown to represent a larger population can the results of a study of the sample be assumed to give reliable information about the larger population. If the sample studied is not *representative*, the conclusions drawn from the research must be limited to the sample studied. This is of central importance to quantitative research.

For example, you might have developed a short questionnaire on attitudes towards nuclear weapons. If you had 20 of your friends, fellow students, and relatives fill out your questionnaire, the results would be limited to that group of 20 people. On the other hand, if you had selected a sample of 20 people that accurately reflected the views of a larger group of 200 (e.g., all the students enrolled in your course), you could draw conclusions about the 200 from the results of the sample of 20 if you are careful about the way you select these 20 representatives. In the first instance, your findings were limited to the 20 people studied. In the second, you could generalize the results to the larger population that your sample represented (your class).

Although sampling soup is easy, sampling groups of people is rather more complicated. The basic problem is to select a sample that accurately reflects a specified larger group. Several techniques for drawing samples from groups of people have been devised by social scientists. The most basic and potentially useful of these techniques will be described in this chapter. The strengths and weaknesses of each will be discussed to help you select a technique appropriate to your research.

It should also be remembered that for some research purposes, sampling is not required. If the researcher is not interested in drawing conclusions for a larger population than that actually studied, sampling is not needed. This is particularly relevant for qualitative research. For example, a psychologist might decide to study her baby's cognitive development. Only one baby (hers) is needed for the study. Why would she not be able to draw conclusions about all babies or even other babies in her family? It is usually dangerous to rely on the observation of a single case to provide an accurate picture of a larger group. It would be like an Australian forming an opinion about all Canadians after meeting one Canadian. Depending on which Canadian was the basis of this "case study," the most amazing and misleading impressions could be formed. In studies of single cases, generalizations cannot be safely drawn. There is no way of knowing whether the case studied will give an accurate impression of the whole.

Another situation in which sampling is not an issue occurs when researchers can easily study all members of the group about whom they wish to draw conclusions. If their interest is in the performance of one history class, or the comparison of two groups of workers—for example, those who did and those who did not hear a speaker on nutrition—then sampling is not an issue. In these instances, the whole population is being studied. As long as the researchers are willing to limit the conclusions to the population they study, sampling is not an issue. If, however, the researchers want to generalize—to draw conclusions about a large group on the basis of studying a few—then a sampling procedure must be selected.

Why do researchers sample? Samples are used to reduce the cost in time, energy, and money of studying large populations. It is often simply not possible or desirable to study everyone. A sample is drawn from a large group in order to gain a reliable picture of that large group by studying a carefully selected smaller number of the population. The way in which the sample is selected determines whether reliable conclusions about the larger group can be drawn.

How to Select a Sample and Participants

What do you want to know? About whom do you want to know it? These are the questions to answer first. Given that it is impossible to know everything about everyone or all groups, selections must be made. First, decide what you want to know. You did this when you formed a research question hypothesis, focused it, and made it operational. You have identified the methodology, devised instruments, and designed research. Once these things are done, turn your attention to the second question: About whom do you want to know?

The first step in sample selection is to identify the population about which you want to know something. Think back to your hypothesis. For example, the hypothesis about amount of study and academic performance relates to students. The largest possible population would be all students in the world at any time past, present, and future. That would be an impossible population to sample. You may decide to limit your sample to students in Canadian post-secondary institutions. That is still a very large and diverse population. You might decide to limit your focus to students in your own institution. Finally, you might decide that making generalizations about all students everywhere is not so important, and you are happy to settle for finding out what is happening in two history classes at your own institution.

Remember: it is perfectly legitimate to select any population as the object of your study.

The population about which you wish to generalize will affect your selection of a sampling procedure. Once you have decided whom you want to draw reliable conclusions about, you are ready to select a sampling procedure. What other practical factors might help you to decide which population you wish to be able to generalize about? Think about time and money. Think also about the type of study you are conducting. If it is qualitative, then generalization is not necessary and the sample can be smaller.

Types of Sampling and Selection Procedures

There are two general types of sampling procedure: random and non-random. A **random sampling** procedure provides the greatest assurance that those individuals selected are a representative sample of the larger group. If a **non-random sampling** procedure is used, the researcher can only hope that those selected for study bear some likeness to the larger group.

Non-Random Sampling Procedures

Non-random sampling procedures include accidental sampling, accidental quota sampling, purposive sampling, and systematic matching sampling. Although useful for many studies, non-random sampling procedures provide only a weak basis for generalization. They are suited for qualitative research studies where the goal is a deeper understanding of the phenomena or situation rather than making inferences to a larger population.

Accidental sampling

Accidental sampling, also known as haphazard sampling, involves using what is immediately available. A professor studies her own students; a psychologist studies his own children. A student studies the interaction patterns of the families of two friends and a cousin. These are all accidental samples. The persons, families, and classes studied were selected because they were available, not because they were known to be representative of some larger group.

Some people confuse accidental sampling with random sampling. Persons met at random—that is, accidentally—do not compose a random sample. Another feature of accidental samples is that the researcher does not know in what ways the sample is biased. How is the sample a misleading representative of the larger population about which information is desired? There is no way of checking this without doing a study of everyone or a study of a properly drawn random sample.

The people on a given street at a given time will be a biased sample of residents of that suburb. Such an accidental sample will not give you reliable information about all residents of the suburb. A questionnaire on attitudes towards abortion given to every tenth person encountered at a suburban shopping centre will not provide a reliable indication of the opinions of residents of the suburb. It will only tell you the opinions of people who shop at that place at that hour on that day of the week. If you are interested in the opinions of the residents of the entire suburb, an accidental sample of Tuesday-morning shoppers will not provide the information.

Similarly, the families you know will be a biased sample of families in your city. They may be members of the same clubs, churches, or political parties or be at similar stages in the family life cycle. In the same way, students enrolled in a particular course or institution will be a biased sample of students. Think of ways in which the students enrolled in your course would be a biased sample of students in your institution. This is why *the results of a study of an accidental sample apply only to the sample studied.*

An accidental sampling procedure is appropriate if you do not intend to draw conclusions about a larger group on the basis of the group you study. It is not appropriate when the researcher wishes to utilize statistical modelling techniques to identify trends. Accidental samples are handy, require little effort, and are useful for many studies. The major disadvantage is that the findings of a study of an accidental sample are strictly limited to those studied, because the researcher does not know in what ways the sample is biased. It is uncertain which

aspects of the total population are included and which are not. Yet a major benefit of the accidental sample is that the researcher can handpick participants who
meet the criteria of providing the best information about the issue of the study.

Accidental quota sampling

In an **accidental quota sampling** procedure, the researcher selects individuals
or groups on the basis of set criteria. A researcher comparing the opinions of
males and females might set a quota of ten males and ten females. This will
ensure that the sample studied has both females and males. Another researcher,
comparing the performance of history classes and English classes, might specify
that the sample must contain the same number of students from each type of
class. Someone interested in the difference between students of different universities, social classes, incomes, or ethnic groups might specify in advance the
number or proportion of each desired in the sample.

Perhaps a more developed example will help. Assume you are interested in
comparing the attitudes towards university held by secondary school students
from different ethnic groups. To make sure that the sample you study has
students from each of the ethnic groups, you might set a quota of five students from each of the ethnic groups you wish to compare. By selecting five
students from each ethnic group—that is, by filling your quota—you make sure
that your sample includes people or groups with certain specified characteristics, in this instance ethnic background.

Quota sampling is useful when a particular group or characteristic is
relatively rare in the population. By setting a quota and selecting people until
the quota is filled, you ensure that the groups or characteristics you want in the
sample are adequately represented in the sample for the analyses you want to do.

Quota sampling, however, suffers from most of the same defects as accidental
sampling. Can you see why? Although the researcher is assured of the presence
of certain categories in the sample—for example, males and females, or Greek,
Nigerian, English, and Vietnamese students—the **representativeness** of the
sample is still not ensured. This is because the individuals or groups are not selected
randomly. The sample may have 25 males and 25 females, but who do these males
and females represent? This is not known. The sample selected may have five
Greek students, five Nigerian students, five English students, and five Vietnamese
students. But it is not known whether the five Nigerian students are an unbiased
sample of Nigerian students. It is not known whether a study of the five Greek
students will provide reliable information about other Greek students. In other
words, it is risky to draw conclusions about a larger group from an accidental quota
sample of that group. Nonetheless, this sampling procedure is often used because
of time and budget pressures. Conclusions drawn are strictly limited to the population actually studied. Tentative implications for others may be suggested.

Purposive sampling

Some researchers believe that they can, using their own judgment or intui-
tion, select the best people or groups to be studied. The "typical" rural school
is selected and studied, and the results are generalized to all rural schools.

The "typical" first-year sociology class is compared with the "typical" first-year nursing class. How are these known to be typical? Unless objective criteria are set out beforehand and each group is shown to meet these criteria, there is no way of knowing. However, there are times when this is the only practical way to draw a sample. If a **purposive sample** is studied, only tentative generalizations about those participating in the study can be made. The conclusions drawn from a comparison of a few "typical" rural schools with a few "typical" urban schools might be phrased in this way:

> The results of this study comparing three rural and three urban schools have revealed the following six major differences. Although it is not strictly possible to generalize from this sample to all rural and urban schools, we think it is likely that these differences are to be found in other instances.

This technique is very appropriate for case study and qualitative approaches in which the intent is not to generalize to a larger population but to examine a "typical" case in order to understand it more fully. Also known as *judgmental sampling*, this procedure is most often used when the topic is new and has not yet been fully explored. According to Neuman and Robson (2009), purposive sampling is appropriate in three instances: for selecting cases that are illustrative of a phenomenon; for selecting "difficult to reach" members of a unique population; or for identifying particular types for investigation in greater detail. In other words, purposive sampling is appropriate for studying extreme cases of a phenomenon.

Palys and Achison (2014) advise that researchers should not place too much emphasis on the opinions or information provided by any single respondent who has been selected using purposive sampling methods. This is because they have not been selected randomly and because purposive sampling is usually done with smaller sample sizes. However, the information they provide may lead you to investigate other aspects of the phenomenon that you had not previously considered.

The snowball technique

The **snowball sampling** technique is used when you need to gain access to certain types of people or to a particular group, but you know only a few people who fit the category and there is no publicly available listing. In this technique, you gather your sample by first approaching those who are available and then asking them to nominate others whom they know, who nominate still others. In this way, your sample grows like a snowball, the most recently formed layer providing the contact with those to be added next. For example, you may wish to interview practising Falun Gong members in order to understand some aspects of their religious practices. But you know only one practising Falun Gong member, and LinkedIn and other networking sites may be unhelpful. You would ask the member you know to nominate others, whom you then ask to nominate still others until you have a sample large enough for your purposes. The snowball technique is used a great deal in qualitative research into less well-organized aspects of social life. It can be seen as a variation of purposive sampling. The conclusion of your study of Falun Gong might be phrased in this way:

> This study of a sample of practising Falun Gong members reveals that those interviewed practise a form of body and mind meditation exercise, come from certain backgrounds, and have been practising an average of X years. While these findings cannot be generalized to all practising Falun Gong members, those interviewed represent about 5 per cent of known practitioners in Toronto.

Systematic matching sampling

In **systematic matching sampling**, individual subjects or groups are systematically matched with others who are similar in all but one critical attribute. It can be effective in at least two situations.

First, it is useful for controlling the influence of variables outside the research hypothesis or research objective. Say you wish to sample Grade 3 students in a large elementary school to find out whether male and female students have reacted differently to a new method of teaching. The school has a great deal of ethnic diversity, and you suspect that the new system will have different effects on students from different ethnic backgrounds. To control the variable "ethnicity," you construct your sample by systematically matching males and females of the same ethnic background. You might arrive at a sample of 10 students, containing a male and female from five different ethnic groups—French, Vietnamese, Italian, Ghanaian, and Indian. You can now compare the differences between males and females for each ethnic "pair" and summarize the general sex differences, noting any variations among the ethnic categories.

Second, a systematic matching sampling procedure is often appropriate when a researcher wants to compare two groups of very different sizes. A study might compare female and male politicians in terms of their goals for social reform. There are currently significantly fewer female politicians than male, so in sampling male politicians for comparison, the researcher needs to be careful. In the current Canadian Parliament, only 91of the 336 members are female, representing 27 per cent of the total (Government of Canada, 2016). The population of males in Parliament is so much greater that they can be expected to be far more diverse than the females, and many would be inappropriate for a sex-based comparison study. Some would have been in Parliament much longer than any of the female politicians, which can be seen in historic records. In 1984, only 9.6 per cent of the seats in Parliament were held by women (Cool, 2013). Because of the greater diversity among male members of Parliament, they are more likely to represent a wider variety economic classes, rich and poor. Since there are fewer females, they are less likely to have incomes that are fully representative of the entire income structure of the country. Also, given their greater numbers in Parliament, men are more likely to represent different marital statuses, such as single, common-law, separated, divorced, or widowed.

Therefore, it is important to "match" the subjects in the sample. If the researcher doesn't do this, then his sample of females will be compared with males who are too different for a reasonable comparison.

We could select 10 female politicians (randomly or non-randomly) and systematically match them to 10 male politicians. Each male would be selected because he matched a female politician in certain features deemed to be important to the consideration of social reform. Examples of such matching features might be age, length of service in Cabinet or on the backbench, education, marital status, and sexuality. Though the claim to representativeness is weak, this sampling procedure is often a suitable compromise when comparing groups of extremely different size.

Summary of non-random sampling procedures

These examples of non-random sampling procedures are given because they are frequently used by researchers. If a non-random sampling procedure is used, the researcher must be aware of the limitations to the conclusions drawn. Technically, the conclusions drawn from a study of a non-random sample are limited to that sample and cannot be used for further generalizations. This means that any tables or calculations created using the results cannot and must not be used to make assumptions or inferences about persons not participating in the study, no matter how similar they might be. Read through some research literature in your library. Can you find an example of non-random sampling being used?

Random Sampling Procedures

Random sampling procedures provide the greatest assurance that the sample accurately represents the population. There are four basic random sampling procedures: simple random sampling, systematic sampling, stratified random sampling, and cluster sampling.

Simple random sampling

This is the ideal method of drawing a sample. It is, however, very difficult to do. A **simple random sampling** procedure guarantees that each element (person, group, university, and so on) in the population has an equal chance of being selected and that every possible combination of the specified number of elements has an equal chance of selection. The mathematics of such selection procedures can be very complex and are beyond the scope of this text.

In order to draw a simple random sample, the researcher must

1. identify the population from which the sample is to be drawn;
2. enumerate and list every element (e.g., persons, households, car owners) in the population or obtain a complete list of participants (and be able to access their contact information);
3. devise a method of selection that ensures that each element has the same probability of selection and that each combination of the total number of elements has the same probability of selection.

Given the virtual impossibility of meeting all these criteria (it is almost impossible to obtain a complete list of anything), it is not surprising that a number of acceptable compromises have been devised. Essentially, the task is to devise some form of lottery in which each combination of numbers has an equal chance of coming up.

The first set of "compromise" random sampling procedures involves studies in which it is possible to identify and enumerate the total population. For example, although possible, it is usually too much work to identify and enumerate the total population of university students in a particular year. On the surface, it seems an easy task, but the reality is that students leave and enroll in university every day. They change programs every day and they leave and return to school every day, so it would be difficult to finalize this list. It would be possible and much more accurate to identify and enumerate the students enrolled in your course. Other populations that are relatively easy to enumerate are the members of a particular club, the students in a history class, the teachers in a school, the children in a particular daycare centre, the people in a home for the elderly, the people whose names are on a voter registration roll, or the students attending any of the provincial high schools in New Brunswick. Previously, telephone directories were useful lists from which to select samples of urban populations. Today, however, the telephone directory may pose particular problems. If the city is large, do you enumerate all the subscribers? What about non-representativeness, since it only includes landline subscribers and usually only one name for each household? In what ways would a voter registration roll be biased? Once identified and enumerated (that is, numbered from beginning to end), a sample may be selected.

Here is an example. You want to study a simple random sample of the 250 first-year sociology students at a particular university. The first step is done. You have identified the population and the university. The second step is to identify and enumerate each element in the population. In this instance, the elements are the 250 students who happen to be enrolled in sociology courses this semester. A list of students must be generated. The students will have to be listed and numbered from 1 to 250:

1. Marjorie Althouse
2. Chris Andersen
3. Lynn Checkley
4. Gino Cortez

. . .

250. Sharlet Zaretski

You have identified and enumerated the whole population to which you want to generalize the findings of your study. It is now possible to move to the next step—selecting the sample. We will deal with issues of sample size later in the chapter. Let us assume that you decided to draw a sample of 50 students from the larger population of 250 students.

An acceptable way of selecting a sample from an enumerated population involves the use of a table of random numbers. A starting point in the table is picked (using a random technique), and those elements of the whole population whose numbers come up as you move down the column from the starting point are selected for the sample. Do this until a sample of the required size is achieved.

To draw the sample of 50 students from 250 sociology students by this procedure, you would do the following. Remember: each student has been given a number from 1 to 250. Table 8.1 is a section from a table of random numbers. Because the numbers you need to select have between one and three digits (or are composed of three digits from 001 to 250), you will use the first three digits of each number in the table (or the middle three digits or the last three digits— your choice). The next step is to select a starting point. This can be done in several ways. An easy way is to close your eyes, point a pen at the table, and start there. An easier way is to let a computer program generate a random starting number (most statistics packages have programs allowing users to generate an infinite number of random numbers, and this is the way that most researchers conduct such sampling strategies). Let's say that we have selected the easy way: closing our eyes and selecting a random number by pointing our pen (note that this is not the most precise method). It is permissible to move up or down the columns, since the numbers are random—that is, there is no pattern in the table. The numbers are in no particular order. Had your pen landed on a number for which the first three digits were outside the range 001–250, you would try again or move to the next number for which the first three digits were in this range.

Table 8.1 • Using a table of random numbers

28071	03528	89714
48210	48761	▷ 02365
83417	20219	82900
20531	43657	45100
94654	97801	▷ 01153
52839	42986	28100
74591	▷ 16100	91478
38921	56913	32675
40759	84027	52831
45980	70523	47985
52182	68194	62783
12890	59208	▷ 00691
08523	74312	▷ 13542

Assume your random selection method resulted in number 161. If you decided to move down the columns, the next number to be selected would be the next number in the range 001–250 that was not 161 (since 161 has already been selected). In this table, it would be element (student) number 023. The next would be student 011, then 006, then 135. You would continue this procedure until you had selected a total of 50 students. You would then have a simple random sample of 50 students, which is more likely to be representative of the population of 250 than a sample chosen non-randomly.

To give yourself practice, start again at number 161, but move up the columns. Which numbers would then be selected? A different sample of 50 would be drawn, but because it was randomly selected, the results of studying it would also be more likely to give reliable information about the whole group than the results of a non-random sample. Indeed, we would expect only the smallest difference between a study of the first sample and a study of the second.

Another (though less) acceptable form of selection is to put all the names or numbers into a hat and draw out the number required. To ensure that each element and combination of elements has the same probability of selection, each time a selection is made the name or number should be returned to the hat. If a number is drawn more than once, it is again returned to the hat, but the number is not "selected" twice. The random selection of a sample of 50 students from 250 according to this method would require that all the students' names, or a set of numbers from 001 to 250, be put into a container. The container would be shaken before each draw. The first 50 students whose names (or numbers) were drawn would form the sample. Please note that this is not a strictly random way of selecting cases. There are several times in history when this process has been used and studies have shown that the numbers or names entered into the draw last are the most likely to be selected—meaning that there is an unequal chance for all elements to be selected. Even batches mixed mechanically over days have this problem, but it is very close to a random sample.

By far the most precise and most accurate method of obtaining a simple random sample is to use a computer program to select the sample. Many computer programs contain functions that can generate random numbers based on user-entered protocol. Users would enter the required number of participants and the range of numbers of available participants. The program would generate a random sample of respondent numbers. When available, this is the preferred method of selecting sample respondents. It is the most random method of selecting respondents (it does not rely on where your pen might fall on a random number table) and is easy to use.

Although these techniques are somewhat laborious and time consuming (with the exception of computer-generated samples), they do provide the most reliable sampling procedures. The simple random sample is the ideal and is the basis from which statisticians have designed the statistical equations used to analyze their data.

Systematic sampling

A **systematic sampling** procedure involves the selection of every nth case in a list. Again, the population must be identified, but it is not necessary to enumerate the list. For example, if you had a list of 400 students in Sociology 101 and you wanted a sample of 80, you might select every 5th name on the list. To draw a systematic sample, you need to know the total number in the group and the number you want in the sample. By dividing the total number by the sample number, you find the interval at which you will select people:

Total population   =   400
Sample desired   =   80
Interval   =   400 ÷ 80 = 5

If the interval is an uneven number, the nearest whole number is selected:

Total population   =   393
Sample desired   =   80
Interval   =   393 ÷ 80 = 4.9 (round up to 5)

The critical step in systematic sampling is to select the first case randomly. To do this, one of the first elements (names, groups, numbers, schools) in the long list must be selected. If the interval is 5, one of the first 5 must be selected as the starting point. If the interval is 10, then you must select one of the first 10, and so on. One way to make a random selection is to put all the numbers (1 to 5, or 1 to 10, or whatever) into a container, shake it, and draw out a number. That number will be your starting point. Or you could use a computer program to generate a random start number. Regardless of which method you use, the first element must be selected randomly. Once the first element is selected, then each nth element (n = interval) thereafter is selected. In the example of students in Sociology 101, the list had 400 names, and the interval was 5. Assume that the number 4 was drawn out of the container. Selection would start with the fourth student on the list (A. Belancourt). You then count down to the fifth next student on the list, J. Cote, and add that name to your sample.

M. Althouse	F. Ennab
J. Adams	D. Ladner
K. Adams	S. Mandal
A. Belancourt*	T. Pearson*
F. Bislimi	F. Plohman
R. Buzdugan	F. Quddus
R. Chaturvedi	V. Rankambe
L. Checkley	A. Sorensen
J. Cote*	J. Van Wijngaarden*
L. Duncan	

If a selected student is unavailable, she is replaced by the preceding student on the list. If T. Pearson is unavailable, then S. Mandal will be selected. When a selected student has dropped out of the course, he is replaced by the next student on the list. If J. Cote has dropped out, L. Duncan will be the replacement. Another replacement strategy is to flip a coin (heads-name before, tails-name after). Note that names are replaced only if the person is genuinely unavailable, not because the researcher might prefer someone else to be in the sample.

As well, replacing names with the next on the list increases the probability that a particular student will be selected. For this reason, systematic sampling is not as precise as other methods of random sampling.

A systematic sampling procedure provides an acceptable approximation of the ideals of the simple random sampling procedure. It helps to overcome **researcher bias** in sample selection. Selection is done independently of the researcher's preferences and prejudices. As long as any biases in the ordering of the list do not occur at the same interval as the sampling interval, a reasonably reliable sample will be drawn by this procedure.

Stratified random sampling

Stratified random sampling is basically a type of quota sampling in which members of each "quota group" within, or stratum of, the sample are selected randomly. You may wish to compare types of schools in terms of the overall performance of students. A simple random sample of schools might not provide enough cases in some of the categories of analysis you intend to use. You might classify the schools into urban, suburban, and rural schools. Having done that, you would identify and enumerate the schools in each group and identify a random sample of each group.

In another example, you might want to compare the attitudes towards the building of additional nuclear power plants held by university students studying math and science to those held by humanities students. Rather than doing a simple random sample of the students collectively enrolled in these faculties at a particular university, you would identify all students in each category, list them separately, and draw a sample from each list using one of the random selection processes outlined above—using a table of random numbers, drawing names from a hat, or using systematic sampling.

The criterion for identifying quota groups or strata will be suggested by your hypothesis. A hypothesis comparing males with females could be studied using a random sample with quotas of randomly selected males and females. Similarly, if the hypothesis compares high-income families with low-income families, it would be possible to use a random sample with quotas of randomly selected high-income and low-income families.

Cluster sampling

The fact that simple random sampling becomes tremendously complex and costly for large and scattered populations has led to the development of **cluster sampling** procedures. They usually involve several stages of random selections. Rather than enumerating the whole population, the population is divided into segments. Then several of the segments are chosen at random. Elements within each segment are then selected randomly following identification and enumeration. In this way, only the elements in the selected segment need to be identified and enumerated.

National samples are usually drawn on a **multi-stage cluster sample** procedure. So are samples of cities. For example, a sample of households in the Montreal metropolitan area might be drawn by first dividing Montreal into segments (these already exist for purposes of the census). A number of segments could be drawn at random. Within each segment, residential blocks would be identified and enumerated and a random selection of blocks drawn. Finally, the residences on each selected block would be identified and enumerated, and a random sample of residences would be selected on the basis of an unbiased rule of selection. In this way, a random sample of Montreal residences would be approximated. Cluster sampling procedures have been devised to provide a reliably random—and hence representative—sample of a large population without having to identify and enumerate the entire population at the outset. In this procedure, only smaller randomly selected segments (clusters) have to be identified and enumerated. Please note that this explanation of cluster sampling is simplified. Students interested in learning more about cluster sampling should consult one of the suggested readings at the end of this chapter.

Choosing a Sampling Procedure

The essentials of the basic forms of sampling have been presented. How do you select a sampling procedure for your research? This depends largely on the population about which you wish to draw conclusions and whether or not you are using qualitative or quantitative methods. If you are happy to limit your conclusion, for example, to the students in your tutorial group and you are using qualitative analytic methods, that accidental sample will do perfectly well. If the demands of time and expense force you to examine a large enough subgroup of a larger population and you want to use quantitative methods to analyze the data, one of the random sampling procedures should be used. The extra effort pays great dividends in the value of your research conclusions. For a relatively small effort, you can dramatically increase the representativeness of your findings and reduce the influence of any known or unknown biases.

Random sampling procedures are particularly important in research that aims to assess the attitudes, values, or beliefs of a population with the goal of being able to say something about the entire population. Public opinion polls usually use some form of random sampling. On the basis of their samples, such pollsters predict how people will vote, what brands of detergent they will buy, and in what direction popular tastes are shifting.

Finally, it is impossible to generalize from most case studies. If a case study is conducted for the residents of a street, it cannot be stated that the street is representative of the suburb, the city, or the province. Case studies include only observations of sections of larger populations and provide the researcher with no observations outside their boundaries.

Determining Sample Size

How large a sample do you need? What is the appropriate sample size for your project? These are very difficult questions to answer. Several basic issues need to be considered in determining sample size.

First, if statistics are going to be used in the analysis and interpretation of data, there are usually requirements for sample size. We will not elaborate on these requirements, since this text takes a non-statistical approach to the research process. Professional researchers must take these considerations into account. If the research involves comparing two groups of people, then the sample ought to be no smaller than 30 (this is for various reasons that are beyond the scope of our discussion). Second, the more questions asked, the more variables controlled for, and the more detailed the analysis of the data,

CASE STUDY

The Importance of Sample Size: Autism and the Andrew Wakefield Case

If you think sample size is not important, consider the very damaging consequences of a widely publicized research project involving autism. Some 20 years later, medical professionals still fight to explain the importance of vaccinating children. Read more below.

In February 1998, Dr Andrew Wakefield and his colleagues had what was considered at the time to be a ground-breaking study on autism published in the prestigious journal *The Lancet*. Their study uncovered a startling link between the measles, mumps, and rubella (MMR) vaccine and the development of autism among children (Wakefield et al., 1998—retracted). His study gained worldwide attention and thousands of parents opted not to vaccinate their children because of fears that their children would develop autism as a result. In 2010, in the face of enormous evidence, *The Lancet* retracted the study and several of the original collaborators have since had their names removed from the article (Eggertson, 2010).

There are many methodological and ethical problems with this research, and whether or not you personally believe the MMR vaccine is linked to autism is not the point of this discussion. The issue is sample size. The original article was based on a sample of only 12 children! These children were selected as part of Dr Wakefield's work, which was funded by lawyers representing the parents in a lawsuit against the makers of the vaccine (Eggertson, 2010). Ethical issues aside, the sampling method is suspect as the researchers used a convenience sample by selecting the first 12 patients who presented with characteristics (MMR vaccination followed by autism diagnosis) that would "prove" their hypothesis. The paper fuelled international hysteria and is cited as the cause of a massive outbreak of measles in the UK in 2008–9 and again in Europe and North America in 2014, in the United States in 2015, and then again worldwide in 2017. The moral of this story is that a sample of 12 patients is far too small to base any generalizable conclusions on. The fact that the children were selected by convenience (had just had MMR vaccination and had been referred to Dr Wakefield's office—a specialist in autism) highly biased this sample. This case illustrates that such an error can have life-altering, long-term public health implications.

the larger the sample will have to be to provide sufficient data for the analysis. In professional research, samples of hundreds or thousands will be drawn to accommodate this demand.

Although large samples may seem more conclusive, it is how the sample is drawn that determines how representative it is. In general, large samples are not necessarily better than smaller ones. We do not have to taste a large amount of soup to determine whether it needs more salt—a small taste will do. In addition, practical considerations of time, money, and effort often combine to keep sample sizes relatively small.

Most of the research you will read about in journals or papers is based on large samples, but we have a few suggestions regarding sample size for student projects. Since the goal of student projects is to learn basic research skills rather than to produce results that are generalized to large populations, several basic compromises are possible. These suggestions for student projects take the form of two basic rules:

1. About 30 individual elements are required in order to provide a pool large enough for even simple kinds of analyses.
2. You need a sample large enough to ensure that it is theoretically possible for each cell in your analytical table to have five cases fall in it. A few examples will make this clear.

Remember the study of snack selection (in Chapter 7)? Workers' snack selections were categorized according to the table in Table 8.2.

Table 8.2 • A dummy table for the categorization of workers' snack selections

Junk Food	Fruit	Other
1	2	3

This is usually referred to as a "dummy" table. It is a table prepared before the collection of data to help to focus the issues of the research, guide data collection, and help to determine sample size. In this case, the data-recording form, dummy table, and final table for presentation of data take the same form. This dummy table has three cells. The minimum sample size for this study would be $3 \times 5 = 15$ (but it would still be preferable to have 30 because of the first basic rule regarding minimum sample size).

This example was also turned into a comparative study between food purchases by machine operators on A-shift and other shifts. The dummy table for such a study would look like Table 8.3. This dummy table has six cells; hence, the sample size required would be $6 \times 5 = 30$. Moreover, this study involves comparing two groups of machine operators. Since each group is accorded three cells in the table, each group requires a sample of $3 \times 5 = 15$. You might select an accidental quota, stratified random, or cluster sampling procedure to draw a sample of at least 15 of each group of machine operators.

Table 8.3 • **A dummy table comparing snack selections of machine operators on A-shift with machine operators on other shifts**

Snack Selection	Machine Operators on A-shift	Machine Operators on Other Shifts
Junk food	1	2
Fruit	3	4
Other	5	6

It is at this stage that you can best see the impact of adding variables to the analysis. It is always a temptation to add a variable. Indeed, you may have good reason to want to assess the impact of a number of variables. Professional research often analyzes many variables. However, adding one variable will increase the sample size required and the complexity of analyzing the data. Again, the use of dummy tables is very helpful in clarifying this for the researcher. Adding one variable to the analysis of workers' snack selections doubles the sample size and doubles the size of the dummy table. If we add the variable "time purchased (before or after shift)," for example, we would require two tables like Table 8.3, one for purchases before shift and one for purchases after shift. The sample size would be 12 × 5 = 60. A combined dummy table for such a study would look like Table 8.4.

Table 8.4 • **A dummy table for a study of workers' snack selections comparing before-shift purchases with after-shift purchases and machine operators on A-shift with machine operators on other shifts**

Snack Selection	Machine Operators on A-shift		Machine Operators on Other Shifts	
	Before shift	After shift	Before shift	After shift
Junk food	1	2	3	4
Fruit	5	6	7	8
Other	9	10	11	12

Adding another variable, such as "marital status," would require yet another doubling of sample size and add further complexity to the data analysis.

What would a dummy table look like for a study of the impact of "study time" on "mark received on a history exam"? In our previous use of this example (in Chapter 7), we used a line graph to present possible results. A second use of dummy tables can now be seen. They help to specify categories of analysis and data collection. The data collection sheet (or mini-questionnaire) suggested for this study (Chapter 6, Figure 6.5) asked the student to keep track of the amount of time spent studying and the mark received in a history examination. For each student, the data summarization form (Chapter 6, Table 6.4) recorded total study time and mark. The number of students required for your sample depends on how you are going to analyze your data. A minimum of about 30 is required regardless of the form of analysis.

However, if you were planning to analyze the data by placing it in a table, the number of cells in the table would also play a role in determining sample size. It would be possible to have a very large table with a row for every mark from 1 to 100. That would require a sample of 500 if only one category of "time spent studying" were used (1000 if two categories of "time spent studying" were used, and so on). Needless to say, that is not suitable for our purposes. Hence, a smaller number of categories for reporting and analyzing both the dependent variable (marks) and the independent variable (time spent studying) must be found. The simplest categorization for marks would be pass/fail, but that might not be satisfactory. You might prefer fail, 50–64, 65–79, and 80–95. That would be four categories of marks (see Tables 8.5 and 8.6).

Table 8.5 • **A dummy table for a study of the impact of number of hours spent studying on examination results using two categories for each variable**

Examination Result	Number of Hours Spent Studying	
	High	Low
Pass		
Fail		

Table 8.6 • **A dummy table for a study of the impact of number of hours spent studying on examination results using four categories for the dependent variable and three for the independent variable**

Examination Result	Number of Hours Spent Studying		
	Low	Moderate	High
80–95			
65–79			
50–64			
Fail			

Then there is the problem of finding categories for "time spent studying." This poses a different kind of problem. Again, you could have a row in your table for each possible value reported from 0 to perhaps 120 hours. This suffers from the same fault as having a column for each possible mark does. Such a table would require $100 \times 120 \times 5 = 60,000$ students in the sample. How are numbers of hours to be categorized? You will not know the range of values until the data are collected. But you might decide to have two categories—high and low. When the data have been gathered, you determine the average number of hours studied. All those above average are categorized "high," and those below are categorized "low." Or you might decide to have three categories—high, moderate, and low.

In this case, you divide the sample into three even groups: those with the highest number of hours, those with a moderate number, and those with the lowest number. It is best to work out these categories before you begin because of the indications for your sample size. Tables 8.5 and 8.6 demonstrate these categories.

In Table 8.5, two categories are used for the analysis of each variable. The sample required for such a study could be 4 × 5 = 20 (30 would be better). In Table 8.6, four categories are used for the dependent variable and three for the independent variable. The sample size required is 4 × 3 × 5 = 60.

The role of dummy tables can now be seen. They focus the research. They help to determine the categories of data analysis. They help to determine sample size. By devising dummy tables before collecting data, the researcher will not collect more data than are actually going to be used. There is no point in collecting data that will not go into the tables. The researcher is also guided in sample selection by decisions about data analysis. In this way, neither too much nor too little data are collected for analysis.

A few more examples may help to clarify this important procedure. What samples are required for longitudinal or comparative studies? Take the example of a "before and after" longitudinal study. In such a study, the same group is studied at two points in time. Hence, the determination of sample size is made by only one of the tables.

Refer back to the example of a longitudinal study on nutrition in Chapter 7. Because the same group is measured twice (or more), there must be a sufficient sample of that group in each measurement. The before and after measures each have three categories, so the minimum sample would be 3 × 5 = 15.

Take the example of the questionnaire developed to assess attitudes towards the building of nuclear power plants (Chapter 6). Data produced by questionnaires have to be categorized just like test results or numbers of hours spent studying. Like test results, scales on a questionnaire have a theoretical range. For the questionnaire on nuclear power plants, the range was from a low of 5 (indicating agreement with anti-nuclear statements) to a high of 20 (indicating disagreement with such statements). It is unlikely that you would want a table with 16 columns for this dependent variable. It will have to be categorized. High versus low agreement and high, medium, and low agreement are two possibilities. If you were comparing two groups—for example, a sample from Atomic Energy of Canada and a sample from the local Greenpeace Canada—your dummy table might look like that in Table 8.7. The sample for this study would comprise a minimum of 10 from each group. This might be achieved by a quota (accidental quota) or a stratified random (random quota) or cluster sampling procedure. Which would be best and why?

Table 8.7 • **A dummy table for a study comparing the views of two groups on the use of nuclear power plants**

Position on Nuclear Power Plants	Atomic Energy of Canada	Greenpeace Canada
Agreement		
Disagreement		

The example of a study of sexist attitudes among private versus public school students provides another opportunity to examine the utility of dummy tables. The questionnaire suggested for such a study is found in Chapter 6. The hypothesis was this:

Students who have gone to private schools are more sexist in their attitudes than students who have attended public schools.

The independent variable is "school social environment," private versus public school. The dependent variable is "sexist attitudes," as measured by responses to a five-item scale. The independent variable has two categories: public versus private school. Hence, the table for analyzing the data will have two columns, one for each category.

How is the dependent variable to be categorized? Again, it is unlikely that one row would be used for each of the 21 possible scores on the sexism scale. This would require a table with 21 rows. An alternative is to reduce the number of categories used to present and analyze the dependent variable. The way the scale was constructed, "agreement" indicated a sexist orientation, and "disagreement" indicated a lack of sexism. The midpoint on this scale was 15. A score below 15 could be taken to indicate low sexism. A score of 15 or higher could be taken to indicate high sexism. This would give two categories for the dependent variable. The break-point in the categories is determined here by the nature of the scale. Since there are two categories for the dependent variable, the table for analyzing data will have two rows.

Table 8.8 presents a dummy table for this study. The minimum sample for this study would be 20: 10 students from each educational context. If the researcher decided to use three categories for the sexism score, the minimum sample would be 30. If the researcher decided to include a category for mixed educational background as well, the sample size would have to increase to 45. Can you see why? Adding a medium sexism category would add another row to the table, with the result that the table would have two columns and three rows and thus six cells. Applying our guide rule of an average of five per cell, we would need a sample of $6 \times 5 = 30$. If the "mixed" category were added to the education context categories as well, the table would have three rows and three columns and thus nine cells: $9 \times 5 = 45$. Make up dummy tables for each of these proposed ways of analyzing the data.

For practical purposes, the sample size of student projects can be guided by two basic rules. First, 30 is the minimum sample size for most studies. Second,

Table 8.8 • A dummy table for a study of the impact of educational background on sexist attitudes among males

	Educational Background	
Sexism Score	Private School	Public School
High		
Low		

if analysis is to be carried out using tables, the sample size must be five times the number of cells in the table. Students should remember that in research that will be used to draw scientific conclusions, usually much larger samples are used. By limiting both the number of variables and the number of categories used to analyze each variable, smaller samples can be used. This will provide worthwhile experience in the research process.

A Warning about Internet Sampling Strategies

How does sampling design influence the results of quantitative research? It turns out that the effect is fairly significant. In quantitative studies, researchers want to be able to generalize the results to the larger population—to the people who did not participate in the research. This is the main purpose of this type of research. Obtaining a large, representative sample should be easy, shouldn't it? It's actually more difficult than you would think.

Many novice researchers, and even some veteran ones, think that collecting data using the internet is a valid way of conducting research. On the surface, internet-based data collection has many advantages. Many people have regular access to the internet. According to the *World Factbook* (2016), 89 per cent of Canadians have regular, at home access to the internet. The internet allows researchers to reach a wide geographic population—from the comfort of your research office. If coverage is this wide, why not use the internet to collect data?

A closer examination of the problems, however, should make us all think twice about relying on this mode of data collection. The first problem is how do we get a random sample of internet users? This is the biggest challenge to this type of research. We could get a list of email addresses, but how do we do that? There's no publicly available list of email addresses and under most provincial and national legislation, these lists cannot be distributed, even to researchers with good intentions, without each person on the list agreeing to the release of this information. In reality, most researchers cannot obtain a list. We might be tempted to use pop-up windows on a website. The participant visits a website and a pop-up asks them to participate in a survey and redirects them to a different site. Less than 10 per cent of all pop-up surveys are ever completed—and the people who participate in such activities are demographically, socially, politically, and economically very different from those who choose not to participate.

Then there's the problem with who has access to the internet. A closer look at internet access reveals large geographic and demographic disparities. It is true that over 80 per cent of the large industrialized nations such as Canada, Australia, Germany, South Korea, and Japan have regular access to the internet, but the vast majority of the earth's population does not have regular unfettered access (Arnett, 2015). According to the World Bank, only one-third of the world's population has access to the internet (Arnette, 2015). And even among those who do have access to the internet, as many as one in five do not regularly use it, mainly because they feel it has no relevance to them. A study in the United States reveals that over 60 per cent of high school dropouts do not use the internet, and 27 per cent of those with a physical limitation cannot use the internet (Zickuhr & Smith, 2012). In Canada, only 75 per cent of rural-dwelling Canadians and only 58 per cent of those with household incomes of less than $40,000 per year have access to the internet (Statistics Canada, 2013). More distressingly, Indigenous Peoples have even lower access. For example, of the 64 bands in the province of Manitoba, only 34 have high-speed internet. Of the remaining 30 bands, six rely on dial-up services, making it nearly impossible to load most of the current webpages. And these figures only account for internet access at band offices and/or community centres. Few private dwellings can afford internet service and, for those who do, since many dwellings are overcrowded, it is not uncommon for 10 to 12 people in a single household to share internet coverage (Government of Canada, 2013). This should give researchers pause as they consider their sampling strategies and how generalizable their results can be!

CASE STUDY

Results of Bad Sample Strategies in Quantitative Research

Despite the warnings, some researchers continue to use non-probability samples for research where they wish to generalize the results to a larger population. The popularity of web-based surveys, which are easy to design, has meant the proliferation of bad, non-probability research masquerading as authentic, generalizable research. As well, the decline in the use of landlines has meant that telephone surveys are becoming more prone to these types of errors as well. People using cellphones as their only source of telephone tend to be younger, less educated, less affluent, male, and members of non-racialized groups (Pew Research, 2018). They also have very different political, social, and cultural opinions.

Much questioning about telephone and internet surveys occurred around the US presidential election of 2016. Multiple polls the night before the election had Hillary Clinton leading Donald Trump by a wide margin (Real Clear Politics, 2017). Only one polling company forecasted correctly that Donald Trump would win the election. The polling world was taken by surprise, yet again, that their predictions were incorrect. Why did this happen? Recall that people who rely solely on cellphones as their only telephone and those who have less access to the internet tend to be those with less than high school education (Pew Research, 2018). One of the major reasons that the pollsters in the United States incorrectly predicted a Clinton win was because the polling methods they used (landline telephones and internet users) systematically excluded people with less than high school education (Bialik & Enton, 2016). This meant that when this group turned out to vote in large numbers, the pollsters had not ensured their voice became part of their polls. To be fair, there were other reasons why the pollsters were incorrect. Another major problem was the underrepresentation of people who do not regularly use the internet in their polling sample. They were simply excluded from internet polls. This group is surprisingly large and mainly older—a group of people who are more likely to vote as well. When a "national" survey uses only one mode of collecting data for their sample, readers should be cautious about the "generalizability" of the results.

Jon Krosnik, a respected survey researcher at Stanford University, has done some significant work on this issue. He prepared one survey but used three methods of sampling. In method one, he used the opt-in/pop-up method on the internet. He even offered a prize to those who participated in the opt-in method. In method two, he used a random digit dialing method to contact participants by telephone. In method three, he was able to obtain a list of email addresses and randomly selected a sample. Method one, the opt-in/pop-up internet sample always yielded the least accurate results. The random sampling of telephone numbers and internet addresses obtained very similar results and they were closest to actual observable results. The rate of error in the opt-in survey was twice the rate as the randomly selected samples (Langer, 2009).

Summary

The way in which the research sample is drawn determines the degree to which you can generalize from the findings of your study. Only randomly drawn samples ensure that the sample is likely to be representative of a larger population. Although other forms of sampling are used, the findings of such studies are limited to the samples studied. Dummy tables are helpful in determining sample size, focusing the questions to be asked in the research, and preparing the way for the later analysis of the data.

Key Terms

Questions for Review

1. Why do researchers use sampling procedures?
2. Why is it risky to rely on the observation of a single case in making generalizations about groups?

3. What are the two basic types of sampling procedure?

4. What are the advantages and disadvantages of each sampling procedure described?

5. What are the steps that must be taken in order to draw a truly random sample? Name two steps that might damage our ability to draw a random sample.

6. What are the critical issues in determining sample size?

7. While it is often necessary for researchers to study large samples in order to examine in detail the influence of many variables, what two basic rules can usefully guide student researchers in determining sample size?

8. Read several articles reporting research results that have been published in professional social and behavioural science journals. What sampling procedures were used?

9. Read an article, a report, or research published in a newspaper, then answer the following questions. If you do not think the article contains enough information, say so. Then guess what might have been done.

    a. How was the sample for this study drawn?

    b. What type of sample would you say it was?

    c. What dummy tables might have been used for this study?

    d. What hypothesis might this study have been designed to test?

    e. What were the basic concepts in this study?

    f. What variables were selected to measure the concepts involved in this study?

    g. How were the data collected?

    h. What conclusions were reached?

10. Could access to a hospital's admissions database be used to draw a random sample of patients to participate in a study of satisfaction with hospital meals? Why or why not?

11. Create a dummy table to study the influence of political party affiliation on gun control legislation. What questions would you have to ask on a survey to obtain the data you need to study this relationship?

12. Why do quantitative studies require larger sample sizes than qualitative studies?

13. What is the rationale for using non-random selection techniques for qualitative studies?

14. Why are studies using internet or cellphones only suspect?

Sources

Arnette, G. (2015, July 10). World wide web? Map resizes countries by number of internet users. *The Guardian*. Retrieved September 8, 2017 from www.theguardian.com/news/datablog/2015/jul/10/world-map-web-users-oxford-internet-institute

Bialik, C., & Enten, H. (2016, November 9). The polls missed Trump: We asked pollsters why. *FiveThirtyEight*. Retrieved September 8, 2017 from https://fivethirtyeight.com/features/the-polls-missed-trump-we-asked-pollsters-why/?ex_cid=2016-forecast

Cool, J. (2013). *Women in Parliament.* Catalogue No. 2011-56-E. Ottawa: Social Affairs Division, Parliamentary Information and Research. Retrieved June 28, 2018 from https://lop.parl.ca/content/lop/ResearchPublications/2011-56-e.pdf

Government of Canada. (2013). *Connectivity profiles by province.* Ottawa: Statistics Canada. Retrieved September 7, 2017 from www.aadnc-aandc.gc.ca/eng/1352223782819/1353504825398?p=mb

Government of Canada. (2016). *Party standings.* Retrieved June 28, 2018 from https://www.ourcommons.ca/Parliamentarians/en/members

Langer, G. (2009, September 28). More on the problems of opt-in internet surveys. *ABC News online* [Blog post]. Retrieved August 27, 2017 from https://pprg.stanford.edu/wp-content/uploads/More-on-the-Problems-with-Opt-in-Internet-Surveys-ABC-News.pdf

Pew Research. (2018, February 5). *Mobile fact sheet.* Retrieved June 20, 2018 from www.pewinternet.org/fact-sheet/mobile/

Real Clear Politics. (2017). *Election 2016 presidential polls.* Retrieved May 30, 2018 from www.realclearpolitics.com/epolls/latest_polls/president/

Statistics Canada. (2013, November 26). Canadian Internet Use Survey, 2012. *The Daily.* Retrieved August 28, 2017 from www.statcan.gc.ca/daily-quotidien/131126/dq131126d-eng.htm

World Factbook. (2016). *North America: Canada.* Washington: CIA. Retrieved June 20, 2018 from www.cia.gov/library/publications/the-world-factbook/geos/ca.html

Zickuhr, K., & Smith, A. (2012, April 13). *Digital differences.* Pew Research Center. Retrieved August 27, 2017 from www.pewinternet.org/2012/04/13/digital-differences/

Suggestions for Further Reading

Dillman, D. A., Smyth, J. D., & Christian, L. M. (2009). *Internet, mail and mixed-mode surveys: The tailored design method.* Hoboken, NJ: Wiley.

Eggertson, L. (2010). *Lancet* retracts 12-year-old article linking autism to MMR vaccines. *Canadian Medical Association Journal, 182*(4), E199–E200. https://doi.org/10.1503/cmaj.109-3179

Fowler, F. (2009). *Survey research methods* (4th ed.). Los Angeles: Sage.

Neuman, W. L., & Robson, K. (2018). *Basics of social research: Qualitative and quantitative approaches* (4th Cdn ed.). Toronto: Pearson.

Wakefield, A. J., Murch, S. H., Anthony, A., Linnell, J., Casson, D. M., Malik, M. . . . J.A. Walker-Smith. (1998). Ileal-lymphoid-nodular hyperplasia, non-specific colitis, and pervasive developmental disorder in children. *The Lancet, 351*, 637–41. [Retracted]. http://vaccines.procon.org/sourcefiles/retracted-lancet-paper.pdf

Weisberg, H. F. (2005). *The total survey error approach: A guide to the new science of survey research.* Chicago: University of Chicago Press.

Suggested Web Resources

MeanThat. (2016, April 3). *Non-probability sampling techniques* [Video file]. Retrieved April 12, 2018 from www.youtube.com/watch?v=Uih7cXuP2tA

Statistics Learning Centre. (2012, March 13). *Sampling: Simple random, convenience, systematic, cluster, stratified: Statistics help* [Video file]. Retrieved April 12, 2018 from www.youtube.com/watch?v=be9e-Q-jC-0

9   Ethics in Human Research

The key to identifying ethical issues in research is to take the position of a participant. How would you feel if you were asked certain questions or observed doing certain things, or if your records and papers were examined for research purposes? How would you want researchers to handle and report on the information they have about you? The ethical issues involved in doing research on humans are very much the same for both quantitative and qualitative research.

Staff and students of Canadian universities, many research organizations, and members of professional organizations are now formally required to conduct their research according to stated ethical principles and to demonstrate this to **research ethics boards (REBs)**. Researchers must submit their research proposal or plans to advisory bodies, which evaluate it based on ethical guidelines. These ethical principles require that participants in the research must be able to give informed consent to being part of the research, the identity of informants must be protected unless they give written permission to be identified in stored data and research reports, researchers must not coerce participants into participating or divulging information, and researchers must keep data for up to seven years (depending on the province) to protect themselves against charges of forging or falsifying data.

The purpose of this chapter is to outline major ethical considerations prior to conducting the data collection. This chapter provides information to students with regard to preparing their submissions to ethics review panels. It is a good idea to contact the board directly and obtain a copy of their guidelines and rules prior to submitting your proposal. This will help you to avoid unnecessary delays in launching your data collection, protect the integrity of the scientific research process, and likely strengthen your research results.

Some of you might be asking, "If ethics is so important, why are we discussing it in Chapter 9?" This is because although **ethics** considerations influence all aspects of the research process, we cannot fully assess ethical implications of any project until the research question has been finalized, the method of data collection identified, the variables or items to be measured are considered, and the population identified. Although ethics involves each of these areas, until these elements are addressed, an application to an ethical review board and approval by a review committee cannot be attained. In short, we must think about ethics throughout the research process, but we introduce it here so that it is not lost in the discussion and learning of new concepts.

The Ethics of Research

Research in the social sciences usually involves dealing with people, organizations, and groups. Unless you are dealing only with data that have already been collected, public records (such as census data), or public documents (such as newspaper articles), you will be asking people questions, observing their behaviour, or collecting other information about them. All our dealings with other people raise ethical issues. We are familiar with the ethical issues relating to our personal lives—issues of loyalty, honesty, and integrity, to name a few. Lately, businesses and corporations are beginning to ask questions about the ethics of economic life. So, too, we need to ask if there are ethical issues in research that need to be addressed.

As with many ethical issues in other areas of life, being thoughtful and considerate of the needs and feelings of others goes a long way towards guiding the researcher. How would you react if you were a participant or member of the group you intend to study? Would you respond well to the questions you intend to ask or the procedures you intend to employ?

Be considerate. You are asking people to do you a favour. You are appealing to their generosity to help you with your work. Not everyone will share your view of the importance of your research. This is true even if you are asking friends, family, or students you know. It is even more true if you are going into the community to do your research. You have a responsibility to the participants in your research to be considerate and not to waste their time. Moreover, you have a responsibility to other researchers not to irritate and alienate the community. If you are inconsiderate or poorly prepared, you let yourself down, waste the time and effort of others, and jeopardize future research.

Part of being considerate is being prepared. Another part is to take up only as much time as is essential. Not only does an unnecessarily long questionnaire waste your time, but it also wastes the time of those to whom it is administered. Ask yourself, "Is this question necessary? Do I really need to know how many children the respondent has?" If the study is about sharing tasks between husband and wife, then yes, you probably do want to ask that question. But if you are inquiring about past achievement in math, you may decide to eliminate the question. Does each question really relate to the hypothesis? Or does it really reflect personal curiosity? Interviews and questionnaires with a clear focus not only produce better data but are also less disruptive and wasteful.

You should also be considerate of participants because you are, to some extent, invading their **privacy**. If respondents sense that you are being intrusive or asking inappropriate questions, they may refuse to cooperate or may sabotage the research by giving misleading information. Your manner and the nature of your research should be carefully designed so as not to offend, embarrass, or annoy those you are studying. They are doing you a favour.

Part of being a considerate researcher is being careful about the way you seek permission from those you wish to study. While it is appropriate to tell people why you are doing the research, it is usually not wise to tell them what you hope to find, since this may bias the information they provide. At the completion of their projects, many researchers offer to tell participants what they found and their conclusions. This often provides interesting feedback for the researcher and those studied.

A consent form signed by you and/or your professor or head of department and the participant is a requirement for conducting most research with human participants. It will help to identify you, provide respondents with a contact if they have questions after the study, and is part of the process required to secure the cooperation of those you wish to be part of your study. The form should describe who you are (e.g., a student at a specified university), how you accessed the person's name, why you are doing your research (e.g., for a degree, a thesis, or a class project), and what the research will require from the person whose permission you are seeking (e.g., completing a questionnaire that will take 10 minutes, an interview lasting an hour, a group interview lasting 15 minutes, participating in an experiment that will involve watching and assessing some videos for half an hour). Providing this information makes it possible for the potential participant to make an informed decision about whether to participate. The consent form, or **plain language statement**, about the research is essential to ensuring that **informed consent** has been given.

A consent form usually concludes with information about what the participant should do if they have any questions or concerns about the research. This clause usually directs the participant to the research ethics board (REB) of the university or another organization responsible for the research, which is useful in situations where the participant does not feel comfortable discussing issues directly with the researcher. Figure 9.1 gives an example of a consent form. Preparing the form is also a good exercise to test whether you have thoroughly thought through your research plan. It will give your professor an opportunity to advise you about aspects of the research that remain unclear or confusing. When students do research as part of their course, their professor is responsible for them and for the conduct of the research. Therefore, it is in the interest of all for students and professors to confer carefully about each research project.

Printed on university letterhead

Consent Form: Title of Project

Principal Investigator: Professor's name
Student Investigator: Student's name
Tel: XXX-XXX-XXXX
Email: researcher@umanitoba.ca

Date

Funding organization or sponsor: Name of group providing financial support for this research (if any)

A. PURPOSE AND BACKGROUND

This project has been funded by [*indicate funding organization if the research is sponsored*]. The research is being conducted by [*indicate professor's and student's names*] at the Department of [*indicate name of department and faculty*], [*indicate university*].

In this research, we want to learn how people find work and whether they use their families and friends to find work. We are particularly interested in studying the work histories of youth without post-secondary education. We want to talk to you about your job experiences to better understand your feelings about Canadian society. A study of youth employment will help us to understand how it may affect you and your well-being, along with its effect on the Canadian economy.

You are invited to participate in this focus group meeting. However, the participation is strictly voluntary. Only if you agree to be part of this study will you be invited to participate in the meeting and answer the questions presented to you.

B. PROCEDURES

You have been selected to participate in this research because you have been identified as a youth without post-secondary school experience. There are two ways that we obtain names for our research. First, we may have obtained your name from a list provided by [*name of organization*]. Second, someone affiliated with [*name of organization*] may have suggested your name.

If you agree to participate in this research study, you will attend a group interview, which will last no longer than two hours, to discuss your experiences looking for work. The group interview will take place at [*indicate location of focus group, date, and time*]. The group meeting will be audio-taped if you permit us.

Continued

Figure 9.1 • **Sample consent form**

C. RISKS

There is no anticipated physical or psychological risk related to participating in this study. Should you decline to participate, your access to employment, settlement, and/or counselling services will not be affected in any way now or in the future. You may choose not to answer any questions and may leave the focus group at any time. Please indicate to the researcher any sensitive question related to your personal information that you do not want to be disclosed.

D. PROTECTION OF IDENTITY AND PRIVACY

Confidentiality will be secured in a variety of ways. Your name and contact information will not be recorded in the interview or used in the publication of any results. This form and any other documents bearing your name will be stored separately from your survey responses, which will be coded with an arbitrary number. When data collection is complete (not later than MM/YY), the list that links participants' numbers with their names will be destroyed, at which point it will be impossible for anyone, including the researcher, to identify data with specific participants. This anonymous data will be stored in paper form for up to 5 years post-publication of the results and for an indefinite period in electronic form. Results from this study will be disseminated through presentations at scholarly conferences and through publication in academic journals. At no time will individual responses be reported.

E. COMPENSATION

You will receive $50 at the end of the group interview as compensation for participating in this research. We will also provide some light refreshments during the group meeting.

F. QUESTIONS

Please contact [*the professor, student*] (please refer to contact information at the top of this letter) if you have any questions about the project.

G. CONSENT[1]

Your signature on this form indicates that you have understood to your satisfaction the information regarding participation in the research project and agree to participate as a subject. In no way does this waive your legal rights or release the researchers, sponsors, or involved institutions from their legal and professional responsibilities. You are free to withdraw from the study at any time and/or refrain from answering any questions you prefer to omit, without prejudice or consequence. Your continued participation should be as informed as your initial consent, so you should feel free to ask for clarification or new information throughout your participation.

The [*name of REB*] and a representative(s) of the University of [*university name here*] Research Quality Management / Assurance office may also require access to your research records for safety and quality assurance purposes.

If you have any questions about this research, feel free to phone or email me (see above). This research has been approved by the [*name of REB*] Research Ethics Board at [*name of university*]. If you have any concerns or complaints about this project you may contact the Human Ethics Secretariat at [*phone number of REB secretary*], or by email at [*email address of REB*].

_____

Participant's signature   Date

_____

Researcher's signature   Date

I am interested in obtaining a summary of the findings from this research project:

No ( )

Yes ( ): If yes, how would you like to receive the results?

By email ( ) Please provide email address: _____

_____

By surface mail ( ) Please provide mailing address:

_____

_____

_____

[1]This section is directly quoted from the University of Manitoba as is part of section D. 2010. *Human Subject Research Ethics Protocol Submissions (Ft. Garry Campus) Guidelines and Checklist for Submissions & Reviews*. http://umanitoba.ca/research/ors/ethics/human_ethics_REB_forms_guidelines.html

A personal card issued by your institution, stating your position (e.g., PhD student) and contact details is an effective introduction to participants (see Figure 9.2). When you give these cards to participants, they can feel more assured of your identity and purpose and confident that you are willing to allow them to verify who you are. This action, which shows prospective participants that you wish to act ethically and do the right thing by them, usually wins their attention and cooperation quickly. Further information, such as the contact information for the REB, can be placed on the reverse side of the card.

Canadian University	If you have any questions about this study, you may contact the Secretary of the Research Ethics Board.
Reece Urcher PhD student Department of Sociology Canadian University 111 Main Street Toronto, ON M2K 2C7 Cellphone: ### ### #### Fax: ### ### #### Email: reeceurcher@canadianu.ca	Telephone: ### ### #### Email: HERB@canadianu.ca Surface Mail: Secretary, Research Ethics Board Canadian University 111 Main Street Toronto, ON M2K 2C7

Figure 9.2 • **A sample card**

Formal Ethical Review of Research

Simply being considerate is not enough. The ethics of all research involving human participants has become a major area of discussion and policy review. Most professional associations, such as the Canadian Sociological Association and the Canadian Association of Social Workers, have devised codes of ethics to guide their members. Read the code of ethics for the professional association related to your intended occupation. These ethical codes are usually available online.

In 2010, the second edition of the *Tri-Council Policy Statement: Ethical Conduct for Research Involving Humans* (*TCPS2*) was passed by the Canadian Institutes of Health Research (CIHR), Social Sciences and Humanities Research Council of Canada (SSHRC), and the Natural Sciences and Engineering Research Council of Canada (NSERC), collectively known as the Interagency Panel on Research Ethics (PRE), the first major update of the original *TCPS* of 1998. Several changes were made to the *TCPS2* in 2014 (PRE, 2014). The purpose of the *TCPS* is "to create a uniform . . . ethics policy for research and a policy that would set the highest common standard for governing the academic or learned research done through these three primary funding agencies" (Kirby, 2007, p. 8). Under the new policy, any research that is funded by CIHR, NSERC, or SSHRC must adhere to these guidelines (*TCPS2*, 2014). As a result, universities in Canada, along with many professional organizations, have adopted these new regulations within their existing ethical framework. One of the conditions of obtaining ethical approval is that researchers (professors and students) must complete an online Course of Research Ethics (CORE) before their application to the REB may be considered. This course takes four to six hours to complete and reviews and tests prospective researchers about their knowledge of ethical research practices.

Following a number of excesses perpetrated by some overzealous or unscrupulous researchers in various fields, procedures have been instituted in all post-secondary institutions for the careful ethical scrutiny of research proposals by REBs prior to the commencement of the research and before funding is approved or passed on to the researchers. First instituted to guide medical research, ethical review is now required for all research involving human participants. The fundamental principles are stated in the *TCPS2* (2014). This document outlines ethics for Canadian research involving humans. REBs use the principles in this statement to guide their consideration of research proposals. All universities now require all research involving humans, including most sociological, psychological, business management, marketing, science, education, and oral history research, to be evaluated by an ethics committee. This includes both funded and unfunded research. Ethical considerations are important and becoming more complicated as more professional organizations adopt their own ethical guidelines and as the provinces have introduced their own, which has added to confusion among researchers. The remainder of this chapter outlines some of the major ethical considerations and is guided primarily by the *TCPS2*. Students are encouraged to also consult the REB guidelines within their own institution, their professional association, and their provincial legislation on privacy and protection of information for details about ethical guidelines.

CASE STUDY

Some Examples of Unethical Research

Not so long ago, researchers paid very little attention to the health and well-being of participants of their research. Canada has a long history of conducting questionable and even criminal experiments against its people. Canada's Indigenous Peoples were subject to many cruel, violent, and downright criminal experiments. In the 1940s and 1950s, several research studies subjected Indigenous children and adults to various inhumane living conditions to conduct scientific and medical studies. In one study, Indigenous children living in Norway House, Cross Lake, God's Lake Mine, Rossville, and The Pas in northern Manitoba were intentionally starved to give scientists a chance to examine the effects of malnutrition on growth and development patterns (Mosby, 2013). In subsequent studies, Indigenous children living on reserves in British Columbia, Alberta, Ontario, and Nova Scotia were refused proper diet and supplements to replicate the Manitoba study (Livingstone & Weber, 2013). Historian Ian Mosby (2013), discovered that scientists, with the help of the Canadian government, had allowed children in several remote Manitoba reserves to starve because they were the "perfect test subjects," meaning that they were not given the opportunity to provide any consent to participating in the study and lacked the political power to question the ethics of the study in the first place, and that because of the racist attitudes held by most Canadians at the time, their poor

Continued

living conditions would continue to go ignored. The scientists "rationalized" the unethical treatment by suggesting that the sacrifices of a few children would lead to significant benefits to the health of future children. Instead, their studies have become part of a massive catalogue of abuse, colonization, and genocide inflicted on Indigenous Peoples within Canada that were encouraged and supported by the Canadian government. In June 2015, the Truth and Reconciliation Commission of Canada (2015) released its long-awaited report on the effects of residential school system on the lives of Indigenous Peoples in Canada. Among its recommendations is recognition of the harm that has been done towards Indigenous Peoples.

The Stanford Prison Experiment, the Milgram Study, and the Tuskegee Study are other infamous examples of questionable ethical practices that students should learn more about. Lest students think ethical practices are less likely to be ignored today, however, the following recent examples shed light on the extent of this problem. Recently, medical ethicists have begun to question a widespread practice among industrialized nations to "offshore" clinical trials. By offshoring these studies, researchers do not have to abide by the more stringent ethical standards imposed on them by professional organizations and regulatory bodies in their own countries or jurisdictions. In 2008, more than 6400 clinical trials were being conducted outside the United States, where funding for these trials originated (Gonzales, 2010). In the 10-year period between 2000 and 2009, over 58,000 drug trials (Bartlett & Steele, 2010) were being conducted in overseas jurisdictions with lighter restrictions on ethical regulations. In countries with less rigid ethical guidelines, it is easier for researchers to conduct studies without requiring informed consent about the true nature of the study or potential risks to participants. An exposé by Bartlett and Steele revealed that many of the participants in such studies believed they were being treated for a disease and were unaware they were part of a clinical trial. Death is not an uncommon event in some of these trials. In New Delhi, in 2010, 49 babies died in a 30-month period during a trial of blood-pressure medication, while in a one-year period in 2008, seven babies died in Argentina after participating in a trial of a pneumonia vaccine. These are just two incidences of extreme abuse and ethical practices in recent medical trials. We must be vigilant in our research practices to ensure that future participants are not harmed by our research.

Basic Principles of Research Ethics

The following principles of research ethics summarize the concerns most REBs focus on in evaluating research proposals.

Principle 1: Researchers must treat with dignity and respect the persons, groups, and organizations who participate in their research

According to the *TCPS2* (2014) guidelines, these issues involve respect for persons, concern for social welfare, and social justice.

People have feelings, orientations, cultures, rights to privacy, and rights to control their lives and information about themselves. The rights of people are greater than the researcher's "need to know." However important you think your research is, you must place participants' well-being first. Sensitivity to others is very important but especially in social science research, where it is precisely that sensitivity that may open new insights into the nature of social situations. You are asking people, "What is it like to be you? What is your perspective on this? How do you respond to this or that situation?" In order to "hear" their responses, you need both to ask sensitive questions and to listen very sensitively to their responses.

Following current discussion of ethics in human research, we refer to people who consent to be researched as "participants," rather than "subjects," for several reasons. First, the term "participant" implies a degree of cooperative activity on the part of those we study. Participants are not passive subjects but cooperate with us in our research. It is important to remember that without the cooperation of participants, we will not get our data. This helps to remind us of our dependence on them and to enhance our respect for them. Remembering that you are dealing with people, not objects, will help you to retain the levels of respect and concern appropriate to humans.

"Participants" is also a useful term because it encompasses groups, corporations, organizations, and neighbourhoods as well as persons. All participants have rights, needs for privacy, and a claim on our respect.

The respect accorded to participants extends to treating the information they provide with great care and not violating their privacy. One way of protecting your informants is to mask their identity by never recording names, by changing the names on your files and using fictitious names in your reports, by assigning numerical codes, and by referring only to grouped data (that is, not to Tom Brown's score individually but to the average score of "young males" in response to a particular question). You can mask the locality of your research by not naming the municipality or organization in which the research was done.

If you are promising participants that you will protect their identities (which is the most common case), your REB will wish to know how you will accomplish this (e.g., de-identifying records and reports of information with codes, keeping records locked in a secure place, encrypting computer data files, etc.).

After gaining permission, you must retain sufficient information, including letters of invitation or recruitment, consent forms, and data, to prove that you actually did what you proposed to do and were given ethical clearance to do so. This is necessary to defend yourself against the possible charge of forging your data and to be prepared for an audit by your REB.

Personal information and privacy

In most social science research, there is no need to collect information that identifies individual participants. Researchers seldom need facts that can identify individual participants to others. However, if you plan to gather and publish such information, you must know the relevant law regarding privacy. Most provinces and territories have passed privacy legislation that binds researchers to protect their participants' personal information. The *Canadian Charter of Rights and Freedoms* also has provisions protecting the privacy and rights of individuals. It is a good idea to become familiar with the privacy legislation in your province. The *TCPS2* also contains general guidelines about protecting individual privacy. Personal information includes information given to the researcher by the participant. It may be answers provided to survey questions or in interviews. It may be health information from physicians' records or academic grades from school. Regardless of the source, "personal information" identifies individuals and must be kept from public viewing at all times.

Depending on the relevant privacy principles, there can be additional restrictions on the collection, use, and disclosure of a type of personal information known as "sensitive information." Sensitive information may include information or an opinion about an individual's race, ethnicity, sexual orientation, criminal record, religious beliefs and affiliations, philosophical beliefs, health information, political opinions, and membership in political parties, trade unions, and professional associations. "Health information" is information or an opinion about an individual's health or disabilities, their health service usage or intended use, personal information they give to health services, and personal information they give when arranging the donation of their body parts.

Before gathering personal information, always consult an expert in privacy regulations. If you research within a government department or private firm, talk to the privacy officer. If you research as a consultant or with a volunteer organization, seek advice from a lawyer. Most universities have units that will provide advice to researchers about privacy laws. Be familiar with the privacy legislation of your province. Otherwise, you may compromise participants' rights and break the law.

The following list contains some guiding ethical principles researchers must abide by as they conduct their studies on human participants.

- **Respect for human dignity:** Researchers must maintain the physical, social, religious, familial, community, linguistic, and cultural integrity of all participants.
- **Respect for free and informed consent:** Participants must be fully informed about the purpose and intended results of the research project prior to signing a consent form. They must not be coerced into participating by any means. Consent, according to the *TCPS2* (2014), is an ongoing process (p. 7). Any changes to data collection protocols must be approved by REBs and participants must be informed and allowed to leave the study.
- **Respect for vulnerable persons:** The *TCPS2* (2014) reminds us that "some people may be incapable of exercising autonomy because of youth, cognitive impairment, other mental health issues or illness" (p. 6). Researchers must take special care in studying these participants. This usually means obtaining consent from parents/guardians or primary caregivers.

- **Respect for privacy and confidentiality:** Privacy is a fundamental right and is protected in various legislative documents both provincially and nationally. Participant information must be kept in secure locations and not shared for purposes outside the intended research. Published documents must remove any identifying information that may compromise the privacy and confidentiality of research participants. The *TCPS2* (2014) outlines various types of directly and indirectly identifiable information (p. 58–9).

- **Respect for justice and inclusiveness:** There is a history of excluding participants from research on the basis of their age, language, ability, gender, race, religion, ethnicity, sexual orientation, and ability. The *TCPS2* identifies this kind of exclusion as injustice. The *TCPS2* (2014) warns us, however, "that particular individuals, groups or communities should neither bear an unfair share of the direct burdens of participating in research, nor should they be unfairly excluded from the potential benefits of participation" (p. 49). This issue is particularly important when considering research with First Nations, Métis, and Inuit peoples, as discussed later in this chapter.

- **Balancing harms and benefits:** Participants in any social science research should not expect to receive any personal benefit. Benefits from most of our research are based on advancement of our understanding of a particular topic or problem and thus are social benefits. Participation in research should not result in harm to participants. Your REB will determine whether or not your research project meets the criteria of low harm.

- **Minimizing harm:** It is the researcher's duty to avoid, prevent, or minimize harm to participants. To minimize harm, research projects should recruit the smallest number of participants and subject them to the smallest number of tests needed to achieve valid data. Minimal risk is defined by the *TCPS2* (2014) as "research in which the probability and magnitude of possible harms implied by participation in research is no greater than those encountered by participants in those aspects of their everyday life that relate to the research" (p. 21). This relatively vague definition may make it difficult for new researchers to determine whether or not their project constitutes "minimal" risk to participants. This is one of the reasons why an independent REB is needed to assess all research.

- **Maximizing benefits:** In most research, the participant receives no direct benefit from participating in the study. The benefit usually occurs in the published research that helps to advance knowledge in a particular field or discipline. Incentives given to participants, if any, should be minimal and not cause undue influence. For instance, giving a low-income mother $1000 to have her child participate in an untested vaccine study may be too high an incentive, given her economic position. The *TCPS2* takes no position supporting or rejecting the use of incentives.

Principle 2: Research must be based on knowledge of the work of others in the area and be conducted and/or supervised by persons qualified to do the work who have the necessary facilities to ensure the safety of participants

It is unethical to rush into the field to collect data before doing a literature review to learn what has been done before, what is known, and what questions remain in the field of study you propose. It is also usually a great help to see how others have tackled the problem you propose to study. It is unethical to carry out poorly designed research since, at the very least, people's time is wasted and, at worst, misleading results might be declared. It is also unethical to unnecessarily replicate studies (unless the purpose is to corroborate evidence) because it is a waste of research funds and the participants' time and goodwill. It is likely that any research you do as a student will need to be cleared by your professor and a thesis/dissertation committee, in addition to an REB.

While many of the skills required for social science research are similar to the ordinary skills of human interaction, their use in research requires careful supervision, particularly when students are learning how to research. In one of the co-authors' experience on an REB, the most problematic research proposals have come from researchers who were just being introduced to the skills of social science research. New researchers require close assistance from their supervisors, who should not allow them to choose sensitive topics that are more appropriate for experienced researchers.

Supervision is also required because in the process of interviewing someone, you may uncover problems that are beyond your ability to resolve—a difficult domestic situation, a deeply troubled person, or some other such circumstance. You are probably not trained as a counsellor or family therapist, or in other helping skills, and hence you have no business trying to solve these problems. You should carry a list of qualified social workers, counsellors, or medical practitioners to whom you can refer people in need. These specialists must be contacted prior to your data collection to ensure they are qualified to assist your participants should they experience ill effects. You may have to report a particularly serious situation to the police or a social worker, especially if the participant is a minor or under institutional care. However, you are only there to collect information relevant to your research project; you are not a helping agent. Your abilities and responsibilities are quite limited. Discuss these issues with the person responsible for your research, or your professor, or your supervisor.

Principle 3: The potential benefits of a research project must substantially outweigh the potential harm to participants

Again, discuss these issues with the person responsible for your research, or your professor, or your supervisor. Your REB can also provide input on these issues. REBs are there to weigh the promised benefits of a project against its potential to harm participants and also to ensure the collection of relevant data. Although researchers have a responsibility to minimize harm, the role of the researcher is different from the role of the therapist or helper. Confusion between therapy and research often leads to serious ethical dilemmas.

Principle 4: Participants in research must be able to make a voluntary, informed decision to participate

Consent

The decision to participate must be based on knowledge of what will be involved, what will be demanded in terms of time, activity, and topics covered, what risks are likely, and where to lodge a complaint should that become necessary. This information is usually provided by means of a consent form like the sample in Figure 9.1, otherwise referred to as a plain language statement. Potential participants must understand such information. This may require translation, careful wording in everyday language, and avoiding the disciplinary jargon that researchers use for efficient communication with each other but that leaves the layperson bewildered.

Written consent from the participant is required in almost all instances of research where humans are participants. Increasingly, REBs are requiring researchers conducting online surveys and self-administered surveys to have all participants sign consent forms. According to the *TCPS2* (2014) consent is assumed when the actions of the participant—such as the return of a completed online survey—indicate consent (p. 46). In these cases, a consent form is not strictly required. Kitchin (2007) agrees with this assessment, given the extreme difficulties in identifying and contacting potential participants on the internet, especially for those researchers conducting a content analysis of blogs, online forums, and discussion groups. When in doubt, however, it is always better to err on the side of caution and collect signed consent forms when possible.

The consent forms are always stored in locked filing cabinets in secure offices. They may be stored for a period of up to seven years (depending on the provincial legislation). These consent forms are always stored separately from the data collected. As a good organizational strategy, consent forms should be separated from surveys, audio or video data, and research notes as soon as the information is collected. That way, if data were compromised, it would not be possible for persons other than the researcher to connect the information collected with specific individuals.

Usually, the risks and discomforts involved in social science research are minimal. However, there are risks that need to be carefully examined. The most important issue here is the risk of the disclosure of information that might be damaging to a person. It is not possible for you to promise absolute confidentiality to the people you interview. There is always a chance that direct quotes may identify individuals. It is your duty to inform all participants of this, no matter how remote the chance. You could be subpoenaed for results if they have a bearing on a court case. Your files are open to searches under the freedom of information legislation current in your province. Before embarking on a project in which this might happen, ask yourself, "How would I deal with it?"

Gaining informed consent poses particular problems for some forms of social research. One such example is public behaviour. This does not usually require consent. Some research is little more than having a conversation with someone. However, that conversation may have proceeded differently if the participant in the research had known the intent of the conversation. In such a case, it would be ethically correct to inform the participant that their responses and opinions will be used in research, but such information might destroy the validity of the research. REBs now assist researchers to resolve some of these ethical issues.

Another issue related to discomfort and risk involves asking questions about sensitive areas. Topics may be sensitive because they are public issues, politically sensitive, or personally painful. For example, interviewing parents a few months after the death of their child from sudden infant death syndrome might be important in understanding the grief process following such a death, but it might be too disruptive to the parents and in fact could affect (positively or negatively) the very process you intended to study.

Voluntariness

While rarely an issue in social science research, it is important never to coerce compliance by offering overly enticing rewards for participation, such as large sums of money or holidays in the sun. At most, participants may receive reimbursement for expenses or some small compensation for the time they give. Most research-funding bodies do not allow for large incentives. CIHR, NSERC, and SSHRC do allow for some compensation but not excessive amounts. It is almost always more acceptable to offer children and youth gift certificates (e.g., to a movie or a bookstore) rather than cash. For some participants, however, cash incentives are not appropriate. In recent research one of the co-authors of this book has participated in, research participants often refused the $50 incentive for an interview lasting two to five hours. The argument made was that the families wished that the research would contribute to changes in policy and practice and that this would be "reward enough." However, it is not ethical for interviewers to allow the participant to refuse (given issues related to bookkeeping and fairness). In these incidents, we advised the interviewers to indicate that participants were not permitted to reject the incentive but that they could suggest that the cash be donated to a charity of their choice.

In some cases of social science research, the investigator may be in a position of power over the participant (e.g., parent/child, professor/student, employer/employee, supervisor/subordinate, parole officer/parolee). When this is the case, particular care must be taken in securing consent. In some cases, it may be impossible to get free consent, and the research may have to be abandoned. In other cases, a neutral third party may be able to secure the consent. Further, an interviewer wearing a lab coat or a clerical collar while conducting an interview may be playing on a symbol of authority to gain the participant's acquiescence. The style of clothing to wear while conducting an interview needs to be considered in terms of the power relations between interviewer and interviewee. The *TCPS2* (2014) advises that "consent should be judged from the perspective of prospective participants, since the individuals being recruited may feel constrained to follow the wishes of those who have some form of control over them" (p. 26). This has to do with issues of trust and dependency. Students who do not wish to participate in research (for course credit, which is common in some disciplines) conducted by their professors, for example, should be given reasonable alternative projects for credit should they wish to opt out of the study. Physicians and nurses should not be involved in the primary health care of their research participants for similar reasons.

However, in most social science research, the most powerful figure is likely to be the participant, who can just walk away, refuse to answer, or give a "safe" or misleading answer. This imbalance of power is central to maintaining the public's trust in participating in scientific research.

Freedom to withdraw

Participants in your research must not only be free to consent to participating at the outset, they must also be reminded that they are free to withdraw at any time without penalty and "need not offer any reason for doing so" (*TCPS2*, 2014, p. 27). This can be very frustrating to researchers, but it is not ethical to pressure participants to complete interviews and questionnaires or to stay for the completion of the experiment. To do otherwise violates the rights and freedom of the participant. Arguing or pleading with participants that their withdrawal will waste your time, threaten your grade in a subject, hold up your degree, necessitate another interview with someone else, or render invalid the questionnaire constitutes pressure and is therefore unethical. Students should bear this in mind when constructing consent forms and approaching potential participants. This also needs to be a consideration throughout the entire data collection exercise.

Principle 5: Research is a public activity, conducted openly and accountable both to the researcher's community and to the participants in the research

Research is a public activity conducted to increase our knowledge of some aspect of the universe. Its very public nature is one of the strengths of knowledge generated by research. Recall the definition of science in Chapter 2. This public nature of research also helps to keep researchers honest and affords a level of protection to participants.

This applies to research teams and covers the rights of co-researchers and assistants. It is important that all researchers and staff involved be as fully informed as possible so that they know what they are part of, what their role in the project is, what the overall goal is, and what procedures are involved. Keeping co-workers and subordinates in the dark is dangerous, inconsiderate, a waste of their input, and unethical. Imagine how you would feel if after working on some aspect of a project, you discovered that its overall goal or basic technique violated your sense of right and wrong. The *TCPS2* (2014) indicates that the principal researcher is ultimately responsible for the actions of her co-researchers, interviewers, and assistants (p. 25).

The research ethics boards at most post-secondary institutions have representatives from a variety of disciplines—from medicine, law, and religion, for example—and from the wider community to provide a public forum for assessing the ethical considerations in specific research projects. As we said in the

In Focus

A Note on Power Dynamics

Although our goal as researchers is to minimize the power differential between the researcher and the participant, there remains a power dynamic. By power dynamic, we mean that the act of conducting research automatically places the researcher in a position of power over the participant. For instance, when preparing the research report, the researcher has the power to identify what quotes are used and who is quoted. The researcher has the power to identify and even determine the issues that are most significant or important and which ones are the least important. They even can choose to leave out issues that they feel are insignificant. Even the act of interviewing has power related to it. An unstructured interview, where the goal is to let the participant identify the issues and direct the flow of conversation, has power attached to it. The researcher still has the authority as "the expert" and the participant provides information.

Even the most seasoned researcher cannot change the way participants perceive their role and contribution to research. We can mitigate some of the issues that cause this power imbalance. We can allow, even in the most structured of interviews, for participants to ask us questions and to add further detail. We encourage participants not to answer any question that they feel is unnecessary or inappropriate, or reveals too much personal information. We give participants the right to end the interview at any time without question or consequence. Good researchers also provide participants with a "sneak preview" of the final report and will allow them to make suggestions or changes to their answers. By including the participant in these aspects of the research process, we respect and value the contributions they make and we can reduce some of the power the researcher has to determine the outcome of the project.

introduction to this chapter, all research involving humans, organizations, and corporations requires the scrutiny and approval of an REB. Much of the research in social science does not raise life-and-death issues; however, many proposals require important advice, caution, or redesign to protect either the researcher or the participants, or both.

Special Ethical Issues in Qualitative and Secondary Data Research

Qualitative research often brings researchers and participants into close contact and creates a need for the interests of both to be balanced. Researchers can improve the lives of participants if they have access to such data, and they need support in their efforts. Because participants provide researchers with personal data, they need to be protected from infringements on their privacy. Research ethics boards consider a number of issues as they seek to support the interests of both participants and researchers.

First, the close and sometimes extended contact between researchers and participants can change researcher/participant relationships and compromise the original conditions under which studies receive ethics approval, especially in relation to questions of authority and trust. REBs require formal relationships between researchers and participants based on clear explanations by researchers and the official consent of participants. During in-depth interviews and participant observation, you and your participants develop a rapport and personal trust, and the relationship can become less formal and more personal. Eventually, participants may reveal personal secrets, trusting you to remain silent. Such confidences are often of little consequence, but participants may confide personal information that will force you to make difficult choices. They may reveal facts that you as a researcher are obliged to report—for example, that they are victims of abuse or perpetrators of crimes. In such situations, you would be faced with a conflict of trust. Either you betray the trust of your participant, or you betray your professional and ethical obligations.

Similarly, in-depth interviews about sensitive issues may stimulate memories that participants find upsetting. REBs often require that researchers make provisions for referring participants to counselling agencies should they have such problems. It is not ethical for you to conduct an interview or series of interviews that leave respondents upset, with nothing in place to meet their need.

Given the personal nature of much qualitative data, REBs seek to protect participants' privacy. You must obtain permission from participants if you wish to quote them in reports. It is acceptable, as long as the participant's consent is obtained, to identify certain people as sources. This may involve quotations that can be attributed to upper management at some organizations, to politicians, and to experts. The issue is that these kinds of identity disclosures are not used very often, and when they are, they are used sparingly. The general practice is to assign pseudonyms to all participants in publications and research reports. Researchers must also take steps to de-identify data—that is, they must remove all references to the identities of participants from tapes and transcripts, such as names and unique characteristics. Lastly, REBs oblige researchers to keep data in secure places, such as locked filing cabinets and encrypted computer files that only they and their supervisors can access. You must have such places ready before collecting data and should officially notify participants in your explanatory statement that you have made such arrangements to protect their data.

REBs also have concerns about observational studies. University and college students must obtain permission from their REB for most observational research. This includes observations of public events such as church services and concerts, and of some online activities where individuals have a presumption that "participants and observers will accord the proceedings some degree of privacy" (TCPS2, 2014, p. 145). When observation focuses on specific organizations, groups, or individuals, REBs require that researchers obtain permission from the intended participants. Therefore, if you wish to observe a local

CASE STUDY

Reflexivity

When reading qualitative research, you might see a new word, "reflexivity." Reflexivity is a process in qualitative research, particularly in feminist methodology, that refers to the understanding that the study of any social phenomenon or problem is always shaped by the researcher's personal experiences, biases, opinions, and outlook. It is not possible for human beings to be entirely "object-ive" about any subject that involves human interaction or behaviour. We "filter" our observations through the cultural, historical, social, and religious mindsets that shape our personal identity. For this reason, social science research, par-ticularly for postmoderinists and feminists, cannot be objective or value-free. We can, as researchers, however, reduce the amount of personal bias and opin-ion that shapes our interpretation of the qualitative data we collect. It is difficult, but becoming aware of our own personal biases, assumptions, and preferences is important as we examine the data and begin to make sense of it. This process is called reflexivity.

It is difficult for some people to learn to be reflexive because we are so en-meshed in our own lives. One analogy is a fish swimming in a fish bowl. The fish knows it is in water but it doesn't appreciate the water it is swimming in until it is removed from the fish bowl. Culture and social situations are very similar. As human beings, we "think" we are aware of our biases, but until something happens that makes us aware of how culture, history, the things we learn, the people we spend time with, and the things we read all influence our outlook, it can be difficult to be reflexive. For some people, travelling to distant places to learn different cultures is one way to become more reflexive. It's like moving your fish into a new fish tank. Being exposed to different cultures, societies, lan-guages, and histories can help us better understand our biases and appreciate differences. For others, simply reading about different cultures or learning a new language can encourage important shifts in the way we think that will help us to begin to appreciate differences in culture or opinion.

Regardless of how you come to realize your own biases, recognizing that not everyone thinks the same thoughts or values the same things as you do and that these differences are based on history, culture, religion, language, and social context is a major step towards reflexivity.

political group or an order of nuns, or monitor an internet chat room, your REB may not give approval until the potential participants supply their written per-mission. If researchers plan to conduct observation studies on premises that are privately owned or have restricted entry, researchers are obliged by their REBs to obtain permission to enter the premises from owners or caretakers. Hence, if you wish to enter factories to observe workers, convention centres to observe visitors, or nightclubs to observe patrons, your REB will require letters of permission from owners or managers. Most research done in shopping centres also requires permission from the manager of the complex.

There are some exceptions to the rules around consent and observation. According to Article 10.3 of *TCPS2* (2014), in situations where those participating have no reasonable expectation of privacy, the researcher must submit a document to his or her REB articulating the need for an exception to informed consent (p. 145). This applies in public places where

- the research does not involve any intervention staged by the researcher or direct interaction with the individuals or groups;
- individuals or groups targeted for observation have no reasonable expectation of privacy; and
- any dissemination of research results does not allow identification of specific individuals (*TCPS2*, 2014, p. 16).

Generally, covertness in all research is unethical unless it is necessary for the research to have scientific validity, the researchers are able to accurately define the extent of the covertness, no alternatives exist, participants are not exposed to any increased harm by the covertness of the project, researchers make immediate disclosures to participants, participants are able to withdraw their data, and the research will not bring notoriety to the research community.

In Focus

Falsifying Data

Falsifying data and results is another unethical practice that, sadly, has been getting lots of media attention lately. One high profile study was featured in the premier interdisciplinary journal, *Science*. In 2014, scientists Michael LaCour, a PhD student in psychology, and his supervisor, Dr Donald Green at Columbia University, published what appeared to be a very important paper. They found that negative opinions on same-sex marriage could be reversed with a simple but short face-to-face conversation between a LGBTTQ canvasser and a potential voter (Wanjek, 2016). Imagine how more accepting society could be of all kinds of differences if all it took was a short conversation! Naturally, everyone wanted the "recipe" or the transcript of the discussion points. Unfortunately, LaCour could neither produce the transcript nor the data that he supposedly analyzed for his PhD thesis and for the published paper. The journal later retracted the study in 2015 when the results were deemed to be fabricated.

It is worth noting that not only was the article retracted with great fanfare, but the lead author, Michael LaCour, had his new job as a professor at Princeton University rescinded. Dr Green has now changed his research practices to provide more scrutiny in regards to his students' work. Falsifying data is not only unethical and damaging to your discipline, it can cost you your job!

Should you wish to consult archives, your REB will require that you obtain permission from the legal custodians. You would also be obliged to inform the custodians of how you intend to use the material and not to use it for any other purpose.

The use of secondary data is also creating increasing confusion regarding ethical requirements. According to the *TCPS2*, "secondary use refers to the use in research of information originally collected for a purpose other than the current research purpose" (2014, p. 64). For instance, one of the co-authors of this book had a student who wanted to survey victims of crime regarding their satisfaction with Victim Services. A database containing contact information and victimization reports was available to this researcher. But since the database was not originally collected for research purposes, the researcher had to contact each individual and obtain permission for the data to be used in the study. More commonly, issues arise from the use of health and tax records for research purposes. There are valid reasons for analyzing this type of information. First, it lowers the research burden on society; the less researchers must "bother" the public to participate in research, the less burden is placed on society. The information contained in such databases may not be readily available to participants. For instance, medical diagnoses and related test results may not be known to the potential participant—but they are readily available in such databases to which the researcher may obtain access.

Under most provincial jurisdictions, as long as the datasets have been anonymized (all identifying personal information has been stripped from the database), researchers are free to analyze their data provided that all of the following apply:

- identifiable information is essential to the research;
- the use of identifiable information without participants' consent is unlikely to adversely affect the welfare of individuals to whom the information relates;
- the researchers will take appropriate measures to protect the privacy of individuals and to safeguard the identifiable information;
- the researchers will comply with any known preferences previously expressed by individuals about any use of their information;
- it is impossible or impracticable to seek consent from individuals to whom the information relates; and
- the researchers have obtained any other necessary permission for secondary use of information for research purposes (*TCPS2*, 2014, p. 64).

Research with Indigenous Peoples

CIHR, NSERC, and SSHRC have developed special ethics guidelines for research about Indigenous Peoples and have devoted an entire chapter in the *TCPS2* to its discussion. Indigenous Peoples have been the subject of extensive research, but much of the historical work done with them has not benefitted them. Much of this research has been conducted by outsiders who have neglected to use methods that appropriately recognize the multiple cultures, languages, religions, and traditions of this diverse people. As a result of these injustices, many Indigenous Peoples are rightly suspicious and distrusting of research, particularly the kind that appears to have no communal benefit.

Like other participants, Indigenous Peoples are subject to the same types of protections we discussed earlier. The difference is that when working with Indigenous Peoples, there is recognition of the harm that has been done to them in the past by ill-intentioned researchers, and recognition that their unique culture, way of life, and contribution to Canada must be acknowledged to best protect their interests when participating in research. The following are some guidelines identified by McNaughton and Rock (2003) and augmented by more recent information from the *TCPS2*.

1. **Decolonizing research:** Current research on Indigenous Peoples should include "Indigenous knowledge, traditions, beliefs and values"; adhere "to Indigenous protocols at all stages"; involve Elders and Indigenous researchers; involve partnership at all stages of research design; and use "Indigenous methodologies as appropriate to local traditions and the subject being addressed" (McNaughton & Rock, 2003, p. 15). Research practices should incorporate their unique worldview that extends "to the interconnection between humans and the natural world" and includes "obligations to maintain, and pass on to future generations, knowledge received from ancestors as well as innovations devised in the present generation" (*TCPS2*, 2014, p. 113).
2. **Equity:** All participants should be treated fairly and equally by researchers. In the past, "abuses stemming from research have included: misappropriation of sacred songs, stories and artefacts; devaluing of Indigenous peoples' knowledge as primitive or superstitious; violation of community norms regarding the use of human tissue and remains; failure to share data and resulting benefits; and dissemination of information that has misrepresented or stigmatized entire communities" (*TCPS2*, 2014, p. 113). To ensure this does not happen again, researchers should ensure that their research will be relevant to the community. Access to data and results by the participants is imperative in terms of the development of community programs and services as a result of research.
3. **Equitable treatment of Indigenous researchers:** Indigenous Peoples should be represented on grant adjudication committees; the merit of non-academic contributions should be considered; Indigenous researchers should be identified as such in projects. Community engagement in the research process is essential as an ethical practice in research with this group. Research should also "support capacity building through enhancement of the skills of community personnel in research methods, project management and ethical review and oversight" (*TCPS2*, 2014, p. 129). This point is related to number 4, which follows.
4. **From obligation to opportunity:** This involves moving beyond the postcolonial critique that has defined much research on Indigenous Peoples

in Canada. Recognition of the rights and self-worth of Indigenous Peoples can help our society move forward. Research on Indigenous Peoples that incorporates opportunity for Indigenous researchers and common research goals may be a first step in social justice. One of the best ways to accomplish this is to apply collaborative and participatory approaches in research and data collection with communities. Another way forward is to mentor Indigenous students in conducting research for their bachelor's, master's, and doctoral studies. If this is not possible, employing assistants and translators from the community also assists in capacity-building.

5. **Partnership with Indigenous Peoples:** Several communities have adopted their own ethics code, based on consultations around the First Nations Regional Longitudinal Health Survey. Known as OCAP, it is based on community ownership of data collected, control over this data, access to data, and "possession of research processes affecting participant communities" (*TCPS2*, 2014, p. 122). SSHRC, NSERC, and CIHR have all created special advisory bodies that oversee research for and about Indigenous Peoples. The idea is to give "Aboriginal [*sic*] scholars and other Aboriginal knowledge-keepers full responsibility for management of research" on Indigenous issues (McNaughton & Rock, 2003, p. 17). In practice, Indigenous communities should be involved in all aspects of the research process, especially when the welfare of entire communities is affected. Indigenous communities must be directly involved when data collection occurs on First Nations, Métis, or Inuit land; when recruitment criteria includes "Indigenous" identity of potential participants; and when cultural heritage or traditional knowledge are the topics of study. The community must also be consulted in the interpretation of data collected in such studies (*TCPS2*, 2014).

6. *Gus-wen-tah* **and joint exploration:** This term refers to the Indigenous way of knowing. *Gus-wen-tah* is also referred to as the Two Row Wampum, "a treaty to express the rightful relationship between the Haudenosaunee (leadership of the nations) and European nations" (McNaughton & Rock, 2003, p. 18). The relationship between "Western knowledge" and the "Indigenous way of knowing" should be equal. Today, the Indigenous way of knowing is not primary in Canadian society. Researchers should work to place the Indigenous way of knowing on an equal footing. This also means the researcher must be knowledgeable and respectful of the cultures in the communities where studies take place. Practices that are acceptable in one community may not be in another.

7. **Joint exploration of knowledge opportunities:** Using the *Gus-wen-tah* may be a way to promote equitable research in the social sciences and humanities.

Researchers must always exercise integrity in adhering to the preceding guidelines. These guidelines already have practical support in protocols developed by the *TCPS2* with respect to research with Indigenous communities. Researchers should engage with Indigenous communities as "collectivities"—

that is, as entities representing their members. It is always necessary to negotiate formal participation and consent with Indigenous communities through their representative bodies (usually band councils and chiefs). As when engaging with individual participants, researchers usually must obtain written consent. However, this may not always be the right/ethical thing to do for some research involving Indigenous Peoples. According to the *TCPS2* (2014), "written signed consent may be perceived as an attempt to legalize or formalize the consent process and therefore may be interpreted by the participant as a lack of trust on the part of the researcher. In these cases, oral consent or verbal agreement(s)" may be substituted in lieu of a signed consent form (p. 46). Research ethics boards usually require that negotiations of this type occur in face-to-face situations. By doing so, researchers observe the guideline of equality. And as they do with any other potential participants, researchers must also respect the right of Indigenous communities to refuse their approaches, especially since Indigenous Peoples have been the subject of many dubious research projects over the past two centuries.

When consent is obtained, researchers must accept the role of "guest" in their "host" Indigenous communities, thereby showing respect and observing reciprocity. Indigenous communities must make the final decisions about the design and conduct of all stages of the research. Communities are then able to retain project ownership, ensure receipt of benefits, protect themselves against exploitation, and preserve their voices and cultural viewpoints in the findings.

For example, communities and researchers must collaborate in the first stage—the formulation of research goals. In order not to perpetuate the exploitive researcher/participant relationships of the past, we must take care to negotiate topics pertinent to each community's needs. Researchers must also present frequent progress reports in formats and language that host communities deem appropriate. This responsibility maintains and respects the partnership and ensures that projects remain true to agreements.

Communities should also participate in decisions about methodology, particularly with respect to issues of cultural sensitivity. For example, a community can stipulate that questionnaires be written in its first language or that the researcher should not interview members of their opposite sex.

Communities may also impose guidelines on the administration of research. A community may ask a researcher to only recruit research assistants from among its members. It may also require a researcher to respect the secrecy of certain knowledge such as that involving sacred ceremonies or songs. A community may also stipulate that findings be presented in its own language and only in the context of its anticipated benefits.

Researchers should respect the knowledge of Indigenous peoples—that is, their interpretations and viewpoints of the world. Indigenous knowledge always takes precedence over that of other cultures, and researchers must acknowledge this in analysis and reporting. If a community attaches special meaning to certain wildlife on its land, researchers must respect this knowledge and, if the community consents, make it a context of their findings. This protocol supports the guideline of equality.

In Focus

Ethical Dilemmas in Research

Sometimes, despite our best efforts and planning, the research process does not go smoothly. Events happen and sometimes researchers uncover unethical situations themselves. Although this does not happen very often, we should be prepared in the event that it does. For example, we may unintentionally discover unethical practices at a business, learn about a criminal event, or discover abuse of vulnerable people. What are we to do in these situations? First, if you are a student, report the situation immediately to your supervisor/professor. They are better trained in dealing with these situations. If you are a researcher, faculty member, or other employed person at a post-secondary institution, report the incident/issue to the research ethics board. The REB will have methods in place to assist you in navigating the situation and determining which, if any, authorities ought to be contacted. This is a legal requirement, and a statement indicating the REB will be contacted when ethical questions arise ought to be included in the consent form (as we discussed above).

Second, seek advice from knowledgeable sources. Do not discuss the issue with your colleagues, friends, or family. Confidentiality remains important, especially when the researcher thinks something is amiss. Everyone deserves the right to a fair hearing of accusations, so it is important that the researcher not disclose this information to anyone other than the REB and professors/supervisors.

Third, document all information. This will be helpful for authorities if additional details are necessary. Ensure that this documentation is kept in a secured place and not easily accessible to your colleagues, friends, or family. Ensure that identifying information is not attached to this documentation.

It is very likely that the authorities will make a decision, based on your report, to investigate the situation. After that, your involvement will likely be minimal. Some researchers have been asked to testify at criminal proceedings, but that happens very rarely. It is unlikely that you will ever uncover unethical or criminal behaviour during your career, but it is important that you understand the steps in reporting issues and protecting vulnerable populations from exploitation.

By entering into a formal contract with the Indigenous community, the researcher formalizes their partnership. In doing so, the researcher observes the guidelines of responsibility and equality. Such contracts should contain clauses on administrative matters. These may include project timetables, principles for project evaluation, methods of obtaining consent from individual members, ways of negotiating changes to research, payments to communities, and procedures for resolving disputes between communities and researchers.

Contracts should also have clauses regarding cultural sensitivities. These clauses may formalize agreement on a researcher's access to culturally sensitive materials, information, and places; the production of images in reports; and appropriate forms of interaction between the researcher and individuals.

There should also be clauses on matters of cultural and intellectual property. The *United Nations Declaration on the Rights of Indigenous Peoples* recognizes that Indigenous Peoples have ownership of their cultural practices, artefacts, and knowledge. For research that incorporates these possessions, communities have legal claims to intellectual property such as final reports, books, cinema, and sound recordings. Canada has signed this declaration, and we are bound by international law to obey it.

This is only a general description of the ethics of researching among Indigenous communities. Even the *TCPS2* acknowledges that its chapter on Indigenous peoples and research is a work in progress. You should look at the official documents on research ethics published by your university and from the major Indigenous associations, including the Assembly of First Nations, the Congress of Indigenous Peoples, the Métis National Council, and the Inuit Tapiriit Kanatami, for additional guidelines. In addition, the extensive discussion of these issues in *TCPS2* is a good starting point.

Ending the Research Project

As part of the process of strengthening our commitment to ethical research, ethics boards, funding agencies, and professional associations increasingly require researchers to provide all interested participants with a summary of the results of the research. The onus is on the researcher to provide participants with an easily understandable summary of the results. Simply giving participants a website address and asking them to monitor the site for results is not acceptable practice. Instead, the researchers are required to send the respondent, either by surface or email, a summary of results at the completion of the project. This task is usually accomplished by a statement and question at the end of the consent form. This question asks participants whether or not they would be interested in obtaining the results of the research. If they answer affirmatively, they are asked to provide their surface or email address for communication purposes. Remember, part of the ethical requirements of any research is to ensure that the identity of respondents remains anonymous. This is why it is important that the consent forms are kept in a secure, locked storage area and that names are not connected to any of the other data stored for the project.

Another project-ending exercise is to submit a final report to the REB. Unlike the lengthy and detailed reports submitted to funders, the REB final report consists of a single question. For projects with "minimal risk," there is a declaration that indicates that the researcher did not experience any problems interacting with study participants. If the researcher has experienced an adverse event, he or she is required to provide details to the REB so they may be kept on file. For projects determined to be "more than minimal risk," the researcher must provide a description of how the study was conducted and to identify any problems or issues that arose during the data collection. Again, this information is kept on file at the REB. In cases where extremely adverse events have occurred, REBs usually require the researcher to produce a detailed report called an adverse event form that identifies the nature of the adverse reaction, procedures taken to alleviate or reduce the adverse action, and a detailed description of how the researcher plans to proceed (i.e., change research protocols or cancel the study).

Summary

For social scientists, the major ethical issues centre on gaining an appropriate form of informed consent, respecting individual privacy and confidentiality, being aware of the power dimension of the relationship between the researcher and the participants in research, and ensuring that the research procedures (variables selected, measurement used, sample selected, and design employed) are adequate to answer the questions being asked. Confidentiality is a particular problem, since it is necessary to keep original data in a readily retrievable form in order to prove that they really were collected, not faked. Further, your files can be subpoenaed if they are relevant to legal proceedings, and you would be liable to charges of withholding evidence if you refused to hand them over or to charges of destroying evidence if you obliterated your files. Therefore, it is not possible to guarantee absolute confidentiality to participants. You can promise to protect the privacy of participants and interviewees by assigning case numbers, changing names, and dealing with group-level data, but there are limits to all undertakings of confidentiality and anonymity.

You must remain aware that there are always ethical issues involved in doing research. As we mentioned in our discussion about respectful and ethical research, particularly with Indigenous Peoples, sometimes you need to discuss proposed research with others not as close to the research as you are so that you may become aware of these issues and can find a way to solve the problems. Some people think that only medical or biological research poses ethical issues. That would be true if social research were inconsequential, if it had no effect. But most social research *is* consequential and therefore does pose ethical issues regarding its consequences for those who participate.

The responsible researcher is considerate, does nothing to injure, harm, or disturb the participants, keeps data collected on individuals and groups secure, accurately records information, and reports the findings of the research in a public manner.

Key Terms

Questions for Review

1. Why is the ethical review of research necessary? Why is this something for which researchers need outside help in the form of a research ethics board (REB)?

2. List some of the ethical issues involved in social research. Read research reported in journals or newspapers and discuss with other students the issues you see. For example, would you like to have been a participant in the research? Why is it unethical to waste other people's time? Is it ethical to conduct poorly designed research? Is it ethical to conduct research in such a way that those following you find it harder to gain access to people for research?

3. Find out the procedures in your university, college, or other institution for the ethical review of research. Try filling out the required form for a piece of research you are considering.

4. Does your professional association have a code of ethics? If so, read it and compare it with the codes of two other professions.

5. What are some of the unique ethical considerations for researching Indigenous Peoples?

6. Define and describe the OCAP principle. How would you put it into practice?

7. What do researchers mean when they mention "decolonizing" research?

8. Who are vulnerable people? Why should researchers be concerned about them?

9. Identify some of the key components of an ethical study.

10. Discuss why researchers need to be concerned about the power that researchers have over their participants.

11. Why don't researchers use the term "subjects" to describe people participating in studies?

12. Compare and contrast some of the ethical issues in qualitative and quantitative research.

13. What is reflexivity? Why is it an important skill in conducting qualitative research?

Sources

Canadian Institutes of Health Research, Natural Sciences and Engineering Research Council of Canada, and Social Sciences and Humanities Research Council of Canada. (2014). *Tri-Council Policy Statement: Ethical conduct for research involving humans (TCPS2)*. Ottawa: Interagency Secretariat on Research Ethics. [Note: cited in text as *TCPS2*]. Retrieved from www.pre.ethics.gc.ca/eng/index/

Livingstone, A., & Weber, B. (2013, July 16). Hungry Canadian Aboriginal children were used in government experiments during the 1940s, researcher says. *Toronto Star*. Retrieved March 9, 2015 from www.thestar.com/news/canada/2013/07/16/hungry_aboriginal_kids_used_unwittingly_in_nutrition_experiments_researcher_says.html

Mosby, I. (2013). Administering colonial science: Experimentation in Aboriginal communities and residential schools, 1942–1957. *Social History, 46*(91), 145–72. https://hssh.journals.yorku.ca/index.php/hssh/article/viewFile/40239/36424

Kirby, S. (2007). Foreword. In H. A. Kitchin, *Research ethics and the internet: Negotiating Canada's Tri-Council Policy Statement* (pp. 8–9). Winnipeg: Fernwood.

Kitchin, H. A. (2007). *Research ethics and the internet: Negotiating Canada's Tri-Council Policy Statement.* Winnipeg: Fernwood.

McNaughton, C., & Rock, D. (2003). *Opportunities in Aboriginal research: Results of SSHRC's dialogue on research and Aboriginal Peoples.* Ottawa: SSHRC.

PRE (Interagency Advisory Panel and Secretariat on Responsible Conduct of Research). (2014, December). *TCPS2: Highlights of changes.* Retrieved June 28, 2018 from www.pre.ethics .gc.ca/pdf/eng/tcps2-2014/Highlights_of_Changes_EN.pdf

Truth and Reconciliation Commission of Canada. (2015). *Truth and Reconciliation Comission of Canada final report.* Winnipeg: TRC of Canada. Retrieved June 21, 2018 from www.trc.ca/ websites/trcinstitution/index.php?p=890

Wanjek, C. (2016, January 1). Bad science: 5 most notable studies retracted in 2015. *CBS News* Retrieved September 27, 2017 from www.cbsnews.com/news/bad-science-studies-retracted-in-2015/

Suggestions for Further Reading

Canadian Institutes of Health Research, Natural Sciences and Engineering Research Council of Canada, and Social Sciences and Humanities Research Council of Canada. (2014). *Tri-Council Policy Statement: Ethical Conduct for Research Involving Humans (TCPS2).* Ottawa: Inter-agency Secretariat on Research Ethics. Retrieved from www.pre.ethics.gc.ca/eng/index/

Canadian Institutes of Health Research, Natural Sciences and Engineering Research Council of Canada, and Social Sciences and Humanities Research Council of Canada. (2014). Chapter 9: Research involving First Nations, Inuit and Métis Peoples of Canada. In *Tri-Council Policy Statement: Ethical conduct for research involving humans (TCPS2).* Ottawa: Interagency Secretariat on Research Ethics. Retrieved from www.pre.ethics.gc.ca/eng/ policy-politique/initiatives/tcps2-eptc2/chapter9-chapitre9/

Crawford, L. (2018, March 23). *Ethics in Indigenous research workshop: Key take-away points.* (Notes from Ethics Indigenous Research workshop, York University, Toronto). Retrieved from www.linkedin.com/pulse/ethics-indigenous-research-workshop-key-take-away-points-crawford/

Haggerty, K. (2004). Ethics creep: Governing social science research in the name of ethics. *Qualitative Sociology, 27*(4), 391–414.

United Nations High Commissioner for Human Rights (UNHCHR). (1997). *Fact sheet no. 9: The Rights of Indigenous Peoples.* Geneva: UNHCHR. Retrieved from www.ohchr.org/ Documents/Publications/FactSheet9rev.1en.pdf

World Health Organization. (2003). *Indigenous Peoples and participatory health research.* Geneva: World Health Organization.

Suggested Web Resources

Canadian Association of Social Workers*Code of ethics*: www.casw-acts.ca/en/Code-of-Ethics

Canadian Psychological Association, *Canadian Code of Ethics for Psychologists* (4th ed.): www.cpa.ca/aboutcpa/committees/ethics/codeofethics/

Canadian Sociological Association, *Code of ethics*: www.csa-scs.ca/code-of-ethics

Lavallee, L. (2016, July 22). *Reconciling ethical research with Métis, Inuit, and First Nations People* [Video file]. Retrieved April 12, 2018 from www.youtube.com/ watch?v=D5qh7MY4el0

National Institutes for Health. (2015, October 17). *A public documentary on the history of research ethics* [Video file]. Retrieved April 12, 2018 from www.youtube.com/ watch?v=9zfrpFwIwug

Retraction Watch website: http://retractionwatch.com/

Teachmepsych. (2017, September 6). *Reflexivity in qualitative research* [Video file]. Retrieved April 12, 2018 from www.youtube.com/watch?v=u9Tccc0Ko68

Phase 2

Data Collection

10 Making Notes, Organizing Data, and Constructing Bibliographies

By now you should be well aware that doing research involves far more than data collection. The research process does not begin, nor does it end, with data collection. Before worthwhile data collection can be done, the researcher must

1. focus the problem;
2. identify and define the basic concepts involved;
3. select variables that relate to each of the concepts under study;
4. devise ways of measuring each of the variables;
5. select a research design that will provide the desired information about the relation between variables;
6. decide on a sampling procedure;
7. draw the sample; and
8. be knowledgeable of all ethical considerations involved in the research.

Unless each of these essential first steps is completed, data collection will often be done in a wasteful, haphazard, and unproductive way, and the resulting data will be flawed at best and useless or misleading at worst.

If preparatory steps are completed with care and attention, however, data collection can proceed smoothly, efficiently, and with little wasted time or effort on the part of either the researcher or the participants in the research. Time and funding are scarce resources for most researchers.

Moreover, someone who is being interviewed has the right to expect the researcher to be organized, efficient, and professional—minimum requirements of ethical behaviour.

You may think that with all the preparation done all that is needed in this chapter are the words *Go to it!* While that is true in a sense, there are still a few important issues to consider.

Attention to Detail

While you are collecting and recording your data, it is essential to pay careful attention to detail in observation. The loss of detail in data collection may make subsequent data analysis impossible or inaccurate, or you may lose precious additional information.

The suggestions in this chapter largely assume that records will be kept in computer databases or computer files. Historically, notes, references, and data organization were collected on paper, lab books, or written on cards. Today, however, most researchers record their bibliography in electronic format and keep their notes in a program that allows them to retrieve notes on similar topics and that records their data for analysis. The logic of these activities remains the same as in the past. Records must be kept, and they must be kept clearly and in such a way that they can be retrieved easily. If you rely on computer storage and retrieval for your information, make sure that you back it up frequently, and you may wish keep back up copies separate from your main working copies to protect yourself against loss as a result of computer hard drive failure or human error.

Keeping a Research Journal

A research journal is a good idea. In some disciplines, it is called a lab book. Whatever you call it, it is important to keep a record of the ideas you have considered. Record the decisions you make and the reasons for the decisions. It is amazing how much you forget in a short time. What decisions did you make as you narrowed the focus of your research project? What forms of the hypothesis and research question did you consider? Why did you select the one you did? Why did you select the variables you did? How did you develop the measure for your variables? What issues did you consider as you chose a sampling procedure and actually selected your sample? A few notes on these issues kept in a research journal (or logbook) will be very helpful when you write your report. They are also helpful in answering questions that people may raise about the research.

Maintaining a Bibliography

Another useful tip is to keep a record of the material you have read or consulted in the course of your research. If you note the bibliographic details when you initially consult the material, you save yourself the effort of tracking them down later. It is best to keep your bibliography and notes in separate electronic files. Then at the end, you will have a complete bibliography in one place and your notes where you need them to write the text of your report. Both notes and bibliography records can be kept on cards or as electronic files. Remember to back up files to prevent accidental loss. Some examples of bibliographic referencing follow.

In Focus

Keeping a Journal

It is always a good idea to begin a journal from the start of your research project. It may be an electronic journal with notes stored on your computer, or it may be an old-fashioned paper notebook. I keep detailed journals for all my research projects, and we require our students to do the same. Journals include information regarding proposal development and record "roadblocks" and problems encountered during project development, data collection methods, and observations and reflections you've made along the way. These notes are particularly important for reference in the methodology section of your research report, thesis, or book. Much of the effort researchers make in recording these notes will become part of this important methodological record of your research. Keep these notes, even after the research is complete: other researchers may contact you upon reading your published research for details on your methodological choices.

Schissel, B. 1997. *Blaming Children: Youth Crime, Moral Panics and the Politics of Hate*. Halifax: Fernwood.

Figure 10.1 • **A sample bibliography for a book**

The information required for a book is author(s), date, title, place of publication, and publisher.

Helly, D. (2004). Are Muslims discriminated against in Canada since September 2001? *Canadian Ethnic Studies, 36*(1), 24–47.

Figure 10.2 • **A sample bibliography for an article**

The information required for an article is author(s), date, title, journal, volume number, issue number (if there is one), and page span.

Campbell, L. D., & Carroll, M. (2007). Aging in Canadian families today. In D. Cheal (Ed.), *Canadian Families Today* (pp. 117–33). Don Mills, ON: Oxford University Press.

Figure 10.3 • **A sample bibliography for a chapter (or an article reprinted) in an edited book**

The information required for a chapter in an edited book is author(s), date, title of chapter, name of book editor, title of book, page span of chapter, place of publication, and publisher.

Eggertson, L. (2010). *Lancet* retracts 12-year-old article linking autism to MMR vaccines. *Canadian Medical Association Journal*, 182(4). Retrieved April 16, 2011 from www.cmaj.ca/cgi/content/full/182/4/E199.

Figure 10.4 • A sample bibliography for information obtained from a website

Rather than providing an example of every possible type of publication, the order of the information required is given in the list that follows. In this way, if you encounter a type of publication you are not sure how to handle, you can work it out for yourself. If you are still confused, ask your professor. There is no single universally accepted format for referencing. Each discipline and every publisher has its own preferences. One of the most popular formats for referencing is APA (American Psychological Association) format. Consult writing and style guides to help you decide which referencing format best suits your discipline. Most disciplines have good reference books available, and it is wise to invest in them. The selection of referencing formats is dictated by two considerations: your academic discipline's preference and the guidelines of the journal or publisher that will eventually publish your research (for example, X Journal prefers APA format, while Y Journal favours MLA). We always prepare our bibliographies with these considerations in mind, and before writing a research article, we consult the publishing guidelines of the journal to which we intend to submit our paper.

Another, more efficient way, of keeping track of your bibliography is to use an electronic program that will automatically generate your bibliography in the style you select. Usually, the user needs to download the program to their computer. Select a program that is compatible with the word processing software you most commonly use. Not all bibliography generators are compatible with all word processing software. Once the program is downloaded, you should be able to use it within your word processing program. In most cases, simply typing the name of the author and year of the publication within the body of your document is enough for the program to locate the source of your information. The program will use the internet to locate the source and automatically produce a bibliography at the end of the document. Users are able to select the citation format (such as APA, MLA, Chicago Manual of Style, etc). Some popular examples are Zotero, EndNote, Harvard Reference Generator, and BibMe.

How do we go about creating a good bibliography or reference list? The following tips will help you out.

1. **The author(s).** The authors are listed as they appear, in the order they appear, with initials or full names as you wish. If the author is a group

or organization—for example, the Canadian Institutes for Health Research—it is listed as the author. If the author is unknown, put "Anon." for "Anonymous" in place of an author's name. If the author(s) is in fact the editor(s) of the book, place "ed." or "eds." after the name of the author(s) as appropriate.

2. **The year of publication.** This should be the date of the edition to which you are referring. Some referencing styles put the date of original publication in brackets after the publication date if the two dates are different. If one author has more than one publication in a year, they are listed in alphabetical order by title in the following manner:

Author (date 1 a)

Author (date 1 b)

3. **The title of the work cited.** Book titles are put in italics. Journal articles or chapters in a book may be enclosed within either single or double quotation marks, depending on the preferences of the journal or publisher.
   a. For journal articles, chapters in books, and articles in newspapers, the title is followed by a statement of the larger source of which it is a part and the pages on which it is found. The form for an article and a chapter in an edited book is given in Figure 10.3.
   b. For books, government publications, newspapers (unless it is absolutely obvious), and encyclopedias, the title is followed by the place of publication and the publisher.

The general rule is that a bibliographic reference must include all the information someone else would need to find the reference quickly and easily. You should keep a separate computer file for each document you consult. Another handy tip is to create a bibliography at the beginning of your project. Add sources as you reference them. That way, your bibliography only requires double-checking (to ensure that all sources are cited or to remove unneeded references) before submitting your paper.

Recording Notes

Note cards (electronic or paper) are useful for keeping track of ideas and information you read in the sources you consult. When it comes time to write your report, you merely need to consult your notes, and you will have all the information you need for a proper quotation and reference. Begin a new note record for each work from which you take notes. Head the record with the name of the author and the date of publication. A sample record is depicted in Figure 10.5. Keeping your bibliography cards and note records in alphabetical order will help you to find material when you need to consult your notes.

Dixon and Bouma (2006)

p.   "_____

_____

_____ "

(direct quotation)

p.   "_____

_____

_____ "

(direct quotation)

p.   _____

_____

_____

(paraphrase or summary)

Figure 10.5 • **A sample note card**

Most researchers today use various kinds of computer software designed for note-taking and retrieval. Most programs allow you to scan your notes using key concepts to locate relevant material. Zotero and EndNote are two such programs.

When taking notes, place quotation marks around direct quotations, and note the page on the note record. If you are summarizing the material in your own words, do not use quotation marks, but make a note of the page(s) on which the summarized material appeared in the source. Keeping track of direct quotes in your notes is very important. Many a student and researcher has been accused of plagiarism, and one of the main culprits is poor note-taking and not differentiating your thoughts from direct quotes in your research notes.

If you quote from a source when writing your report, you will have the information needed for a proper reference on the note card, from which you will draw the quotation. One convenient form of referencing, called the Harvard (or scientific) system, uses the following format. The author's name, the year of publication, and the page number(s) are given in the body of the text. In the bibliography at the end of the report, the full information is listed. Readers wishing to find out more about a reference need only consult the bibliography under the relevant name and date. This reduces the clutter of bibliographic detail. All journals, publishers, and academic disciplines have set guidelines for researchers when they prepare journal articles, chapters, and reports. These manuals and guidelines will assist researchers in determining the preferred method of citing direct quotations.

Dixon and Bouma (2006, p. 42) report that:

_____

_____

_____

If a direct quotation is used, the quotation is placed in quotation marks. The following forms are also used:

According to Dixon and Bouma (2006, p. 86–8):
"_____

_____

_____"

or
"_____

_____" (Dixon & Bouma, 2006, p. 92).

The reference is placed before the full stop, not after it. Long quotations (five lines or longer) are usually indented.

Data Collection Sheets

Data collected for each "unit of analysis" should be recorded separately. A unit of analysis can be any of the individual or collective elements of the entity being researched. You will need one data record for each unit of analysis—for example, each person, group, or hour of television in your study. This is required for later analysis of the results. Therefore, you must keep separate the data collected on each entity studied—that is, each person or group. For example, do not ask for the responses of more than one person on a single questionnaire form (at least not without a proper organizational system embedded within it). It will be impossible to disentangle the results later.

To collect your data properly, you must first ask what the unit of analysis in your research is. Is it the individual, the (university) class, or the group? It is possible for the same hypothesis to be researched at different levels of analysis. For example, in studying the impact of the amount of time spent studying on the result of a history examination, the unit of analysis was the student. Each student in each class completed a questionnaire, so the researcher had a record of hours spent studying and the exam result for each student. In contrast, the class was the unit of analysis in the experimental study of the relation between the amount of time a class had to read material and a test of the class's comprehension of that material. This study design was described in Chapter 7. Classes were given different amounts of time to study the material, and the average results for the classes were compared. In that case, a data sheet for each class was all that was required.

Similarly, in the study of workers' snack selections (in Chapter 7), machine operators on A-shift were used as the unit of analysis. The proportions of the selections made by all A-shift machine operators of junk food, fruit, and other snacks was the datum collected. The machine operators on A-shift received the talk on nutritious snack selection, and the results for the shift were recorded. Only one data-recording sheet for each shift, not each worker, was necessary.

By keeping separate records of each unit of analysis, you effectively manage data for both analysis and review. When conducting analysis, you can easily recover data for each unit, allowing you to distinguish between cases that follow trends and those that do not. Further, if you suspect that some of your data is incorrect, you can review each unit individually.

In summary, keep careful notes as you collect your data. Be careful and considerate with those you study. Be careful and meticulous in carrying out your research with precision and in recording your findings accurately.

Questions for Review

1. What eight steps need to be taken before a researcher can collect data?
2. What information should researchers record in their journals?
3. What information should be kept on bibliography cards for
    a. a book?
    b. an article?
    c. a chapter in a book?
    d. a website?
4. What is a "unit of analysis"? Why is it important to know this in preparing data collection sheets and data-recording sheets?
5. Why is it important to develop an organized and systematic method of recording notes for your project?
6. Prepare two examples of correct citation
    a. using a direct quotation
    b. paraphrasing
7. What style of referencing is most commonly used in your discipline?

Suggestions for Further Reading

Beins, B. (2012). *APA style simplified: Writing in psychology, education, nursing and sociology.* Malden, MA: Wiley-Blackwell.

Berg, B. L. (2001). Writing research papers: Sorting the noodles from the soup. In B. L. Berg, *Qualitative research methods for the social sciences* (pp. 268–86). Needham Heights, MA: Allyn & Bacon.

Bryman, A., Teevan, J. J., & Bell, E. (2009). Writing up social research. In A. Bryman and J. J. Teevan, *Social research methods* (2nd Cdn ed., pp. 313–24). Don Mills, ON: Oxford University Press.

Suggested Web Resources

Baker, J. R., Brizee, A., & Velázquez, A. (2018, February 14). Writing a research paper. *Purdue Online Writing Lab*. Retrieved April 12, 2018 from https://owl.english.purdue.edu/owl/resource/658/01/

Carleton University Library. (n.d.). *Writing the research paper video* (Adapted from Dalhousie Libcast writing guide on term papers) [Video file]. Retrieved April 12, 2018 from https://library.carleton.ca/help/writing-research-paper-video

SUNY–Empire State College. (2018). *Steps in writing a research paper* [Video file]. Retrieved April 12, 2018 from www.esc.edu/online-writing-center/resources/research/research-paper-steps/

11 Summarizing and Presenting Data in Quantitative Research

You have collected your data and you have prepared your literature review. Now what are you going to do with the stacks of questionnaires, data sheets, or completed interviews? You will have made some tentative decisions about this when you prepared dummy tables earlier. Nonetheless, when you are confronted with a pile of data, new problems emerge, and further decisions will have to be made—namely, how they are to be summarized and presented. This chapter provides an introduction to presenting data collected using quantitative research. Chapter 12 examines how qualitative data is analyzed and presented. Remember, there is no "contest" between quantitative and qualitative data. The selection of data collection strategies depends on the theory used and the research question asked.

Since this text presupposes no knowledge of statistics on the part of students, complex methods of data summarization and presentation will not be covered. It is strongly suggested that students wishing to make statistical inferences about correlation and causation consult the statistical readings presented at the end of this chapter and to consider attending specialized instruction in this area. This book also assumes that the projects undertaken will be very limited in scale so that in-depth computer analysis of data is not required. Most of the techniques described in this chapter can be completed manually or by using standard computer software. Regardless of the method of data collection you choose, a standard "common sense" approach to data summarization and presentation is necessary in projects that involve both very simple and very sophisticated analysis. It is worth covering the basic rules of this approach to illustrate the common sense involved.

Summarizing and organizing your data involves four steps:

1. Identify the data to be included and excluded from your report.
2. Select the categories in which the raw data can be summarized.
3. Code the data—that is, sort them into the categories.
4. Present the data in a form that helps you to draw conclusions.

Including and Excluding Data

Although data are collected in detail, they usually cannot be reported or presented at the same level of detail. In other words, it is unlikely that you will be able to report all of the data that you have collected. Selecting data for inclusion and exclusion is always very difficult. There are, however, some ways to make this easier. If you have not overburdened the participant (that means not asking too many questions), then there shouldn't be much data to exclude. There will be times, however, when even the best-designed questions are flawed. One of the authors of the current text recently surveyed recently arriving refugees to Canada. She asked questions about their temporary accommodation (some stayed in hotels for one or two months before their permanent homes were located). Despite the existence of a filter question (one that "filters" out the people to whom the question does not apply), many of the refugees who did not stay in temporary accommodation answered the questions. It meant that it became nearly impossible to code the refugees who stayed in temporary accommodation from those who did not. Even though the answers to this question were important to the funders and to the project, the researcher was forced to ignore these questions because the distribution of the answers was false. This is one instance where data can be rejected—due to incorrect data. In this instance, some of the interviewers did not follow the instructions on the survey (which clearly stated that refugees who did not stay in temporary accommodation were not to be asked a certain series of questions). These kinds of errors can also occur in online surveys when the filter questions are not properly programed or in paper-pencil surveys when participants do not read the instructions.

At other times, data might be excluded because of a mathematical problem called a "constant." A constant occurs when 90 to 100 per cent of the answers to the question are the same response. It means there is little to no variation in the answer—everyone who participated in the survey answered the same way or had similar feelings about a question. For example, say you found in your survey of students that 97 per cent of them when asked strongly favoured the introduction of a fall semester break. That means that only 3 per cent of your sample disagreed. This is almost unanimity. In a statistical sense, there's not much we can do about this data. If we compare the responses between agricultural and nursing students, it is unlikely we are going to get any statistically significant difference in opinion—which means comparing them is not useful. It would likely be that 97 per cent of nursing students and 97 per cent of agriculture students agree that the fall semester break is a good idea. Constants cause major statistical problems, some of them beyond the scope of this book. At most, one could report that with almost uniform agreement, all students agreed that a fall semester break was a good idea.

Categories

The next step in summarizing and presenting data is to construct tables, graphs, or charts for the data you are planning to use; averages and percentages are then calculated. To do this, you must first categorize the data. We saw this earlier in the case of research into the effect of the amount of study time on academic performance. Assume that the data presented in Table 11.1 were recorded on the data summary sheet suggested in Chapter 6 (Table 6.4).

As it stands, no conclusions can be readily or reliably drawn from this data summary form. No pattern emerges from a quick scan of the data. In this form, the data are too detailed and difficult for your readers to digest. More inclusive categories are required for reporting both the amount of time spent studying and its result on the examination. A possible starting point for constructing categories is determining the extreme scores and the average scores.

What are the extremes

- for amount of time spent studying?
  most ____ least ____
- for result on examination?
  highest ____ lowest ____

Scan the list and record the results.

What is the average

- for amount of time spent studying?
- for result on examination?

The average, or the mean, is calculated by totalling the measures (number of hours or result on examination) and dividing by the number of measures (in this instance, students).

$$\text{Mean, or average, history result} = \frac{\text{Total number of history results}}{\text{Number of students}}$$

Several ways of categorizing these data are now possible. The students could be classified into those who studied more than the average and those who studied less than the average. Similarly, the students could be classified into those whose results were above or below the average. Other ways of classification might include separating those who passed from those who did not. The results could be separated into high pass (65–100), pass (50–64), and fail (49 or less).

Table 11.1 • **A completed data summary form for a study of the relation between hours spent studying and result on a history examination**

Student Number	Number of Hours Spent Studying		Examination Result	
	Raw Score	Code	Raw Score	Code
1	30		98	
2	25		99	
3	10		50	
4	12		44	
5	20		65	
6	22		68	
7	25		80	
8	30		75	
9	30		80	
10	20		60	
11	24		65	
12	19		55	
13	18		54	
14	21		58	
15	22		60	
16	24		62	
17	28		70	
18	26		70	
19	27		65	
20	24		60	
21	18		58	
22	19		57	
23	25		68	
24	20		65	
25	21		60	
26	14		45	
27	20		35	
28	22		50	
29	26		55	
30	10		40	

Once the categories are selected, the data are coded. That is, the raw data are reclassified into the more inclusive categories. Let us say that you decided to use the categories of "above average" and "below average" for both number of hours spent studying and for examination result. Go back to Table 11.1 and codify the data—after each raw score indicate the category into which it fits. For example:

Table 11.2 • A completed and codified data summary form

	Hours Studying		Result in Examination	
	Raw Score	Code	Raw Score	Code
Student 1	30	AH	98	AR
Student 2	25	AH	99	AR
Student 3	10	BH	50	BR

AH = above-average hours   AR = above-average result
BH = below-average hours   BR = below-average result

In this way, the raw data are codified and can be more readily analyzed.

If your calculations agree with mine, the average number of hours spent studying was $652 \div 30$, or 21.7 hours. Hence, students who studied more than 21.7 hours were coded as "AH" (above average), and those who studied less were coded as "BH" (below average). How many students were there in each code?

Number coded AH = 16
Number coded BH = 14

How about the examination results? What was the average result? My calculations were $1871 \div 30$, or 62.4. Students who scored over 62.4 were coded "AR," and those who scored below 62.4 were coded "BR." How many students fell into each category?

Number coded AR = 13
Number coded BR = 17

You have codified your data and established the frequency of students appearing in each code. You are now ready to present your data in a form that will show the relationship between the two variables.

You can see that if you used different categories, the coding would look different. To give yourself practice, copy out Table 11.1 and codify the data results using high pass (65–100), pass (50–64), and fail (49 or less) as the categories. Whatever categories you choose, your aim is to reduce the raw data to a more manageable set of categories. Decide on the categories, and then code the raw data into those categories.

The first two steps have been done. Categories have been selected and the data codified. How are they to be presented? The hypothesis guiding this research asserts that there is a relationship between the amount of time spent studying and the result of an examination. This means that the way in which you present your data needs to show the strength of the relationship between the two variables. There are several ways to do this. They are presented in the following tables.

Tables

The most basic form of data presentation is "tabular presentation."

Table 11.3 • **A table for presenting the data from a study of amount of time spent studying and result on an examination**

Result on History Examination	Amount of Time Spent Studying (Number of Students)	
	Above Average	**Below Average**
Above average		
Below average		

To calculate the numbers to put in Table 11.3, it is necessary to **cross-tabulate** your data. That is, you have to locate each case of data collected (in this case, each student) in the appropriate box of the table. For this example, you would take each student listed on the data summary sheet in Table 11.1 and place a check mark in the appropriate cell (blank square) of a table like Table 11.3. Student 1 was categorized as "above average" in both variables, so check the upper left-hand cell of the table. Student 2 was also categorized as "above average" in both variables, so place another check mark in the upper left-hand cell. Student 3 was categorized as "below average" for both variables, so place a check mark in the lower right-hand cell of the table. When all the data have been cross-tabulated in this way, your preliminary table should look like Table 11.4.

Table 11.4 • **The relationship between time spent studying and result on a history examination (preliminary table)**

Result on History Examination	Amount of Time Spent Studying (Number of Students)	
	Above Average	**Below Average**
Above average	✓✓✓✓✓✓✓✓✓	✓✓
Below average	✓✓✓✓✓	✓✓✓✓✓✓✓✓✓✓✓

Next, add up the check marks in each cell, and put that number in the cell. What do your results look like? They should look like those in Table 11.5. Eleven students were above average in both examination result and amount of time spent studying. Five were below average in result but above average in study time. Twelve were below average on both variables.

The numbers at the right side and the bottom of Table 11.5 are called **marginal totals**. They are the same as the totals you calculated earlier for the **frequencies** of each variable. They serve as useful checks to make sure that your coding and cross-tabulating were done accurately. It is amazing how many errors can occur at this stage of the research process. The marginals must add up to the total used for the construction of the table. They must also add up correctly both across the rows and down the columns. It may seem tedious, but it provides a critical check on accuracy, and the marginals are also used in the calculation of various tests of statistical significance (an issue that is beyond the scope of this book; for additional references, please see the end of this chapter).

Table 11.5 • The presentation of the results tabulated in Table 11.4

Examination Result	Amount of Time Spent Studying (Number of Students)		
	Above Average	Below Average	Total
Above average	11	2	13
Below average	5	12	17
Total	16	14	30

How would you interpret Table 11.5? It shows a very clear relationship between the two variables: the more there is of one (study time), the more there is of the other (marks on an examination), with few exceptions. Note that these tabulations are not equivalent to stringent statistical measures that examine relationships. The strongest evidence is provided by statistics that indicate the direction and strength of the relationships between the independent and dependent variables. Students are strongly advised to consult texts listed at the end of this chapter for more advanced readings in statistical modelling.

Although interpreting Table 11.5 is relatively straightforward, it is almost always better to present the tabular results as percentages because most audiences understand these figures. There are two ways of doing this. Since each accurately reflects the data but does so in a slightly different way, the selection depends on which mode of presentation is easiest to interpret. Table 11.6 presents the findings in Table 11.5 as percentages of the total, 30. In all tables giving the results as percentages, it is very important to indicate the total number upon which the table is based. That is why "$n \times 30$" (which means the total number is 30) is placed where it is. It is nearly a universal convention to use the lower-case, italicized "n" to refer to the number of cases in a table or graph. Thirty is usually considered the minimum number of cases for the use of percentages in a 2 × 2 table like the one in Table 11.6. The more cells a table has, the higher the number of cases should be.

Table 11.6 • The relationship between amount of time spent studying and result on history examination

Result on History Examination	Amount of Time Spent Studying (%)	
	Above Average	**Below Average**
Above average	36.6	6.7
Below average	16.7	40.0

$n = 30$
100%

Table 11.7 presents the findings in Table 11.5 in column percentages—each column adds up to 100 per cent. When you create a table like Table 11.7, you show the impact of the column variable (in this instance, amount of time spent studying) on the row variable (result in history examination). This is correct because amount of time spent studying was your independent variable and examination result, the dependent variable. This technique is, by far, the most preferred method of presenting tables in the social sciences.

When you construct and interpret tables, it is crucial to keep in mind which is the independent and which is the dependent variable. Failing to do so can lead to nonsensical interpretations of data. In this example, "time spent studying" was the independent variable, and "examination result" was the dependent variable. Table 11.7 would be read in this way. Among those students who spent an above-average amount of time studying, 68.7 per cent received above-average examination results and 31.3 per cent received below-average results. In contrast, among those students who spent a below-average amount of time studying, 14.3 per cent received an above-average result in the examination and 85.7 per cent received a below-average result. We therefore conclude that the amount of time spent studying had a definite and positive effect on the examination results of this group of history students; our hypothesis is confirmed or accepted.

Table 11.7 • The percentage of students spending an above- or below-average amount of time studying who scored above or below average on their history examination

Result on History Examination	Amount of Time Spent Studying (%)	
	Above Average	**Below Average**
Above average	68.7	14.3
Below average	31.3	85.7
	100%	100%
	$n = 16$	$n = 14$

As a general rule, if you are presenting your data in tables using percentages, it is best to percentage the independent variable across the dependent variable (as in Table 11.7). In this way, you display the influence of the independent variable on the distribution of the dependent variable, which is of course what you are trying to show. A good rule to follow is to place the independent variable in the columns and the dependent variable in the rows. The percentages would be calculated where each column would total 100 per cent.

If you look back over Tables 11.4 to 11.7, it should become clear that the interpretation would be the same in each mode of tabular presentation of the data. Tabular presentation of data is very basic and very useful. To give yourself practice at tabular analysis, take the data in Table 11.1, and recode the exam result data into the three categories of high pass (65–100), pass (50–64), and fail (49 or less). Construct tables by cross-tabulating the data again. Present the tables numerically and as percentages of the whole, row percentages, and column percentages.

There are other ways of presenting data as well. Remember, data are summarized and presented so as to clearly demonstrate the strength of the relationship between the variables under study. Other ways of summarizing and presenting data include several kinds of graphs, the scattergram, and the use of means (averages).

Graphs

Bar Graphs

To prepare a graph, it is necessary to perform steps 1 (selecting categories) and 2 (coding the data) of data summarization and presentation. It is also necessary to cross-tabulate the data in some way. Take, for instance, the **bar graph** or histogram. In both methods, the amount of space given to each variable is proportional to that variable's portion of the sample. Figure 11.1 shows a bar graph presenting the data in Table 11.5.

Essentially, this graph presents the information in the top two cells of Table 11.5. It shows a bar graph based on the frequency distribution of the data (the numbers falling into each category of analysis in the test). Figure 11.2 is a bar graph that gives all the data in Table 11.5.

Bar graphs can also be used to present percentage data. Figure 11.3 presents the data in Table 11.7 in the form of a bar graph. In this instance, a table presented as column percentages is converted to a bar graph by making the space in the graph proportional to the percentage of each cell. The essential feature of a bar graph is that the size of the bar is proportional to the size of the variable. Again, it can be seen that different methods of presenting the same data, when used correctly, do not lead to different conclusions.

Pie Graphs

Pie graphs are appropriate when analysis examines the proportion of variable categories to all variable categories over the whole population. In other words, pie charts are used when we want to examine the frequency distribution of a single variable. For example, we will construct a pie graph for the variable "ethnicity" when it is measured for a class of students. The composition of each

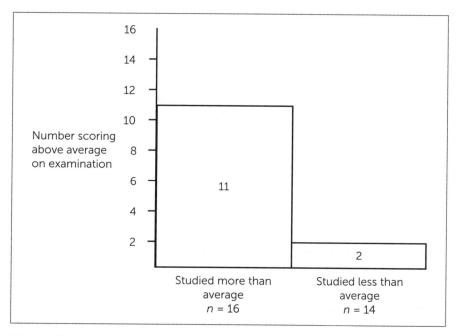

Figure 11.1 • **A bar graph showing the relationship between hours studied and history examination result**

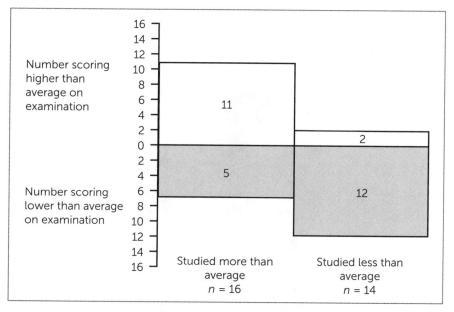

Figure 11.2 • **A bar graph showing the relationship between amount of time spent studying and history examination result**

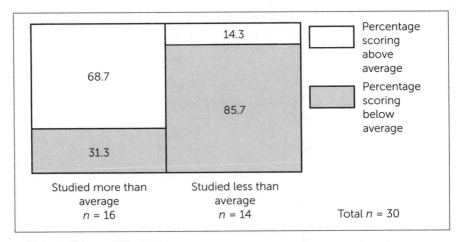

Figure 11.3 • A bar graph depicting the relationship between the amount of time spent studying and history examination result

category of the variable might be as follows: Chinese, 10 per cent; British, 10 per cent; Canadian, 60 per cent; Filipino/a, 8 per cent; other, 12 per cent. Accordingly, the pie graph would look like Figure 11.4.

Each group occupies a "wedge" proportion of the total area of the pie graph equivalent to its proportion of the total class population. In Figure 11.4, the size of the wedge to represent the Chinese must be 10 per cent of the circle area. Pie graphs can be easily constructed by using commonly available computer

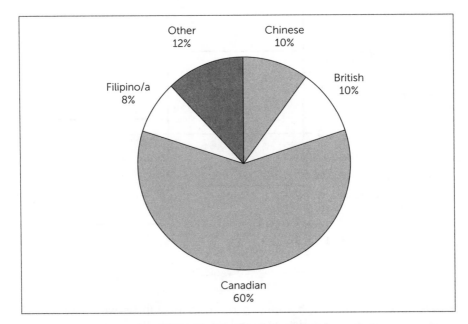

Figure 11.4 • Ethnic makeup of class (fictitious data)

programs or by drawing a graph by hand, as follows. The wedge size we require here is obtained by calculating 10 per cent of 360 degrees (there are 360 degrees in a circle). Ten per cent of 360 degrees is 36 degrees. Using a protractor, count 36 degrees, place a dot at 0 and at 36, then draw lines to the centre of the circle, and you have a wedge of the pie equal to 10 per cent of the circle. Repeat this for each group. The next group, the British, would also require 36 degrees. Starting where you left off (at 36 degrees), count off 36, place a dot at 72 degrees, and draw a line to the centre of the circle.

This procedure may seem tedious, but it provides important visual information about the frequency distribution of important dependent and independent variables in your study. You may find it easier to use one of the many available computer programs designed to produce accurate pie, bar, and line graphs from data. This visual presentation of data is also an easier way for many audiences to understand your results.

Figure 11.5 is a similar pie graph that could be constructed for the population of Canada. A comparison of the two graphs would show the distribution of ethnic groups enrolled in your course compared with the distribution of such groups in Canada. The fact that the percentages are given as well as the visual impression of the different sizes of the various wedges helps us to interpret these graphs. When presenting such data, labels that include the percentages are a good addition to the graph.

It should be noted that such differences are more precisely displayed in simple tables, such as Table 11.8.

The pie graph is not particularly suited to presenting the type of data with which we have been dealing in the examples above. Pie graphs are difficult to compare. They are usually used in journalistic reporting and for presenting financial data, such as government funding allocations, rather than in scientific reporting.

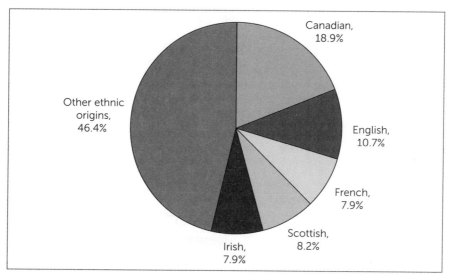

Figure 11.5 • **Selected ethnic origins for Canada, 2016**

Table 11.8 • Selected ethnic origins,[1] Canada, 2016

Ethnic Origins	Total Responses[1]	Percentage
Canadian	11,135,965	18.9%
English	6,320,085	10.7%
French	4,670,595	7.9%
Scottish	4,799,010	8.2%
Irish	4,627,000	7.9%
Other ethnic origins	27,288,200	46.4%
Total	58,840,855	100%

[1]Respondents who reported multiple ethnic origins are counted more than once in this table because they are included in the multiple responses for each origin they reported. For example, a respondent who reported English and Scottish would be included in the multiple responses for English and for Scottish.
Source: Statistics Canada. (2017). *Immigration and ethnocultural diversity highlight tables—Canada, 2016 Census*. Retrieved from www12.statcan.gc.ca/census-recensement/2016/dp-pd/hlt-fst/imm/Table.cfm?Lang=E&T=31&Geo=01&SO=4D

Scattergrams

The **scattergram** is another way in which data can be summarized and presented. A scattergram is produced by pinpointing each instance of measurement on a grid defined by the two axes of a graph. Figure 11.6 shows such a grid.

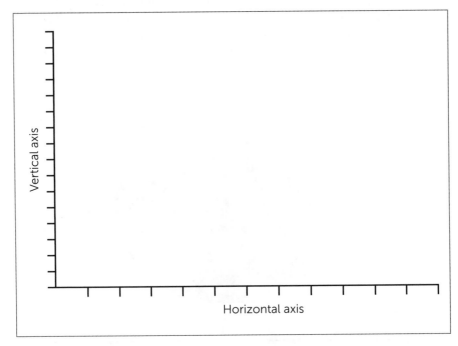

Figure 11.6 • A scattergram grid showing horizontal and vertical axes

The two lines along which the units are marked are called axes, and the space between them is defined by the grid formed by the intersecting lines drawn from each unit point along the two axes. The first step in constructing a scattergram is to decide on the scale of units to be used on each axis.

Data are not categorized and coded before constructing a scattergram. Instead, the scale of each axis is adjusted to accommodate the range of the variable being analyzed. Remember, we suggested that you analyze the data from the study of the impact of amount of time spent studying on examination result. We asked you to identify the range of each variable by noting the extremes. This is a very important step if you wish to construct a scattergram. Re-examine the data presented in Table 11.1:

- What is the range of the values recorded for the variable "time spent studying"?
  Highest _____   ◄———►   Lowest _____

- What is the range of the values recorded for the variable "result on an examination"?
  Highest _____   ◄———►   Lowest _____

The scale of units along each axis of the scattergram must be able to sensibly record the full range of collected data. In this instance, the scale of the horizontal axis, the one used to indicate hours spent studying, must range from 10 (the lowest reported) to 30 (the highest reported). The range for the vertical axis, the axis dealing with examination results, must go from 35 to 99. Figure 11.7 presents a grid upon which a scattergram for the data presented in Table 11.1 could be constructed. The scattergram is constructed by putting a dot on the grid in the place defined by the two pieces of data for each student. Using graph paper makes this task much easier. The axes are drawn and units marked along them. Now a dot is placed on the grid for each student. Student number 1 studied 30 hours and received a 98, so place a dot at the intersection of a line drawn up from the 30 position on the horizontal axis with a line across from the 98 position on the vertical axis. The positions of students 1 to 5 are given as examples.

Using a sheet of graph paper, make a scattergram of all the data in Table 11.1. Normally, the intersecting lines are not drawn on the table. Rather, two rulers are used to indicate where the lines intersect, and only the dot is placed on the grid. Place two dots close together where two data points are the same. The result is a pattern of dots. What does the pattern of 30 dots tell you?

Most conventional computer software can produce accurate scattergrams that can be used in published research papers and reports.

Line Graphs

A **line graph** is almost the same as a scattergram except that consecutive points are joined by lines, making up one complete line joining all the data points.

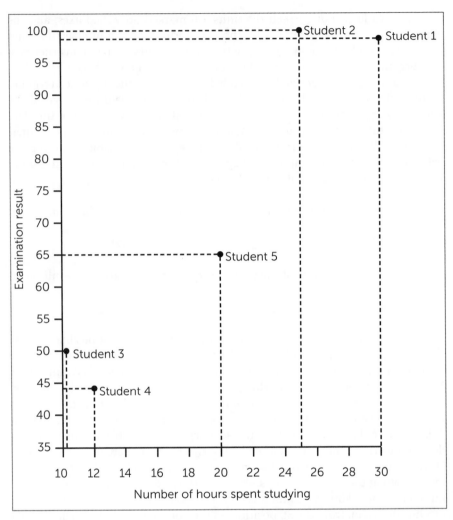

Figure 11.7 • **A grid for the construction of a scattergram for data on impact of amount of time spent studying on examination result**

The data tabled in Table 11.9 can be presented by a line graph (as in Figure 11.8). The independent variable "year of entry" is placed on the horizontal axis. The dependent variable "number of immigrants entering" is placed along the vertical axis. The units are clearly marked along each axis. Then the data points are marked, as for a scattergram. The data points are joined by a line that begins at the first dot on the left and moves to the next dot to the right.

As an exercise, convert your scattergram of the data on the relationship between "number of hours spent studying" and "examination result" (refer back to Table 11.1) to a line graph. To do so, start with the dot on the far left and move to the next dot on the right. You will encounter a problem. What do you

Table 11.9 • **Number of immigrants entering Canada by year of entry, 1985–2016**

Year	Total Immigrants	Year	Total Immigrants
1985	84,345	2001	250,640
1986	99,355	2002	229,049
1987	152,083	2003	221,348
1988	161,583	2004	235,825
1989	191,553	2005	262,241
1990	216,454	2006	251,642
1991	232,815	2007	236,754
1992	254,809	2008	247,247
1993	256,678	2009	252,179
1994	224,394	2010	280,687
1995	212,869	2011	248,747
1996	226,073	2012	257,903
1997	216,038	2013	259,023
1998	174,198	2014	260,404
1999	189,952	2015	271,820
2000	227,455	2016	296,395

Source: Citizenship and Immigration Canada, *Permanent residents—IRCC monthly updates 2017 data*. Retrieved from http://open.canada.ca/data/en/dataset/f7e5498e-0ad8-4417-85c9-9b8aff9b9eda?_ga=2.255898507.1411109611.1506961188-396949903.1467818064

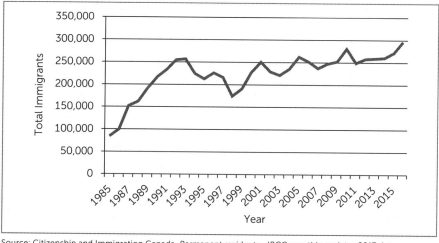

Source: Citizenship and Immigration Canada, *Permanent residents—IRCC monthly updates 2017 data*. Retrieved from http://open.canada.ca/data/en/dataset/f7e5498e-0ad8-4417-85c9-9b8aff9b9eda?_ga=2.255898507.1411109611.1506961188-396949903.1467818064

Figure 11.8 • **Trends in immigration, 1985–2016**

do when there is more than one dot in a vertical line? Which is the "next dot to the right"? In such a case, the average is calculated, and the data point is put at the average position. For example, you will begin with a problem in the data in your scattergram when you find that there are two data points in the vertical line above 10 hours of studying. One received a result of 50, the other a result of 40. The data point for a line graph would be placed at 45. In this way, a line graph "smooths out" some of the detail of a scattergram. The advantage is that it makes the pattern clearer, but the disadvantage is that it hides some of the variation.

There are several critical points to remember in constructing line graphs. First, the units of measure must be clearly specified, labelled, and marked on each axis of the graph. In Figure 11.9, the vertical axis is marked in hours (0–6) and labelled "number of additional hours."

Be aware that units of measure affect the appearance of line graphs and can make them misleading. Large units can underemphasize change in relative terms, and small units can overstate the magnitude of change. The following example will demonstrate this. There is a lot of talk these days about hate crime in Canada, particularly against ethnic, religious, and sexual minorities. The data on the number of hate crimes in Canada for the years 2009 through 2015 are presented in tabular form in Table 11.10. The data given in this figure are from Statistics Canada.

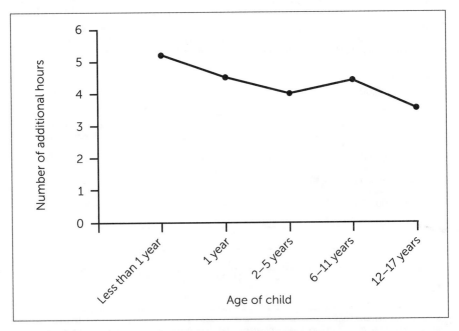

Figure 11.9 • **A line graph depicting increased number of hours spent on housework because of presence of child at different ages**

Table 11.10 • **Hate Crimes in Canada, 2009–2015**

	2009	2010	2011	2012	2013	2014	2015
Total Canada	1473	1401	1322	1414	1140	1295	1362

Notice, however, that two ways of presenting those data in a line graph give very different impressions. Figures 11.10 and 11.11 show the same data recorded in line graphs using different scales of units. Do they look the same? They are both accurate, but they give different impressions.

They express the data differently because of the difference in measurement scale for the vertical axis. As an exercise, make line graphs for several entries from the data presented in Table 11.9. Use different scales to see what difference this makes.

This effect can be particularly confusing in graphs that have two vertical axes with different scales. Although there are legitimate reasons for using this device, it can be very misleading. Figure 11.12 gives an obvious example. It shows line graphs of annual environmental spending by City A and City B. Say that both cities commenced allocating funds for the environment in 2006. The graph seems to show that City A has been increasing its spending on the environment at a much faster rate than City B. But is that correct? Read the graph carefully, and keep in mind that the lines are drawn to axes of different scales, according to which spending for City A is expressed in smaller units ($100,000s) than data for City B ($millions). The same spending increases appear to be more dramatic for City A than for City B.

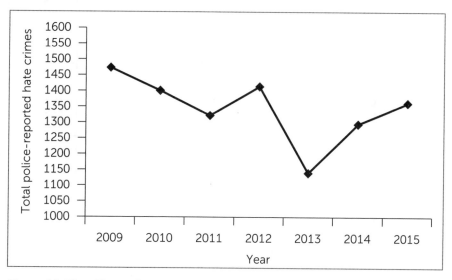

Figure 11.10 • **Hate crimes in Canada from 2009 to 2015, small scale (rising and falling)**

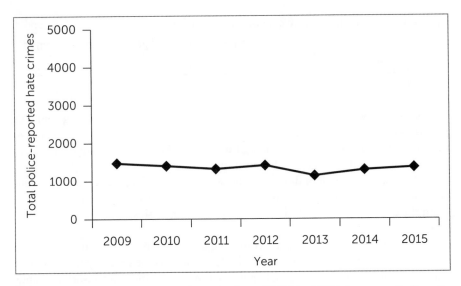

Figure 11.11 • **Hate crimes in Canada from 2009 to 2015, large scale (hardly changing)**

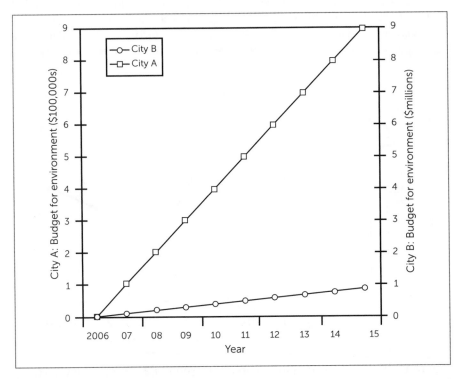

Figure 11.12 • **A misleading line graph using different units on two vertical axes to compare growth in environmental spending**

Thus, an examination of the graph will show that the dollar amounts spent by the cities were the same each year. Spending in both cities increased by the same amount ($100,000 for City A, $0.1 million for City B) every year between 2006 and 2015. In 2015, both cities spent $900,000. Spending on the environment was the same in both cities despite the different appearances of the lines plotted against the different scales.

Finally, line graphs are very useful for comparing the trends or performance of several groups or persons. Figure 11.13 is a hypothetical line graph comparing the monthly phone calls received by three telephone counselling services in one year. The raw data are presented in Table 11.11.

Table 11.11 • **Phone calls received by three fictitious telephone counselling services**

Month	Service A	Service B	Service C
January	205	920	860
February	255	750	620
March	300	605	275
April	350	410	350
May	520	300	360
June	620	275	380
July	880	275	400
August	925	275	450
September	620	290	350
October	540	420	300
November	480	590	580
December	320	830	690

These three services have different patterns of demand. The graph in Figure 11.13 shows these differences more clearly than the columns of numbers in Table 11.11.

Service A receives more calls in summer than in winter. It may serve a holiday region where social problems increase every summer and during a school holiday period when tourists arrive. Service B experiences a smooth pattern of demand, which begins at a relatively high level early in the year, bottoms out mid-year, and gradually increases as the end of the year approaches. The area covered by Service B might be a place where social problems change with the traditional holiday season. During the Christmas and New Year season, social problems increase, perhaps because of money shortages or increased alcohol consumption. The general "mood" of the area calms after the New Year, and the demand for counselling services decreases, remaining stable until September, when spending and alcohol use begin to increase in anticipation of Christmas.

Service C experiences increased demand in the winter months and a small upswing in the middle of the year. It may serve a northern area of the country where decreased daylight has been shown to increase bouts of depression, thereby increasing the number of calls to the counselling service.

The value of a line graph comparing the use of the three counselling services can be seen in Figure 11.13. Such presentation of data is very useful in policy analysis because it displays comparative information clearly. What issues does Figure 11.13 suggest for a government administrator allocating funds among the three counselling services? Think about how you would allocate the funds, and justify your decision based on the graph.

Scattergrams and line graphs can be very useful ways of summarizing and interpreting data. They are frequently used in articles, books, and research reports.

To construct a line graph, you must

1. select categories for your data;
2. code the data into the categories;
3. select a scale of units for each axis;

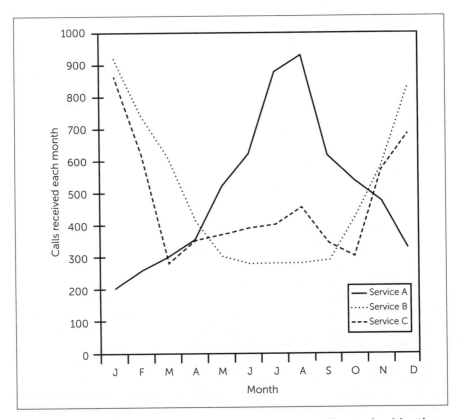

Figure 11.13 • **A line graph comparing the phone calls received by three fictitious Canadian counselling services**

4. plot the data points; and
5. link the data points with lines.

There are several computer programs available that will produce line graphs.

Means

Means, or averages, are often used to compare groups. Means are a useful way to summarize and present data. The average performance of groups, the average rates of consumption, or the average incidence of a particular event may be compared.

To calculate an average, you add up the individual data and divide by the number of individuals. For example, earlier in this chapter you calculated the average number of hours spent studying and the average examination result.

Means could be used to summarize and present the data from our study of the impact of the number of hours spent studying on examination results. The class could be divided into two groups, those who studied more than the average and those who studied less than the average. Once this is done, the average examination result for each group could be calculated. First, divide the students into two groups. Remember, the average time spent studying was 21.7 hours.

The data in Table 11.12 would simply be reported in this way. The group of students who studied more than the average received an average result of 70.3, and the group of students who studied less than the average received an average result of 53.3.

As an exercise, calculate the average number of hours spent studying for each of two groups of students. First, do it for those who received above-average results, and then do it for those who received below-average results.

We saw that the move from a scattergram to a line graph involved losing a certain level of detail in the presentation of the data. When groups are compared using means, all variation internal to each group is lost:

* scattergram: presents most information;
* line graph, bar graph, or pie graph: present less information;
* mean: presents least information.

Using the data in Table 11.11, calculate the average number of calls received monthly by each counselling service. Service A's average monthly total was 501.25 calls, Service B's average was 495.0 calls, and Service C's was 467.92 calls. This example shows one potential problem with an average: it does not show the variation in the measures. Although Services A and B averaged almost the same number of calls per month, they experienced different trends of monthly increases and decreases in calls.

While averages are very useful, they must be used and interpreted with care. The average tells us nothing for certain about an individual in a group. It is not legitimate to infer that the average for a group applies to any specific individual. For example, the average household income of residents in a particular

Table 11.12 • **The calculation of mean test scores for two groups of students**

Group A Studied More than Average		Group B Studied Less than Average	
Student	Mark	Student	Mark
1	98	3	50
2	99	4	44
6	68	5	65
7	80	10	60
8	75	12	55
9	80	13	54
11	65	14	58
15	60	21	58
16	62	22	57
17	70	24	65
18	70	25	60
19	65	26	45
20	60	27	35
23	68	30	40
28	50		
29	55		
16	1125	14	746

Group A average =1125 ÷ 16 = 70.3   Group B average =746 ÷ 14 = 53.3

suburb might be $100,000 per year. But there are many combinations of household income that would lead to that average. For example, one household earning $910,000 and nine each of $10,000 would result in an average income of $100,000. Some averages can be almost meaningless.

Conversely, we are often interested in group performance and not so interested in the outstanding cases. The average is a useful indication of a characteristic of a group. Trends in averages, like trends in percentages, are particularly useful. For example, a local electricity supplier, in predicting energy supply requirements for the month of July, will rely on the trends in average energy consumption for the previous 20 Julys. It will not be interested in the variations in individual household consumption.

Case Study

Example of a Quantitative Research Report

Most research projects produce several "outputs." These outputs consist of journal articles, book chapters, books, and research reports. The research report is an important reporting mechanism. It provides an overview of central findings from the research project to the funders and key stakeholders of the project. Almost all funding agencies require a final research report to be submitted in order to fulfill the requirements of accepting funding. As discussed in Chapter 9, the research report also serves as an ethical requirement of keeping research participants informed of the results of the study.

Reports vary in length and content. A copy of a research report that was the result of a national longitudinal survey of newcomer families and their children is a good example of a simple quantitative research report. The New Canadian Children and Youth Study followed more than 4300 migrant families over a period of eight years during their initial years of settlement in Canada. The Prairie Research report contains simple tabular and graphical results of this study. It provides a good template for producing your research report. Readers can consult this research report by visiting the website of the Prairie Metropolis Centre Working Papers Series.

Summary

Once your data are collected, they are ready to be summarized and presented. To do this, you must select categories in which to summarize your data. Although you did some preliminary thinking about this when you constructed your dummy tables, the final selection is done when your data are in hand. Once you have selected categories, the data are coded into the categories. Then the data are cross-tabulated in some way to show the relationship between the variables in question. We have looked at tables, graphs, and means as the basic techniques for summarizing and presenting your data.

Key Terms

Bar graph	228	Marginal total	226
Cross-tabulate	225	Mean	241
Frequency	226	Pie graph	228
Line graph	233	Scattergram	232

Questions for Review

1. What are the three steps involved in summarizing and organizing your data?
2. Why is it necessary to categorize your data?
3. Why is it important to remember which variable is the independent and which is the dependent when constructing tables for the presentation and interpretation of your data?
4. In which part of the table should the independent variable appear? In which part of the table should the dependent variable appear? In what direction should you calculate the percentages?
5. What does it mean to cross-tabulate your data?
6. Describe the difficulties associated with your graphs.
7. What is a scattergram?
8. What are the advantages of using means (or averages) rather than line graphs or scattergrams in presenting data?
9. What is a constant? Why should it be removed from your report?

Suggestions for Further Reading

Babbie, E., &. Benaquisto, L. (2010). *Fundamentals of social research* (2nd Cdn ed.). Toronto: Nelson.

Gray, G., & Guppy, N. (2007). *Successful surveys: Research methods and practice* (3rd ed.). Toronto: Harcourt Brace.

Healey, J. (2004). *Statistics: A tool for social research* (7th ed.). London: Wadsworth.

Miles, J., & Shevlin, M. (2001). *Applying regression and correlation: A guide for students and researchers*. Los Angeles: Sage.

Munro, B. H. (2004). *Statistical methods for health care research* (5th ed.). Philadelphia: Lippincott Williams &Wilkins.

Palys, T. & Atchison, C. (2014). *Research decisions: Quantitative and qualitative perspectives* (5th ed.). Toronto: Thomson Nelson.

Roberts, L., Edgerton, J., Peter, T., & Wilkinson, L. (2015). *Understanding social statistics*. Don Mills, ON: Oxford University Press.

Roberts, L., Kampen, K., & Peter, T. (2009). *The statistics coach*. Don Mills, ON: Oxford University Press.

Tabachnick, B., & Fidell, L. (2016). *Using multivariate statistics* (6th ed.). Boston: Allyn & Bacon.

Suggested Web Resources

Howtech. (2016, September 19). *How to create charts in Excel 2016* [Video file]. Retrieved April 12, 2018 from www.youtube.com/watch?v=Xg0Z5qPteGw

Schultz, J. (2012). *Analysing your questionnaire* [Video file]. Retrieved April 12, 2018 from www.youtube.com/watch?v=c5ClF8RlGb4

Presenting Results Using Qualitative Research

The Qualitative Research Process

Qualitative research has its own demands and integrity, although there are some similarities with quantitative research, which we discussed throughout the book. Although the qualitative approach shares some requirements with quantitative research, there are subtle and not-so-subtle differences in the way the research issue is conceived and the data collected, analyzed, and reported.

One of the major differences between quantitative and qualitative research is that once the basic decisions are made in quantitative research, there is little opportunity to alter them in the light of early findings. Once a questionnaire is designed and distributed, it cannot be changed. Once an experiment has been carried out, there is no opportunity to alter the methods to take advantage of spontaneous, unexpected observations. However, qualitative research allows more continuous reflection on the research in progress and more interaction with the participants in the research, and there is usually more room for ongoing alteration as the research proceeds and new, unexpected observations are made. For example, if early observations or interviews reveal that one approach is not working or that additional issues need to be considered, later interviews and observations can be adjusted accordingly. One way of expressing this is to say that in qualitative research, the researcher is more interactive with the data-generating process, whereas in quantitative research, once it is set up, the research proceeds according to a predetermined plan.

As the following section reveals, the stages of reporting on qualitative research can be similar to quantitative research—but the steps also reveal significant differences in the process of conducting qualitative research. It is important to keep these differences in mind since the fundamental assumptions of qualitative research differ significantly from quantitative research. It is worthwhile to reinforce the steps in the qualitative research process here because so much of the process is embedded within the writing and reporting of results.

Phase 1: Essential First Steps

Selecting a Problem

As with the research procedures outlined in earlier chapters, selecting a research problem is the first stage. Each of the examples in Chapter 3 could have led to a qualitative research project, and the ways they were developed usually presumed that qualitative approaches to the issue had been taken to some extent. Take the first example of family decision-making. The prompting situation was this:

> **An important family decision**
> The Khan family has to decide whether to send their daughter to a public school or a private school.

There are many research focuses that this situation might stimulate. What is the nature of family decision-making? What kinds of issues arise? Whose arguments carry more weight—males' or females'? Young people's or older people's? Or you might focus on the differences associated with attending a public or a private school. You could select a more quantitative approach by asking questions such as "What proportion of girls attending public schools, as opposed to private schools, go on to university?" Or you could ask a more qualitative question such as "What is it like to attend a public school or a private school?"

As with all research, it is necessary to focus when doing qualitative research. It is not possible to answer all the questions. If you focus on the nature of family decision-making, you might go to the library and look up information on various databases. In doing this, you will, in part, be checking to see whether much is known about family decision-making. You will also assess the nature of the research already done, which may lead you to do some basic qualitative research to find out the themes and issues in family decision-making. Or you may feel that previous research has focused on different groups from those you have had in mind—for example, Americans in 1980 rather than Canadians in the twenty-first century. The literature search will help focus the research.

On completing the background reading, you may be ready to state the goal, objective, or central question of the research. This will play the same guiding role as the hypothesis in quantitative research. It states your aim, goal, or focus. For example, you might express your goal as one of the following research objectives:

> **Objective**
> To ascertain the themes that emerge in family decision-making about a daughter's education.

Objective
To describe the way the Khan family decided where to send their daughter, Sumita, to school.

Objective
To find out what it is like to be the subject of family decision-making about one's education.

There are other ways to state a research objective about family decision-making, but each of the above objectives provides a sharper focus and describes a qualitative approach to the general issue raised in the area of "family decision-making."

Sampling in Qualitative Research

Qualitative research is usually less concerned with generalization to large populations than with understanding what is going on in specific settings. However, you must not forget that the findings of any research project are limited by the nature of the sampling procedure. Sampling issues in qualitative research involve the deliberate selection of subjects, locations, groups, and situations to be observed or interviewed. Sampling issues therefore focus on how well the subjects and situations provide "windows" on social processes. Qualitative research will not be able to tell what proportion of female managers feel a certain way about their work environments, but it will be able to present in detail what it is like for women to work in selected types of managerial environments. We need quantitative sampling procedures to be able to make observations that can describe the entire population. With qualitative sampling, we need to locate people or cases that best illustrate the phenomenon we wish to study.

Sampling will also be an issue in the selection of locations, time frames, and points of orientation for observational research. Each of these selections will affect what is observed, so they must be made intentionally and described in the report so that readers will understand the nature of the observations upon which the research is based.

Phase 2: Collecting, Summarizing, and Organizing Data

At this stage, some key differences between quantitative and qualitative research become more apparent. One is the degree of focus on the topic and the degree of commitment to the given research method before gathering data. In quantitative research, much effort goes into preparing questionnaires, setting up experiments, or selecting groups for comparisons. This is done to ensure comparability of data and to make data summarization more efficient. Also, such preparation lowers the chance that you will have a problem with data collection once you start. Quantitative researchers must know the research topic very well to foresee problems.

In qualitative research, however, one of the key aims is to provide the maximum opportunity for the researcher to learn from the participants with an emphasis on giving participants a strong voice. This requires flexibility in data collection. Where quantitative research produces a relatively small amount of data focused on predetermined issues or variables and with no opportunity for the individual voices of participants to be showcased, qualitative research tends to produce large amounts of information that can only be focused after data collection. Generally, quantitative research progresses through a series of distinct stages—problem-focusing, choice of measurements, design of data collection instruments, and data collection. By comparison, in qualitative research these stages blend together and may be repeated or conducted at the same time at the researcher's discretion. Qualitative researchers continually progress back and forth through the stages, sensitizing themselves to the situation, so that they can eventually give a fuller description of "what is going on." As initial information is collected, good qualitative researchers revisit their data collection instruments and revise them accordingly. These revisions tend to take place frequently and throughout the entire data collection stage.

Data Collection

Qualitative research usually involves one or more of the following data-gathering techniques: observation—including *participant* and *non-participant* observation—in-depth interviewing, focus groups, and the use of textual material.

Observation

Observation is a basic qualitative research technique that requires discipline, planning, and alertness. There are two basic forms of observation: *non-participant* and *participant*. Three general focuses of observation are relevant to both forms:

1. the whole situation—for example, the "whole situation" of a committee meeting can be aggressive, conciliatory, or defensive;
2. the participants in the situation—for example, at a committee meeting, people from different factions will express different points of view and different interests;
3. what the researcher perceives given his own preconceptions and values—for example, you may be surprised, personally, when a committee conducts itself in an unexpected way. It is important that you be aware of how you perceive and appreciate events. Later, when reviewing observations, you will be able to distinguish your opinions about events from the events themselves.

In **non-participant observation**, the researcher stands back from the situation and observes—for instance, when a researcher sits in a corner at a committee meeting to find out how the committee arrives at decisions.

As an example, say you were doing a project for which the research goal was to describe the job-search experiences of first- and second-generation youth in Canada. Part of this project could be an observational study of a section of Winnipeg's census tracts (neighbourhoods, as defined by Statistics Canada) in terms of the employment counselling services available and the types of individuals using these services. Your purpose is to observe the social situation when racialized youth utilize these services and compare their experiences with youth who are not racialized. You hope that this will give some indication of the social situation that racialized first-and second-generation youth face every day. Using appropriate introduction procedures, you identify a suitable employment counselling agency in the census tract and obtain their permission to observe some of their job-search sessions, knowing that youth from various backgrounds will use their services at some point during your observation.

One of your tasks is to observe the "whole situation"—that is, the whole social situation at the employment counselling centre, which includes every person: young or old, racialized or not. The whole situation might contain "social tension" or "social harmony"; it might be "loud," "quiet," "energetic," or "subdued." The environment may seem very "multicultural" because it contains people of a range of races and ethnic dress. You should be alert for changes, particularly if they occur when racialized youth participate in sessions.

Second, you must observe the participants, who in this case are racialized first- and second-generation youth and everybody else. There are two things to observe: how participants act and how these actions express intentions, group feelings, or states of social relations. When observing how participants act, the researcher may see that some groups of non-racialized participants stare at the racialized youth or pay them no special attention. Others might sit in sex, gender, or race groups. You should interpret these actions. If the group mixes (i.e., there is no pattern in how the participants sit), you may discern that race and gender are not as important in the employment counselling groups as you might have anticipated. If non-racialized youth sit apart from racialized youth or refuse to engage them in conversation, you might need to ask participants about the types of people they prefer to spend their time with.

Last, it is also important to observe and record how you personally react to the situation and the participants. Entries about "how I felt," "what I thought," and "what I was reminded of" provide a vivid recording of the observation experience. Self-observation can also make you aware of biases or wrong preconceptions. If you felt surprised to see racialized groups sitting apart from one another and from non-racialized groups, you should consider why this seemed unusual. It may signal that you have misconceptions about race and ethnicity, which, if not corrected, could lead to misinterpretations of other events and actions.

It is also necessary to find a suitable observation point. This would be a place from which you can observe things critical to the research objective without disturbing participants. If you are observing a job seminar at an employment counselling centre in a certain census tract in Winnipeg when youth are present, you would need a place from which you could discreetly observe facial expressions and body language. This will allow you to appreciate how racialized and non-racialized youth react to one another. A seat at the back of the room may be suitable. Then again, if people see you watching them and taking notes, they might feel self-conscious and not act or speak in their usual manner.

Even if you are observing in an unobtrusive manner, participants may notice you watching and taking notes and ask about your activity. Your research ethics board (REB) will probably ask you to prepare printed information for such inquiries. This might be a one-page summary of the project, including the title, project number, your student number, date of REB approval, project description, supervisor's contact details, and complaints instructions. Such a document can quickly inform others of the purpose of the project and demonstrate its legitimacy.

Participant observation occurs when the researcher becomes a participant. The distinction between researcher and participant blurs, since the researcher observes not only what is going on among the regular participants but also their own reactions as a participant. In effect, the researcher shares some aspects of the standpoint of regular participants.

If you are researching the first job experiences of racialized youth in Canada, you may become a participant by attending and participating in some of the job seminars held at the employment centre. You would not only observe other people—racialized and non-racialized youth—but also actively participate in the activities of the respondents, and observe and record your own actions and reactions. In other words, you become part of the group in order to obtain detailed personal accounts and reflections from group members. You may feel physically uncomfortable while doing this, or very self-conscious, or hardly different at all. Such data would directly inform you about one aspect of what it is like to be a youth looking for work in Canada.

Participant observation has three possible disadvantages. First, your presence may affect the situation and cause other participants to feel self-conscious or even "trespassed" upon. People sometimes become upset if others pretend to be like them. Second, you might be unable to observe much of the situation while participating. For example, while you are talking, it may be hard to take notes about the reactions of others around you. Third, if you are significantly older than the participants, it may be difficult for you to "blend in" with the youth. As well, it will probably be impossible to observe the youth in an actual job interview. Last, certain forms of participant observation are likely to be subject to scrutiny by an REB. These issues are considered later in this chapter.

What are some of the issues to consider when choosing between participant and non-participant observation? Some argue that participant observation is far superior and that the only way to get to know what something is really like is to be "part of the action." However, as we have seen, researching "what it is like to be an unemployed racialized youth in Winnipeg" raises several issues.

You have two choices. First, you could be a non-participant observer, watching and taking notes at job-search seminars and résumé-writing courses and observing job-counselling sessions. Alternatively, you could be a participant observer and take part in the job-search seminars, résumé-writing courses, and job-counselling sessions along with the other youth.

What level of participation is possible or desirable in observational data collection? What information leads to the best data to answer your research question? The possibilities range from absolute non-participation (such as observation from a distance with a concealed video camera) to fully involved participant observation. The decision depends largely on the research question and the attitudes and permission of participants involved in your study.

First, the research question itself can determine what level of participation is appropriate. If you wish to research how charity collectors obtain donations, you can make an informative range of observations by simply watching and listening as collectors solicit donations; there is no real need for you to participate. If, however, your goal is to discover what it is like to be a charity collector, then participation would be appropriate, and you could expect to gather more relevant data by working as a collector.

Second, the research setting may lend itself more to either participation or non-participation. For example, if you are researching the society of a prison, there would be little advantage in doing participant observation. Unless you work undercover—which would be dangerous—other inmates and prison staff would never treat you as "one of the regular prisoners," and you would never observe the situation from the prisoners' viewpoint. However, through non-participant observation, you and the prisoners could interact without encroaching on each other's social space. You would also be free to interact with prison staff to appreciate how they affect the society of the prison.

Conversely, there are situations in which participation is the only option. If you wish to observe the crowd at a local dance bar, you are unlikely to gain entry without wearing appropriate clothing. You would have no choice but to participate.

The last issue is your research ethics board's policy on participation. REBs are likely to delay projects involving unacceptable or risky types of participation. For example, REBs are not likely to approve participation in dangerous activities. If you proposed to hang out with a violent street gang or take part in illegal drag-racing, your REB would almost certainly refuse the project because these activities are not safe. REBs will also oppose participation that may offend people because it seems culturally insensitive. For example, the wearing of a *hijab* or *qamis* by a non-Muslim may upset some Muslims, and most REBs would ask for reassurance that such a form of participation would cause Muslims no offence. Participation is also unacceptable to REBs when the researcher is likely to obstruct people in their regular roles and duties. Should you propose to participate in paramedic activities, your REB would certainly question the project because, without training, you would probably endanger people's lives.

Similarly, REBs are likely to be negative about non-participation that leads to possible identification or the recording of personal information without participants' consent. For example, for many REBs, the observation of people via hidden cameras is unacceptable because participants can be identified and they have no opportunity to consent or refuse.

Most professional organizations have a code of ethics that practitioners are expected to follow. The Canadian Sociological Association has a *Statement of Professional Ethics* by which all research sociologists are bound; it was revised to reflect the new guidelines introduced by the Tri-Council (see Chapter 9). Regardless of whether or not you are a sociologist, the code of ethics provides useful ethical guidelines for researchers in the social sciences.

Data recording

The most basic technique for gathering data in either type of observation is note-taking. There are three issues to consider in note-taking: first, the separation of observations and personal reactions; second, how to divide attention between observing and note-taking; and last, notation.

It is easy to get events and personal reactions to events confused and then take notes that do not separate the two types of observations. Therefore, you should note events and your reactions to them separately. For example, while observing a group of youth gang members in Winnipeg, you may see a white youth make unwanted contact with a racialized youth. Following is an inaccurate way to record the incident:

> At this point, a white youth bumped into one of the Vietnamese youth. This deliberate act was the first example of unfriendliness today.

Such an observation is a mixture of objective fact and reaction. A collision took place, as someone else could verify, but you do not know for sure that it was the outcome of a deliberate and unfriendly act. Unless you separate your interpretations and observations, your notes will indicate that the collision was indisputably deliberate.

A simple way to keep observations and reactions separate is to divide pages as in Figure 12.1. On notepaper, draw a vertical line about one-third of the way from the right side. Use the "two-thirds" column to record observations and the "one-third" column to record personal reactions such as opinions and emotional reactions. In this way, records of events show observations and feelings separately but on the same page.

Second, you should not allow note-taking to distract you from the important task of observing. This can happen if you decide to take notes about everything you experience and feel. You may try to write too much and be distracted from the observation situation while frantically creating volumes of notes. Hence, it is better to spend most of your energy observing while taking notes on the things that seem most significant at the time. Your close observation will provide comprehensive memories of the situation, and you will be able to write up other details immediately afterwards.

Last, you should feel free to use any style of notation that is comfortable for you. You might use longhand, shorthand, abbreviations, diagrams or symbols, or foreign words. As long as the act of note-taking is not a distraction

What you observe	Your reactions/thoughts

Figure 12.1 • **Data-recording sheet for recording observations**

from the situation and your notes are legible, you should feel free to take notes however you wish. Laptops, while small and handy for taking notes, may be highly distracting and perhaps ought not be used, especially when connecting with participants is important. That said, laptops are becoming ubiquitous even in the poorest societies and may not pose a problem. The best suggestion is to use your own judgment. If you feel the laptop is imposing an artificial barrier between you and your participant, or if you think the participant is becoming suspicious that you are using the computer's recording device without their permission, it is best not to use the laptop. In addition, during participant observation, it may not be practical to write down or record data, so a good memory is the most important data collection tool. It may be necessary to schedule a time, such as lunch break, to rapidly write notes from memory.

A popular set of tools for gathering observational data are audio-and visual-recording devices such as tape recorders and camcorders. They provide comprehensive records of situations, and the tapes can be reviewed many times. Tapes also allow you to re-observe a situation and refocus on events that had seemed unimportant.

While making recordings, you should also take notes to document the experience of observing the situation as it happened. It is also important to observe or listen to recordings with discipline. Recordings do not observe for you, they do not distinguish between significant and insignificant events, nor do they record your perceptions. Finally, be aware that under current principles of research ethics in Canada and for your discipline or profession, it is only appropriate to make recordings when participants give permission (see Chapter 9).

In-depth interviewing

In-depth interviews provide the best opportunity to find out what someone else thinks or feels. The idea of in-depth interviewing is to get a "window" on reality from the point of view of a participant and to allow them to tell their story as they wish, identifying the issues that are important to them. The common approach is to ask only very general questions so as to encourage participants to "open up" and lead the interview and give their perspectives with as little influence from the researcher as possible. Usually, researchers have a list of general topics but are ready to discuss others that the participant identifies as important.

Another feature of in-depth interviews is that they often take several hours and may extend over more than one session. This allows participants to talk as exhaustively as they wish. Hence, some people call them "extended interviews."

In-depth interviews are usually more productive if you gain some rapport or mutual sense of comfort with participants. You should conduct in-depth interviews in places that are safe and comfortable for both you and the participants. It is important to be discerning in your style of language and to be careful not to use words that might cause participants to feel offended or patronized. Similarly, you should select your dress carefully, wearing clothes that do not cause offence. Ties or suits, for example, may cause factory workers to see you as a member of the same social class as their employers. Dressing too casually, however, may be inappropriate for other research participants.

Also, it is important not to ignore participants' cultural practices. In some cultures, for example, women do not shake hands or remain alone with males who are not family members. Being aware of such practices not only prevents offence but also demonstrates respect, which participants are likely to return.

Two problems often occur during in-depth interviews. First, because participants have a lot of freedom in how they respond to general questions, they often drift to topics unrelated to the research. Listening to some idle talk is polite and can also be productive, particularly when it generates rapport. However, it is important to redirect discussion back to a research topic; otherwise, you will collect very little data.

One strategy is to show interest in the participant's discussion before redirecting them back to the research topic. For example, you might be interviewing racialized youth about their job-search experiences in Winnipeg. One male participant begins talking about a recent job interview but drifts into a discussion of a car he saw on a recent trip to the supermarket. You might get the discussion back on track with the following:

> That's interesting. It sounds like an amazing car! I'd like to know more about that car when we finish. Just getting back to what we were discussing before, I'd like to hear you talk a bit more about what it's like to be a young immigrant man trying to find work in Winnipeg.

Communicate to the participant that you respect them enough to engage in friendly conversation and then gently restate the original question. Note that if you ever indicate that you will chat about other subjects later, it is respectful and considerate to do so. Participants usually ask for nothing in return for their time, and you can show appreciation by sharing some friendly talk.

A second common problem is the tendency of some participants to provide only brief answers. Some people just tend to answer "yes," "no," or "maybe" without elaborating, thus rendering little data. Such responses often occur when questions do not invite participants to talk at length or reflect on personal experience. Take the following question that might be asked in an interview with a racialized young woman:

What is it like to be young and looking for work in Winnipeg?

It would not be surprising for participants to give short replies like "All right," "It was easy," or "I don't even think about it." A short answer is sufficient, given the form of the question, and further, the question contains no explicit request for the participant to reflect on her experience. The question stands a better chance of eliciting an extended answer if it asks participants to tell a story about themselves. For example:

Can you tell me about your personal experience of looking for work in Winnipeg?

Could you describe what it's been like for you to look for work in Winnipeg since you first came here to live?

Before conducting interviews, researchers should consider whether their questions invite short or extended answers and make appropriate changes.

Sometimes there is no success regardless of how you prompt a participant because she may be a person of few words or she may find the question sensitive. Once you realize that you will not get an elaboration, move to the next question. You must respect the right of participants to answer questions as they wish. Participants are not obliged to answer questions and may complain to your REB if they feel pressured. Also, if participants generally tend to give only short answers to a particular question, this may be an indication that the question touches on a sensitive subject.

One way of documenting an interview is to take notes of your dialogue with the participant and then do a "write-up" immediately after the interview is over. However, any delay undermines the record's accuracy and reliability, so write-ups should be done immediately.

Another common method is to tape-record interviews and then do a transcription. This allows a thorough collection of the interview data, which you can review as many times as you wish. However, transcriptions do not record gestures and body language. So it is valuable to take notes while recording an interview and document a participant's physical reactions. Transcribing interviews is

Case Study

How In-Depth Interviews Help Researchers Gain More Detailed Information

It's worth our while to stop for a moment and consider one of the real strengths of the in-depth interview. One of its most powerful attributes is the ability of the researcher to ask participants for more information. Think about it. If the participant tries to evade answering the question or gives confusing or nonsensical information, the researcher can ask for clarification. We must be careful about using this procedure. We do not want to badger or pester the participant. After all, it is their choice to answer a particular question or not. Instead, have the interviewer explain the reason they are being asked the question. If the participant still does not agree to answer the question then indicate your thanks and move on to the next question. That said, explaining the reasoning behind asking the question often helps ease the mistrust that a participant might have and they may willingly answer the question after they have been provided with sufficient explanation of why it is being asked and how the data is being used.

Let's use an example from the research presented in the Appendix. In this study, we were trying to understand the job-search process from the point of view of young people in Canada. We asked the following question of a racialized young woman:

What is it like to be overlooked for a job promotion?

In this example, it would not be surprising for participants to give short replies like "It was terrible," or "I felt so disappointed." Questions asked in this way sometimes encourage short answers. To get participants speaking about their experiences and feelings, a better way to ask this kind of question is like this:

Can you tell me about your personal experience of being overlooked for a job promotion? Could you describe what it's been like for you experience being passed over for a job promotion?

It is this kind of phrasing that encourages participants to respond with life narratives or examples. The role of the interviewer, in this instance, is to encourage participants to elaborate on their responses or to ask for clarification if something requires elaboration, seems confusing or out of place. Instead of eliciting responses like "It was easy to find a job," what we found was that participants would say things like "It was really difficult to find this job, now that I think about it. When I first graduated, I tried to get a job like the one I currently have [as HR manager]. I wasn't even given an interview. I watched my white friends from university get similar jobs, but for me, I had to start at a lower salary and responsibility range. It took me eighteen months to get promoted to HR manager, even though some of my white friends got similar jobs right out of university."

By asking questions in this way, we were able to get participants to reflect on their job search histories and to compare their results with those of their peers—without even asking them to compare themselves. Now we have a nice record of how participants come to view their labour force histories without asking a leading question.

a time-consuming task. It may take four to five hours to transcribe an hour-long interview. While you may be able to hire a transcriber, this is very expensive, particularly if a project has a large number of interviews.

Rather than doing in-depth interviews, it is sometimes preferable to issue questionnaires containing "open-ended" questions—that is, questions that request extended responses. If participants are literate and accustomed to expressing themselves in writing, it may be practical to ask for written answers. For example, a study of professors could ask, "Please tell us your thoughts and concerns about the ethical treatment of children during research interviews." Such "open-ended" questions (in this instance, without references to specific aspects of "ethical practices") give respondents the freedom to discuss the things they perceive as important.

Life narratives

A modification of the in-depth interview is to ask people to write or record their life stories. In the field of oral history, a disciplined expertise has been developed in using this technique to gather material about what life was like in various places and times by asking people to narrate their life stories and recollections of significant events. Researchers can audio-record the narrations and produce written reports of life stories in the participant's narrative voice, like a piece of autobiographical writing.

The main purpose of collecting life narratives is to give the participants the opportunity to tell their own stories, their way. It is therefore critical not to impose your own viewpoints on the data—for example, by omitting events that are unimportant for you but important for the participant. It is also possible to misrepresent the participant by emphasizing events that are consistent with your own political, social, and moral concerns. It is important to be aware of these possibilities, particularly if you and the participants have different political, social class, cultural, ethnic, or educational backgrounds. Therefore, participants should view and appraise your edited versions of their life stories. They can comment, suggest changes, and verify that the report is representative of how they remember and feel about events.

Life narratives may include more than just biographical materials. They may include an examination of journal and newspaper articles written during

Case Study

An Example Using In-Depth Interviews

One of the book's authors has a graduate student who is very interested in understanding the conditions and experiences of immigrant women experiencing domestic violence in Canada. Domestic violence, also called "intimate partner violence," is a very personal and traumatic experience, one that most women are reluctant to discuss with anyone. It can be more difficult for immigrant women to discuss such matters for, in addition to the other feelings of trauma that victims experience, immigrant women have the added fear that they and their families will be deported if their abuse is reported to police. The student and her supervisor discussed many strategies for answering the research question. It became clear that the only way this research could be done was to conduct in-depth interviews with immigrant women who had successfully left abusive situations, along with in-depth interviews with police and social workers who have helped them. It is a method that has been used elsewhere (Social Planning Council of Perth and Huron, 2013). Bramadat's (2015) in-depth interviews with immigrant women survivors of domestic violence reveals that their fears are well founded. One woman was not able to report the physical violence she experienced because interpreters were not available. She was unable to leave her abusive partner for nearly three years. Another participant reported that her children were removed by child welfare authorities because her husband made (false) claims that she had physically abused the children. Three years later, this participant is still fighting to regain custody of her children. This kind of information could not have been collected from a survey instrument. Rather, it was gathered by extensive interviews, and grew out of a development of trust between the researcher and the participant. In addition, none of this information could have been "predicted," so questions about this type of experience could not have been added to a questionnaire. Only through in-depth discussions and narrative life histories can this type of information become available. Had Bramadat not interviewed survivors of domestic violence, we would have been unaware that for some immigrant women, translation services prevent them from disclosing abuse and that the threat of having their children taken away is real.

the time period to contextualize the era. They may also involve interviewing those who are intimate with the subject matter. Minutes from meetings, personal notes, and other artefacts may augment the data collected in the life narrative. The process is different from content analysis, since "the data are used to build the chronology and resultant life history" (Kirby, Greaves, & Reid, 2006, p. 158). With this in mind, Kirby and her colleagues suggest the following steps: (1) identify important milestones and personal events; (2) gather information about the person using a variety of different sources; (3) tell the history chronologically; (4) corroborate your version other historical materials; and (5) repeat steps 1 through 4 until you are certain that the life history accurately reflects what actually happened.

Focus groups

Focus groups combine the strengths of in-depth interviewing and observation in a group context. In a focus group, a small number of people, say between 4 and 12, agree to meet for collective discussion with the researcher, who acts as **facilitator**.

Focus groups are used increasingly as a way of learning about public opinion on a variety of issues. It would be possible to recruit a focus group of racialized youth to talk about their experiences looking for work and ask them to discuss issues they perceive as important. Other types of people may also attend, such as non-racialized youth or youth who have employment. This would generate data on a cross-section of views and provide observations of different parties reacting to each other's ideas. A drawback of focus groups is that they are more time-consuming for the participants. All participants must take time to listen to the responses of others. The advantage, however, is that by listening, all participants can create their own conversation, asking different questions and allowing the researcher to gather information on issues she might not have anticipated earlier in the study. For researchers, the focus group is actually a time-saving, data-rich method.

Note-taking can be very difficult when administering focus groups, simply because so much is usually going on. The best way to collect data is to make a video-recording with a camera mounted in a non-intrusive place or to audio-tape with a digital recorder. The recording should capture the dialogue of individual participants and their interactions. Video-recordings also document body language and gestures, which can be valuable data. Remember that use of any recording device must be approved by your REB.

Facilitators are the people who introduce the research topic to participants, ask questions, direct conversations, and record the results. Usually, the focus group facilitator is the primary researcher. However, it is increasingly common for researchers to hire focus group facilitators. Regardless of who directs the focus group, it is a very good idea to provide a focus group schedule to the facilitator. The schedule consists of a list of discussion questions that must be covered during the focus group activity. The facilitator must be prepared to probe and ask additional questions when the focus group delves into topics that are tangential to the original research question. Usually, this additional information is interesting and helps to provide a fuller depiction of a research topic. Occasionally, however, the line of questioning may be unnecessary and unhelpful in understanding a problem. For this reason, the focus group facilitator should be intimately familiar with the research project, the researcher's intentions, and the primary research questions.

In Focus

Organizing a Focus Group

Organizing a focus group can be a challenging exercise. In today's busy world, it can be difficult to identify a meeting time and place that is convenient for potential participants. One way of negotiating this is to offer potential respondents more than one time and location in which to participate. For example, offer a focus group in the morning, one in the afternoon, and another in the evening to accommodate those with shift work. When your research involves a single organization, speak with human resource managers to see if it is possible to hold the focus group during work hours and at the workplace. That may increase the likelihood of participation among potential respondents.

Ensure the focus group facilitators have good organizational skills. One of the most important jobs of facilitators is to make participants feel welcome in the focus group. Remember that not everyone is comfortable with participating in research. Facilitators should welcome participants as they enter the room. Good focus groups offer beverages and snacks to participants as a way of "breaking the ice." Facilitators should introduce themselves and at the start of the focus group introduce other participants to one another. Focus groups are usually audio-recorded. The facilitator should mention the names of the participants before they speak or encourage participants to introduce themselves each time they talk so that it is easier for the transcriber to attribute responses to particular individuals.

Facilitators introduce the purpose of the focus group prior to asking the questions. A good facilitator does not dominate the conversation, but ensures that the topics of interest are discussed prior to ending the focus group. Good facilitators are able to gently redirect conversations that veer too far away from the researcher's interests. Sometimes a separate note-taker attends the meetings with the facilitator. That helps the facilitator concentrate on asking the questions while the note-taker can focus on observations and recording devices.

It is usually best that the focus group facilitator act as transcriber. The transcriber takes the audio or video information and records it word-for-word into a computer program. This becomes the primary textual material from which the researcher draws the analysis. The transcriber, having conducted the focus group, can more accurately record the conversation, especially if the recording is of poor quality. If this is not possible, a professional secretary should be hired to record the notes. Each hour of interview can take at least three to four hours to be transcribed. Professional secretarial staff with superior typing abilities may be able to transcribe at a faster rate, saving the researcher time but costing more money.

It is a good idea to provide refreshments for participants, since discussions tend to be long, especially on topics that are important to the participants.

It is not uncommon for focus groups to last more than two hours. Focus groups on less sensitive or personally important topics, such as discussions among high-school youth on about their after-school employment, may last only half an hour. Length of time is dependent on the number of questions asked, the number of participants, and the centrality of the research question to the individuals who attend the focus group.

Focus groups have also been used for non-research purposes, such as by television networks developing new programming and by marketers developing new products. Some of these groups do not use scientific methods of data collection, however, which has had a negative effect on research. Increasingly, participants are reluctant to take part in such endeavours without the assurance that their data will be used for research purposes. It is a good idea, then, for researchers to clearly identify themselves as such. Materials given to the participant should clearly indicate the university or institution the researcher is affiliated with. This may increase the chances that the individual will participate in the research. It is also required as an ethical practice.

Textual material

The use of textual material, including written records, is described at length in Chapter 6 with respect to a quantitative form of research, **content analysis**. Here the researcher counts frequencies of themes, phrases, or ideas. However, texts can also be a source of data in qualitative research. Rather than just counting the number of times themes occur, researchers use the themes to construct a picture of what it is like to experience a given situation.

For example, documents can be used to answer the question "What was happening in this time and place to these people?" Letters, diaries, and minutes of meetings are useful sources of data about what it is like to experience particular situations. When using documents, it is important to keep in mind the identities of the people who wrote them, who was to receive/read them, and for what purpose they were written. Such information specifies the perspectives of those who participated in the creation of the text and makes it easier for new readers to understand how to situate the data within its historical, cultural, and social context.

In conducting a content analysis, the researcher must first identify the kinds of text that are appropriate for answering the research question. Are newspapers the best source of information? If so, which newspapers? What year? How many weeks? Are editorials included or excluded? These are important questions to consider prior to embarking on the assembly of textual materials.

Once these questions are addressed, the researcher needs to develop an analytical framework to make sense of the mass of materials collected. One way to go about this is to look for key words or phrases that appear in the material and count how many times they appear. Another is to count how many times a particular phenomenon is described positively and negatively. Material can also be organized according to the author or the name of the newspaper, or even chronologically. Recall the literature review you conducted prior to collecting the textual materials. What themes are identified by this literature? This will give you a good beginning from which to identify your own themes. Be warned, however: the literature review should serve as a guide only. You are likely to discover many other themes not previously considered in the course of your research.

In short, textual material may be the main data collected for a qualitative research project or it may supplement data collected in other ways. There are many cases in which content analysis can be used as the central data collection strategy. For example, a research project conducted by one undergraduate student involved an examination of the materials produced as part of the Bouchard-Taylor Commission on reasonable accommodation in Quebec. It was not practical or possible for her to travel to Quebec to interview all those who participated in the commission's hearings, given the time and cost constraints she faced as an impoverished student trying to complete her honours thesis. So instead, she collected all the newspaper, editorial, and opinion articles she could; scoured federal, provincial, and municipal government websites; and conducted a content analysis identifying the main arguments and contradictions of the debate.

Content analysis is an especially important form of data collection when the original participants are no longer alive to participate in interviews. In other cases, the content analysis supplements data collected in other forms. The project examining the job search strategies of Canadian youth, described in the Appendix, has a content analysis component. In addition to the data collection strategies discussed in that section, the researchers examined government and educational materials that are given to youth job seekers to give context to the number, type, and availability of services. This information assisted the researchers in preparing a fuller view of the school-to-work transitions of Canadian youth.

Organizing and Summarizing Qualitative Data

Once you have made your observations, recorded or written up your interviews or focus group interactions, or collected your open-ended questionnaires, what do you do with the data? Qualitative research tends to produce vast amounts of information, which you must first organize and summarize.

Organizing data

As in content research, qualitative researchers look through interviews, textual data, and observational data for recurring themes or issues. They identify these and organize them into systems of categories, a practice called "coding." Following is a simple example of coding. When asked a question on the topic of employment, "Why don't you work?," a young woman might answer thus:

> I prefer to concentrate my time on studying and to have a less hectic schedule instead of working while going to school.

There are two dimensions to the thematic content of the sentence—the topic and the issue. The topic is "Looking for work," as given by the question. In response, the participant raised the issue of her preference to focus on school and studying rather than balancing a work schedule with schooling.

The next task is to "code" the theme—that is, apply a label designating the topic and the issues. A simple way to code the above statement is therefore:

1.1 Looking for work: Personal preferences

The word or phrase before the colon identifies the topic; the words or phrases after it identify the issues. The code is also given a number for easy indexing, in this case 1.1. In this example, "Looking for work" is Topic 1 and "personal preference" is Issue 1 for the topic; hence the full code is "1.1." There are many ways to code themes, and you should devise or adapt ways that make the greatest sense for you.

As you read interviews and create new codes, write the code numbers on the pages of the interview transcripts where they occur. While doing this, also write a "codebook"—that is, a list of codes, indexed to the interviews in which you identified them (see Figure 12.2). When finished, the codebook will be a useful tool for analysis, giving you a structural overview of how you have perceived the data. The codebook will also indicate how often codes occur, thereby showing their relative importance according to your own reading of the data. Lastly, the index of interviews and page numbers will allow you to quickly review and extract coded text.

It is valuable to review a coding scheme at least once. This generally leads to a refinement of the coding and greater familiarity with the data. If possible, another researcher should review the coding to assess its coherence and ensure a greater depth of understanding of the data by the researcher.

You can create a codebook on a computer with a simple spreadsheet or word processing program. There are a number of software packages designed especially for coding and analyzing textual data. Students should gain some skills with these programs if they intend to pursue research as a career.

Topics: Issues	Interviews: Page numbers					Total
1. Looking for employment						
1.1 Racial discrimination	Int. 1: page 4	Int. 8: page 5	Int. 17: page 2	Int. 6: page 3	Int. 10: page 1	5
1.2 Language barriers	Int. 1: page 2	Int. 9: page 3				2
1.3 Age discrimination	Int. 14: page 1	Int. 1: page 2	Int. 13: page 1	Int. 6: page 3	Int. 5: page 2	5
1.4 Prior work experience	Int. 1: page 1	Int. 2: page 1	Int. 23: page 5	Int. 3: page 2		4
2. Social networks						
2.1 Family connections in Winnipeg	Int. 6: page 1	Int. 8: page 1	Int. 19: page 2	Int. 23: page 2	Int. 25: page 1	5
2.2 Cultural connections in Winnipeg	Int. 7: page 1					1
2.3 Friendship networks in Winnipeg	Int. 9: page 6	Int. 8: page 5	Int. 17: page 4	Int. 22: page 4		4
etc.						

Figure 12.2 • Codebook: Immigration to Winnipeg

Phase 3: Analyzing Data

Having organized your data, how do you analyze or "make sense of it" so that you can write about "what is going on" with the benefit of an informed understanding? Most importantly, how do you develop your sense of having "been there" or having "been close" to the situation so that you can look at the data with the sensitivity of someone who knows the situation personally? When a person has visited a remote place, they can describe it with reference to personal experience—the sights, sounds, smells, social values, and customs. The visitor is "sensitized" to the place and can analyze its social situation by referring to his first-hand knowledge of "what it was like" to be there. Similarly, you have to develop the same type of sensitivity to the situations you research.

If you have done participant research for an extended period, your sensitivity may be adequate. Then again, if you have used less intimate methodologies like non-participant observation or interviews, you may need to develop extra sensitivity through immersion in the data. Read and reread interview transcripts and notes, review and re-review sound or visual recordings and photographs, and continue to revise the coding.

As your sensitivity increases, take notes of your changing impressions. The notes will eventually expose "forms" in the data. Patterns and relationships between actions and social structures will become perceptible, allowing you to explain "what is going on" or "what it is like" in the situation. For example, after a thorough reading of interviews with racialized youth in Winnipeg, you may "see" systems of support within the racialized communities that participants never describe explicitly but take for granted. Their dialogues could contain assumptions of reciprocal duties of support to certain people—family, clergy, friends, schoolteachers—but participants may never make direct references to these duties. You may also perceive social problems to which most participants refer only in their jokes. Participants may make jokes because they cannot get work in Canada or because they believe their jobs are inferior to those of non-racialized youth. These jokes, however, may indicate a general problem for racialized youth in the labour market.

Fundamentally, you should approach all qualitative analysis with a view to developing sensitivity to the data. This way, you can discuss "what is going on" or "what it is like" to be in a situation just as though you had been inside it—or as close to it as possible. In addition to developing sensitivity, you can employ a number of frameworks to make sense of data from particular analytical perspectives. Descriptions of two appear below: the "action/cultural" framework and the "typical actions" framework.

Action/Cultural Framework

The **action/cultural framework** makes reference to cultural or social facts in understanding social actions. It often requires extra data about the culture of the people within the research situation. Therefore, it may be necessary to consult history books, religious texts, or company mission statements.

For example, if you are a non-racialized person researching racialized youth in Canada, you may want to understand the social context of discrimination in

Canada. The immediate answer, as you would be told in interviews, is that racial and ethnic discrimination is rampant in Canadian society. This answer provides only a superficial understanding, however, and raises the further question "Why do racialized youth believe that racism is prevalent in Canadian society?" If you look more closely at the culture, social norms, and history of Canada, you will find that racism and discrimination do exist in Canada and are influenced by events of both the past and the present. An examination of Canadian history reveals extensive racial discrimination in the job experiences of racialized and immigrant peoples. For example, the Chinese were prohibited from working in industries other than the railway, construction, manufacturing, and service sectors. Ukrainians, Poles, Hungarians, Russians, and others faced significant ethnic discrimination when applying for jobs in Canada. More recent evidence reveals that racism still exists in the Canadian labour market today. For instance, Frances Henry and her colleagues have done extensive research revealing that racialized youth, particularly young men from Caribbean countries, are less likely to get job interviews and job offers (Tator & Henry, 2006; Henry & Ginsberg, 1984). Therefore, another way to understand youths' experience of racism is to contextualize their comments within historical and current events and the results of research conducted in Canada.

Typical Actions Framework

This analytic approach considers how people construct their social lives. It examines what actions are generally understood as "**typical actions**," which make social life possible. For example, typical actions by which Muslims recognize other Muslims are attendance at Friday prayers, abstinence from pork, wearing the *qamis* or *hijab* (for some), and the standard greeting of "*Assalamualaikum.*" These are typical actions that, for Muslims, signify qualities of Islamic identity. Muslims recognize each other through these actions and have socially defined interpretations of the meaning behind each.

In a study of Canadian Muslims, a significant issue among participants could be their relations with non-Muslims. In analyzing any friction between the communities, the researcher might search interviews for Muslims' negative interpretations of the "typical" actions of non-Muslims. The participants may note that many non-Muslims stare at their *hijabs* and *qamis*, assume that all Islamic marriages are "arranged," and express a lack of understanding of abstinence from alcohol and that some non-Muslims attempt to stop the building of mosques in their suburbs. Likewise, the interviews may indicate typical actions that Muslims interpret as friendly. Interviews may contain several references to participants' feelings of solidarity with non-Muslims at work or to the prayer facilities for their children in public schools. Repeated references to such types of social actions indicate what it is like to be a Muslim in Canada and how Muslims construct the social actions of others. The recognition of both negative and positive interpretations of typical actions by non-Muslims would be the basis for a rich description and set of explanations of this group.

Reporting on Qualitative Research

Qualitative research does not always lead to clear conclusions. As with quantitative research, it is important that when reporting results, you remind yourself of the question or research objective that guided the research. It is that question that you must now answer, that research objective about which you must now draw conclusions. If you asked "What is it like to be a racialized youth in Canada?," your conclusion, based on your data, will express a response to this question. If the research objective was "to describe how a family made an important decision," then you will summarize the findings and observations in terms of themes, interaction patterns, sequence of argumentation, patterns of power and submission, or whatever you found. This will allow you to describe what is involved in the situation and to interpret it for readers.

Reporting on qualitative research involves careful description of what was observed and heard, "what it was like," and how people felt, reacted, and behaved. This may involve data summarization and categorization into themes or patterns, or it may involve description and interpretation of observations. Generally, qualitative research "tells a story." It is more difficult to report, since the communication of such research means trying to make sense of the experiences of a number of different research participants. How do you write a coherent research report on the varied experiences of 30 participants or 175 participants? The Appendix provides an example of how this is done in practice. Here are some guidelines.

The report always begins with a statement on the research question and a description of the theory or theories used to inform your research. Remember that literature review you conducted prior to collecting the data and formulating your research question? This is another point at which it is helpful in the research process. The literature review serves different purposes in qualitative research depending on the topic. If the topic is new and not much has been written about the phenomenon, then the literature review will be short. When embedding your findings within the literature in that case, this part of the process may also be short. If research on your topic has been widely published in the literature already, then the literature review will include a discussion of how your findings either support the existing literature or how your findings contribute to our understanding of the topic.

In qualitative research, the literature review and production of the research report are symbiotic. The researcher must constantly return to the literature review when analyzing the results to better situate the results of the project within the existing literature. Kirby and her colleagues tell us that this takes a significant amount of time to accomplish and that the writing occurs in stages. It may require the researcher to do a little work at one time and then put it aside for a while. Writing in stages can help to ensure that "the analysis is solid, steady, and unlikely to change" (Kirby, Greaves, & Reid, 2006, p. 236).

In contrast to quantitative research, data in a qualitative project can take many forms. Typically, there is a research report. This informs funders and readers of the results of the study. However, it may contain material very different from that in a quantitative report. Reports for projects involving **unstructured interviews**, for instance, typically include long quotations embedded within deep theoretical analysis. Other data may include "**photojournals**"—examples of photos taken by respondents, followed up by detailed interviews. Projects may include maps showing where individuals spend time. It may include examples of the participants' work. The researcher should contact the publishers and funders well in advance to ensure that they are able to provide the technical or financial assistance necessary to reproduce photos and other pictorial materials in the report. Further, it will likely take the researcher a bit more time to analyze such data in order to make connections between the visual material and the interview material.

Kirby and her colleagues (2006) provide some tips on reporting on qualitative research. While your analysis must address the research question, it is not possible to give equal attention to all themes that come out of the data. Some themes may be more poignant or more illustrative or occur more often than other themes. Do try to provide as much attention to these themes as your respondents do. Do not overemphasize points that the participants do not spend as much time discussing.

Data reduction is another tricky issue. Many researchers may be tempted to report on every single detail raised by every participant. This approach is inadvisable and often leads to a lengthy report filled with tangential information. Instead, select only the most illustrative examples. Tied to this concern is the issue of "forcing the data analysis." Kirby and her associates suggest that all materials included in the research report should directly relate to the research question. Ensure that all data contribute to answering the research question in some way. If you are tempted to add parallel material, keep your description short and perhaps use this material towards the end of the report as illustrative of possible trends but not definitely linked to the research topic.

Finally, be careful in the way you convey the voices of the participants in your report. It is important for the "voices" of participants to figure prominently in the report, but do not use their words as your own: ensure that your voice and opinion as researcher are reported separately from those of your participants. The point of most qualitative research is to project the voices, opinions, and ideas of the participants. If their voices are not part of the research report, you are not doing a good job of explaining their reality. As well, ensure that you clearly attribute quotes and research materials to the correct participants.

It has been our experience that preparing the results of a qualitative research report is more time-consuming and less intuitive than it is for quantitative projects. For this reason, you should allow more time to prepare your report. Consult Tuhiwai Smith (1999) and Kirby, Greaves, and Reid (2006) for assistance with the process.

Key Terms

Questions for Review

1. What are the basic data-gathering techniques in qualitative research? What are the advantages and disadvantages of each?
2. What is involved in the summarization of qualitative data?
3. In qualitative research, the subject of the research participates more in the project than in quantitative research. Discuss.
4. Look up your discipline's professional code of ethics. What does it say about the practice of qualitative research?
5. What advantages does transcribing your own interviews have in conducting research?
6. Why must we take into account culture or history when undertaking any social research?

Sources

Bramadat, J. (2015). *The role of Canadian laws and social policies in perpetuating intimate partner abuse among newcomer women in Canada* (Unpublished master's thesis). Department of Sociology, University of Manitoba.

Henry, F., & Ginsberg, E. (1984). *Who gets the work? A test of racial discrimination in employment.* Toronto: Urban Alliance on Race Relations and Social Planning Council of Toronto.

Kirby, S. L., Greaves, L., & Reid, C. (2006). *Experience research social change: Methods beyond the mainstream.* Peterborough, ON: Broadview.

Social Planning Council of Perth and Huron. (2013). *A study of violence against women.* Kitchener, ON: Social Planning Council of Perth and Huron. Retrieved March 9, 2015 from www.communitybasedresearch.ca/resources/649%20VAW%20Huron/Final_VAW_Report.pdf

Tator, C., & Henry, F. (2006). *Racial profiling in Canada: Challenging the myth of "a few bad apples."* Toronto: University of Toronto Press.

Tuhiwai Smith, L. (1999). *Decolonizing methodologies: Research and Indigenous Peoples.* New York: Zed Books.

Suggestions for Further Reading

Canadian Sociology Association. (2010). *Professional code of ethics.* Retrieved April 18, 2011 from www.csa-scs.ca/code-of-ethics

Denzin, N. (2004). The art and politics of interpretation. In S. N. Hesse-Biber and P. Leavy, eds., *Approaches to qualitative research: A reader on theory and practice* (pp. 447–72). New York: Oxford University Press.

Richardson, L. (2004). Writing: A method of inquiry. In S. N. Hesse-Biber and P. Leavy, eds., *Approaches to qualitative research: A reader on theory and practice* (pp. 473–95). New York: Oxford University Press.

Suggested Web Resources

Cotton, S. (2016, January 10). *Content analysis coding* [Video file]. Retrieved April 12, 2018 from www.youtube.com/watch?v=wilBzZLjZ1M

Löfgren, K. (2013, May 19). *Qualitative analysis of interview data: A step-by-step guide* [Video file]. Retrieved April 12, 2018 from www.youtube.com/watch?v=DRL4PF2u9XA

Mod U-Powerful Concepts in Social Science. (2016, November 1). *What does coding look like?: Qualitative research methods* [Video file]. Retrieved April 12, 2018 from www.youtube.com/watch?v=phXssQBCDls

Schultz, J. (2012, August 14). *Analysing your interviews* [Video file]. Southampton Education School. Retrieved April 12, 2018 from www.youtube.com/watch?v=59GsjhPolPs

Phase 3

Analysis and Interpretation

13 Drawing Conclusions

You have now reached the point where you have analyzed and interpreted the findings of your research. You have clarified your thinking, formed a hypothesis, and gathered data. Now what? Essentially, it is time to draw conclusions about your hypothesis on the basis of the evidence you have collected and to provide some guidance about policies and practical implications of your findings.

A proper conclusion is grounded on careful analysis and interpretation of data gathered in the light of the basic question being researched. Data have been collected and presented, but they still require evaluation and analysis. Four basic questions guide the activities of data analysis and interpretation:

1.   What did you ask?
2.   What did you find?
3.   What do you conclude?
4.   To whom do your conclusions apply?

What Did You Ask?

The first step in drawing conclusions is to remember what it was you asked. It is surprising how easy it is to lose sight of the purpose of a piece of research. Before leaping to conclusions, it is useful to remind yourself about the questions that originally motivated you to do the research. You may have made many interesting discoveries as you gathered data or prepared your data for presentation. But what was the central issue? In this regard, it is very important to repeat your research question or thesis statement. This not only reminds you of the purpose of your research, but it serves to remind the reader about what you have accomplished.

If you kept a research journal, you should look back to remind yourself of your original questions. Some will seem very broad and unfocused now. You may be able to see how, in the process of clarifying your thinking and narrowing the focus of the research, you tackled a manageable part of a much larger issue. Try to clarify now how you see both the larger issue and the role your research plays in that larger issue.

The clearest statement of what you are asking is your research question, your hypothesis, or your research objective. Recall the process by which you narrowed the focus of your project and formed the hypothesis or objective. Now look at these items again. How does your thesis statement, research question, or hypothesis relate to the larger issues? Use the examples we have used in this book.

We have spent a lot of time on research involving hours spent in study and exam results. The hypothesis stated:

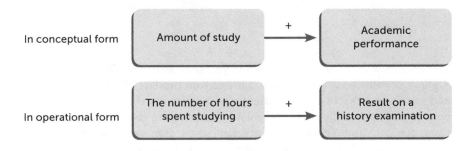

What was the background of this hypothesis? In Chapter 3, it was observed that some students get better marks than others. This prompted a series of clarifying questions. Refer back to Chapter 3 to remind yourself of the other possible explanations that were put forward. It should become clear that your hypothesis and hence your research will tell you something, but not everything, about the general issue. There were other factors, but these were not explored. Hence, any conclusions you draw will be limited to the factor you examined. Your research pertains to the general area but deals specifically with one isolated factor. When asked "Why do some students get better marks than others?," you cannot conclude, "Because some study more than others do." You know that there are many possible factors, including hours spent studying. Your research deals with only one. You could conclude that "amount of time spent studying seems to be a factor in examination results." Your research deals with one aspect of the overall issue. Be careful to ensure that in drawing a conclusion, you draw attention to the general issue and the way your research relates to it.

The first step in drawing a conclusion is to restate the general issue and the hypothesis, showing how the hypothesis relates to the general issue. For qualitative research, we depend on the general issue as there is no hypothesis generated in this type of research.

Another hypothesis used as a quantitative example throughout this book concerns the relationship between a talk on "healthy snack selection" and the selections that workers actually make in the cafeteria. Reread the sections of Chapter 7 in which this example is first developed. Then answer these questions:

1. What is the general area of concern?
2. What is the conceptual hypothesis?
3. What is the operational form of the hypothesis?
4. How does the hypothesis relate to the general area of concern?

Here again you see the importance of stating conclusions in a way that clearly relates to both the specific hypothesis and the general issue. There are many ways that the nutritional status of workers could be studied. In this case, snack selection in the cafeteria was chosen as the focus. First, a general observation study was done to discover the patterns of selection. Then an experiment was conducted to ascertain whether a talk on healthy snack selection would change workers' snack selection patterns. The conclusions of such research would relate to the general areas of worker nutrition, cafeteria operation, and nutrition education. How does the specific hypothesis tested relate to each of these areas? In this way, the conclusions of a small study are related to larger issues.

The first step in drawing conclusions is to clarify the way your research relates both to the hypothesis and to the larger issue. You did not start collecting data on the number of motorists who had run red lights for no reason. What were the reasons? How does your research relate to these reasons? If you did research comparing the degree of sexism among different groups of males, why did you do so? To simply conclude that levels of sexism among males who had attended private schools were higher or lower than or the same as those among males who had attended public schools may be correct, but it is too limited. Relate the findings of your small study to the larger context of which it is a part. This means returning to your literature review to see how your results support or refute others' findings.

What Did You Find?

Once you have reminded yourself of what it was you were asking and how your hypothesis or research objective related to that general area of interest, you can ask, "What did I find?" Yes, the data your study produced are by now displayed in tables or graphs or expressed as averages. But what do you think they say? They do not analyze or interpret themselves. You would be surprised how many of your readers may lack the basic skills to read a table. It is your job to identify the significant findings from each table in your research report. Without doing this, your important findings are likely to be ignored.

There are several basic aspects to answering the question "What did you find?" First, the data need to be interpreted. Second, the data must be related to the hypothesis, research question, hypothesis, or research objective. Third, you need to evaluate the data. We will discuss each of these aspects.

First, what do your data, as presented, say? This involves expressing in words what the tables, graphs, or averages say. We spent some time on this in Chapter 11. Look again at Table 11.7. It is followed by a simple statement expressing in words the relationships between the data in the table. That is an example of interpretation.

Now turn to Figure 11.1. What does it "say"? The interpretation of this figure might be written in this way:

> Among those 16 students who studied more than the average amount of time, 11 (or 68.7 per cent) received an above-average result on the history examination, while among those 14 students who studied less than the average amount of time, two (or 14.3 per cent) received an above-average result.

Interpreting your data means restating the relationships depicted in your tables, graphs, or calculations of averages as clearly as possible in words.

How would you interpret the data presented in Figures 11.4 and 11.5 and make a comparison between the ethnic composition of the students attending one course and the ethnic composition of the Canadian population? The interpretation of these data depends on the question being asked. Let us assume that the question was this:

> How does the ethnic composition of Course X compare with that of the Canadian population?

An interpretation of the data in the two figures might be as follows:

> The data shows that the ethnic composition of the class enrolled in Course X is different from that of the general Canadian population. The ethnic composition of Course X shows a greater proportion of people of "other" ethnic origins (including Chinese and Filipino/a) and a lower proportion of people of Canadian origin than is the case for the population of Canada as a whole.

When you interpret the data, you simply restate in words what is presented and summarized in the table, graph, or averages. You do not try to explain the data, nor do you draw conclusions from them. If the results are unclear, you report that the data are unclear.

As an exercise, try to interpret the data presented in Table 11.9. Remember, interpreting the data means restating in words the relationship between the variables presented in the table, graph, or average. Finally, interpret the data presented in Table 11.10.

Once you have interpreted the data, you are ready to relate your findings to the hypothesis or research objective. That is, what do these data tell you about your hypothesis? Is the evidence "for" or "against" the hypothesis? What are the implications of the findings for the narrowly defined research question?

This is usually straightforward. Problems emerge if the data are unclear and there is no strong trend one way or the other. If this is the case, your analysis should state that the implications of the data for the question, or the hypothesis, are unclear.

At this stage, it is best to report the implications of the data without discussion or comment. Either the hypothesis is supported or it is not. Ambiguous findings cannot be taken as support, but they ought to be mentioned in your interpretation. It is important to remember that a hypothesis is never proved to be absolutely correct. Rather, a hypothesis is tentatively accepted or likely to be correct given the evidence, or it is not accepted given the lack of evidence. If you would like to investigate correlations and causation further, this would be an appropriate time to consult more advanced statistical methods to answer your question or to prove your hypothesis. Tests of significance and model building are powerful ways to support or refute your hypothesis. When using advanced statistical methods, however, pay attention to the data interpretation as many readers will be unfamiliar with these strategies. Good writers can make complex statistical models easy to understand for all readers.

Once the findings are stated and related to the hypothesis or research objective, it is time to evaluate the data and to acknowledge the limitations of your study. General issues are critical here. First, the operationalization of the variables would doubtless have not entirely satisfied you. Again, if you kept a research journal, you would have noted limitations in it. These limitations can be noted either at this point in the report or earlier in the discussion of variable selection, decisions regarding research design, sample selection, and data collection. You may have questions about the instrument (questionnaire) or the interviewers. The limitations of your sample are to be noted.

The most important limitations involve the possible influence of the variables that you are unable to control or measure. Possible alternative explanations for the relationship between the independent and dependent variables need to be noted. You may have suggestions for future research. It may be that your findings were not clear and you suspect the interference of some variable. It is useful to note this.

Your findings may be surprising or unexpected. It is here that you can comment on this and suggest explanations. Your findings may conflict with the findings of others. This can be discussed.

Acknowledge the limitations of the study, whatever they are. This shows that you know what you might have done if you had had more time, money, or other resources. It also shows that you know your conclusions are made tentatively in the light of the limitations of your research. It may seem counterintuitive, but seasoned researchers realize the importance of clearly identifying the limitations of their study.

What Exactly Do You Conclude?

A good conclusion has two levels. First, it clearly states in simple terms what the data reveal, especially in relation to your hypothesis and the existing research on this subject. Second, it relates this simple statement to the larger issues and existing research. This can be seen as the reverse of the process by which you narrowed your attention in the first stage of the research process.

Here is a sample conclusion for the research on study time and marks:

Conclusion

A study of 30 students in a history class in a university in X revealed that those who spent more than the average time studying tended to receive above-average results in a history exam. While there were some exceptions, the data as presented in Table 11.7 show a clear trend in this direction. It is safe to conclude that these data provide evidence that support the hypothesis.

Thus, it is likely that amount of time spent studying is one among other factors that affect academic performance. Other factors such as IQ, social life, nutritional status, and specific study habits may account for some of the exceptions in this study. Further research is required to establish how widely this finding applies. Further research should compare students at other universities, the effect of time spent in studying on the examination results in other subjects, and the results of other methods of examination.

This conclusion clearly states the relationship demonstrated by the data. It supports this statement with references to the data summaries and graphs. Next, it states the implications of the data for the larger issue and future research. The first part of the conclusion restates what the data reveal about the operational form of the hypothesis. Data do not interpret themselves; you have to interpret them. Do the data support the hypothesis? Do they reject the hypothesis? Or is the situation unclear? Then the implications of the findings are drawn for the conceptual form of the hypothesis and, finally, the larger issue. The role of a conclusion is to restate the findings of the study and then to state the implications of the findings for both the hypothesis and the larger issue.

Take the example of the study comparing sexist attitudes among those attending private versus public schools. The hypothesis (see Chapter 6) was as follows:

Those students who have gone private schools are more sexist in their attitudes than students who have attended public schools.

The dummy table suggested for this study is found in Table 8.8. Let us assume that Table 13.1 presents the data from a study of 60 males, of whom 30 had attended private schools and 30 had attended public schools.

Given the data in Table 13.1, what would you conclude about your hypothesis? Is it supported or rejected, or are the results unclear? The data in Table 13.1 do not immediately present a clear picture. They are not compelling. There is too little difference: there are only four more people who attended private schools as opposed to public schools who score high and low on the sexism score. A conclusion drawn from a study based on these data might read as follows.

Table 13.1 • **Findings from a hypothetical study of sexism among males**

	Educational Background	
Sexism Score	**Private School**	**Public School**
High	24 (80%)	20 (67%)
Low	6 (20%)	10 (33%)
Total	30 (100%)	30 (100%)

Conclusion

In an attempt to determine whether educational background played a role in the development of sexist attitudes among private and public school attendees, a questionnaire was administered to two groups of students. One group had attended private schools for all of their schooling; the other group had attended public schools. Does an educational context in which private school attendees have to interact with members of the opposite sex regularly produce lower or higher levels of sexist attitudes?

The results of our research indicate that students from both educational contexts show high levels of sexist attitudes as measured by the sexist-attitude scale used in the study. Students from private schools are slightly more likely to have highly sexist attitudes. The differences between these two groups of students are not sufficiently large to conclude that the hypothesis is clearly supported. While the data are in the hypothesized direction, the relationship is too weak to draw any firm conclusions.

While educational context may well have an effect on the development of sexist attitudes among private and public school students, it cannot be concluded that this is so on the basis of this research. Additional research and more advanced statistical analysis are required to ascertain whether the relationship is stronger or weaker in other schools. It may well be that the general level of sexism in our society is such that educational context has little effect on the development of sexist attitudes among students. Again, the role of the conclusion can be seen. It relates the specific findings back to the hypothesis and then to the general issue. Researchers wishing to investigate this issue further are advised to calculate an appropriate test of significance for the information provided in this table (beyond the scope of this book) and/or to increase the size of the sample in future investigation to get a clearer picture of the relationship between type of school attendance and sexism.

As an exercise, write a conclusion for this research given the findings in Table 13.2. In writing your conclusion, be sure to

1. restate the general aim of the research;
2. restate the finding of the research;
3. indicate whether the hypothesis is supported or rejected, or whether the result is unclear;
4. explain the implications for the larger issue; and
5. make suggestions for future research.

Table 13.2 • **Findings from another hypothetical study of sexist attitudes among males in two educational contexts**

| Sexism Score | Educational Background | |
	Private School	Public School
High	14	5
Moderate	10	10
Low	6	15
Total	30	30

In the conclusion, you state what the data, as summarized and presented in your tables, graphs, or averages, tell you about the hypothesis you formulated. The implications are then drawn for the larger issue. This is also true for a research objective. However, research objectives are not accepted or rejected. The data are simply summarized in words and a conclusion drawn.

Take the example of the simple observation study of one baby's growth. Once the data have been collected and recorded, the simplest conclusion would be that the baby had grown by the addition of X cm and Y g. But there is a background to this study. You could look up the average growth rates for infants and compare this baby's growth record with that standard. Then a conclusion about one baby's growth in comparison with the average could be made.

Since no specific comparisons are being made, though, and no data on other factors are kept, no other conclusions can be drawn. If the purpose of the study had been to compare the growth rates of different infants—for example, one group that had been breastfed with another that had been bottlefed—then the conclusion could be drawn.

An appropriate conclusion for a study of infant growth guided by a research objective might take the following form:

Conclusion
The purpose of this study was to observe the growth of one infant over a period of 8 weeks in order to see, in a specific infant, the general

patterns of growth as described in the textbooks. The specific measures were of growth in length and weight. Other aspects of growth and development were observed but not systematically recorded.

The baby I observed grew by X cm and Y g during the 8-week period of observation. The baby was 8 weeks old at the beginning and 16 weeks old at the end. A growth of X cm and Y g is well within the bounds of normal growth for infants of this age.

This observation has also made me aware of the complexity of observing infant growth and development. I would suggest that in future observations of this type, the following be considered . . .

Although a conclusion about a hypothesis is not drawn, the conclusion of a study guided by a research objective may well make suggestions for future research. For example, take an observation study guided by the following research objective:

To discover what factors are considered by the person(s) in charge of meal planning in the selection and preparation of food.

The researcher might conclude at the end of the research as follows:

Conclusion

An observation study conducted in a single household revealed that the following factors were taken into consideration in the selection and preparation of food:

- cost
- preferences of family members
- availability
- preparation time required
- preparation skills required
- nutritional quality
- balance and diversity in foods
- kilojoule content of foods

Although cost was the predominant factor in the single case study household, closely followed by preferences of family members, this may well vary from household to household. Future research into the factors shaping household decision-making about food should ascertain how the importance of these factors varies among households.

Although we interviewed each member of the household, we discovered that one person is generally responsible for meal planning and preparation. Given our experience in this household and our observations within similar families, we suspect that this person is not always the mother. This means that future research can focus on one member of each household but that care is required in selecting which member to interview. We also suspect that a questionnaire could be devised to measure the relative importance of various factors.

The researcher here used the observations of a single case study as the basis for many suggestions for the next stage of research on this issue. She could well have made other comments. Further observations regarding the amount of time spent in meal preparation, meal planning, and shopping might also have been made. The researcher might have commented on the accuracy of the information available to the participant and the suitability of the meals planned to the purposes outlined by the participant.

Thus, although research guided by a research objective does not lead to conclusions about hypotheses, the results are summarized and related to the general issues behind the research. Suggestions for future research may also be made.

This introduction to the research process has deliberately avoided covering more mathematical forms of analysis and the more complicated aspects of qualitative data analysis and interpretation so that you can become familiar with the essential logic and flow of doing research without the burden of learning complex statistical modelling and qualitative data analysis at the same time. However, conclusions that are drawn using less complex techniques and are reliant solely on the reporting of percentages or direct quotations from interviews are very limited. There are a number of computer programs available that allow students—even students who consider themselves weak in mathematics—to make quite complex statistical analyses. There are even programs to help researchers organize and report qualitative results. Consult your professor to determine whether your data are suitable for statistical analysis, and check out what programs and statistics and qualitative research courses are available at your institution.

To Whom Do Your Conclusions Apply?

The question "To whom do your conclusions apply?" can be answered in both a narrow sense and a broader sense. The narrow interpretation is that your conclusions are limited to the sample studied and to the population it represents.

If you studied a representative sample of history students in your university, your conclusions are limited to history students in your university. If you observed one family, your conclusions are limited to that family.

The narrow interpretation of the applicability of conclusions is based on the limitations imposed by the sampling procedure selected. This narrow interpretation refers to the data—to the "facts" produced by the research. Take the example of the study of sexist attitudes among private and public school students. The data in Table 13.1 relate to two groups of 30 students from different educational backgrounds. The specific findings are limited to those students. That is, the finding that two-thirds (67 per cent) of students attending public schools scored high on sexist attitude, while four-fifths (80 per cent) of students attending private schools did, is limited to those males. If those students were a representative sample of a larger population, then that finding would apply to that larger population. It is not permissible to conclude that, in general, 67 per cent of students attending public schools and 80 per cent of students attending private schools will score high.

The conclusions regarding the data apply to those from whom the data were collected or to the larger population of which they are a representative sample.

On the other hand, research is done to gain some understanding about larger issues. Some of the conclusions refer to the implications of the research findings for those larger issues. This is the broader sense of the applicability of the conclusion. In drawing conclusions, the researcher moves from the narrow conclusions about the findings of the study to the implications of those findings for the larger issues. It is in this sense that conclusions have a broader applicability.

Again, take the example of the study of sexist attitudes among students. The data in Table 13.1 were too close to allow us to conclude that educational context made much difference between those two groups. Then the conclusion discussed the implications of the findings for the larger issue. When drawing the implications, a much more tentative style of expression is adopted: "It may well be that. . . .", "Additional research is required. . . ."

The sample conclusion for the study of 30 history students demonstrates the shift between the narrow conclusion and the drawing of implications. First, it summarizes the empirical findings (the data), then it continues, "Thus it is likely that amount of time spent studying is one factor among others. . . ."

Thus, in drawing conclusions, the first step is to restate the empirical findings. This part of the conclusion applies narrowly and strictly to those studied or to the population of which they are a representative sample. Then the implications of the empirical findings for the more general issues are discussed. In this part of the conclusion, the findings are related to a broader context and made more generally relevant. However, the discussion of implications is done tentatively. In this way, the conclusion can be seen to have a narrow aspect (the summary statement of the empirical findings) and a broader aspect (the discussion of the implications of those findings).

Questions for Review

1. What four basic questions guide the activities of data analysis and interpretation?

2. Interpret in words the data on the effect of age on school attendance, highest level of education, and receipt of employment insurance in Canada presented in Figures 13.1 to 13.3. Note that your task is simply to restate in words what is presented in the graph. Do not try to explain, moralize, or draw conclusions. Simply state what each graph "says."

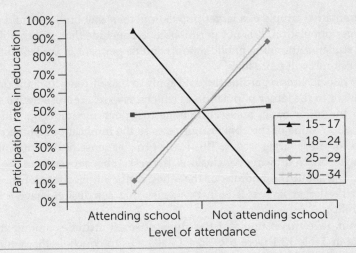

Source: Statistics Canada. (2018). Table 37-10-0101-01. *Participation rate in education, population aged 15 to 29, by age and type of institution.* Retrieved from www150.statcan.gc.ca/t1/tbl1/en/tv.action?pid=3710010101

Figure 13.1 • **Effect of age on school attendance, Canada, 2016**

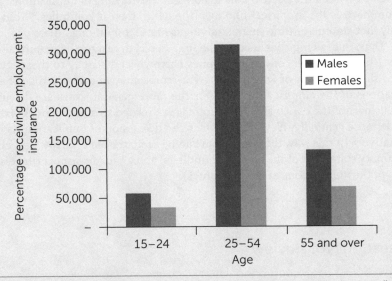

Source: Statistics Canada. (2018). Table 14-10-0014-01. *Employment insurance beneficiaries by census division, monthly unadjusted for seasonality.* Retrieved from www150.statcan.gc.ca/t1/tbl1/en/tv.action?pid=1410001401

Figure 13.2 • **Percentage of employment insurance receivers by age and sex, Canada, 2018**

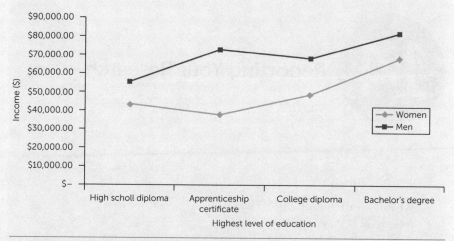

Source: Statistics Canada. (2017, November 29). *Does education pay? A comparison of earnings by level of education in Canada and its provinces and territories.* Retrieved from www12.statcan.gc.ca/census-recensement/2016/as-sa/98-200-x/2016024/98-200-x2016024-eng.cfm

Figure 13.3 • **Average Income of Canadians aged 25–64 by highest level of education and sex, 2015**

3. Why is drawing policy and practical considerations after conducting only a superficial or basic analysis of qualitative or quantitative data not advisable?
4. Why is it important for the writer to explain and interpret the results of their research?
5. Identify the elements of a good interpretation of data.
6. Why is it important to interpret data?
7. Why is it important to acknowledge the limitations of a study?
8. How does the sampling procedure you choose influence the conclusion you draw?

Suggestions for Further Reading

Miller, J. E. (2004). *The Chicago guide to writing about numbers: The effective presentation of quantitative information.* Chicago: University of Chicago Press.

Remler, D., & Van Ryzin, G. (2011). How to find, focus and present research. In D. Remler & G. Van Ryzin, *Research methods in practice: Strategies for description and causation* (pp. 489–516). Los Angeles: Sage.

Suggested Web Resources

Government of Canada. (2018). *Open data portal.* Retrieved April 12, 2018 from http://open.canada.ca

Thibideau, R. (2014, April 15). APA *writing style: Writing the results and discussion sections* [Video file]. Retrieved April 12, 2018 from www.youtube.com/watch?v=tEOQdldAS-E

14 Reporting Your Research

By now you have focused on a research issue, identified and measured variables, drawn samples, selected research designs, collected data, summarized and presented data, drawn conclusions, and discussed implications. You are now ready to write the research report. If you have kept a research journal, you will probably have a mountain of notes and records. These will be valuable to you in writing the report. This mountain of records and notes may also be daunting!

We have not said anything about the research report or other ways of communicating your findings until this time because it is the last activity in one cycle of the research process. Although your assignment might be to write a research report, that task occurs once the research is complete. Not everything that is done during the research is included in the research report. Rather, the research report summarizes the activities so that they are clear to the reader and so that the reader could repeat the research. In most cases, it is impossible to include absolutely all of your findings in your report, no matter how thorough you want to be.

The report is not the only way that data and results can be communicated. Often, researchers are asked to present their results to a public audience. The contents of such presentations depend on the nature of the audience. If the audience is the lay public, then discipline-specific jargon must be avoided. If the audience is knowledgeable about the topic, then extensive reviews and an introduction to the problem are likely not required. In all cases, as has been our experience, however, when numbers are involved, concentrating on simplifying the message is very important. One way this is done is through transforming tables into graphs. Another way to do this is to be prepared to make statistical explanations as simple as possible. For qualitative data, one of the most important ways to report your results is to summarize your findings succinctly in ways that your audience can understand and relate to.

Beyond the report and presentation, you will likely need to communicate your findings in other ways. Professors and students will want to publish in peer-reviewed academic journals. The content of such articles is highly dependent on the nature of your discipline and the guidelines of the journal. Every journal has guidelines for authors, and sadly, they are all different. Be sure to follow the instructions precisely or you risk having your paper rejected before it undergoes peer review. You may also want to communicate your findings in a research poster. Posters contain an overview of the research project, including the research question, hypotheses or goals, a very brief literature review, findings, and interpretations of findings. Posters are small and don't allow for much elaboration, so the trick for researchers is to be able to adequately communicate a significant amount of information in a very short space so that readers are not left with questions.

Still another way to communicate findings is by putting them on a website. This is a very useful tool for disseminating research—particularly for research participants, as they often lack access to the reports, academic journal articles, and conferences at which the results are presented. At the conclusion of the interview, participants can be given a website address and email notifications once the findings are posted. Often, researchers provide executive summaries rather than full results to research participants. This is because many times, research participants are not interested in reading long, jargon-laden research documents. However, if your research population is highly motivated or is knowledgeable about the subject (a strong possibility, given our increasingly educated society), consider providing them with access to the full and final report as part of your communication with them.

What Is Worth Reporting?

What should go into your report? How much is worth telling? The research report communicates your research to others. This is as true of your report as it is of articles published in research journals and books that report research, but the contents of both may differ. To communicate your research, it is necessary to make clear what you did, why you did it, what you found, and what you concluded from your findings. Readers must be able to tell what you did and understand why you did it the way you did. Readers can then decide whether they would draw the same conclusions given the data you present. They could also conduct the research again to see if the same results were found.

A General Outline

The research report should take the following general outline in this order:

1. Statement of problem
2. Review of relevant literature
3. Statement of hypothesis or research objective
4. Selection and operationalization of variables
5. Description of research design

6. Description of sample selection procedure
7. Description of how data were collected
8. Data presented and summarized in words
9. Conclusion, limitations, and implications
10. Bibliography or references
11. Appendices

A research report need not be very long, although the requirements may differ according to the guidelines specified in your research contract. One paragraph should be adequate to introduce the problem. A brief statement of what the literature review revealed about the problem is all that is required for simple reports and can be part of this first paragraph. More extensive reports should have longer, more detailed literature reviews. References to the material reviewed must be included and proper, consistent citation techniques must be used. The length of the research report may be dictated by the funding agency that supported your research. Some prefer shorter reports rather than longer ones because their staff have limited schedules and may need to evaluate many research reports. It is increasingly likely that your final report will also contain an executive summary—a short synopsis of the major findings of your research. Executive summaries precede the text of the report and give casual readers a shorter version of the text to read should they not wish to read the entire report. Sadly, it may be the only part of the report that some people read.

The section below is a discussion of a sample research report. The important thing to remember is the form and what is covered. The length and degree of detail in the report depend on the size of the research project and on the guidelines provided by the funder and/or the requirements of the assignment.

The Problem

State succinctly the question or problem your research deals with. Some call this "the human problem"—that is, the ordinary daily, policy, or intellectual issue that inspired you. Youth homelessness, marital breakdown, how to care for the elderly, the impact of legislation to prevent sexual harassment, and how people who live in Toronto are different from people who live in St John's are examples of such issues. They are unformed, large, wide-ranging issues, the sorts of concerns that awareness of everyday life brings to the minds of social scientists. It is advisable to introduce your major research question or statement towards the end of this section.

The Review of Relevant Literature

The literature review section of a research report takes the ordinary human issue and locates it in a body of theory and previous research. This helps to transform the human issue into a researchable question or hypothesis. For example, reviewing past work on youth homelessness will tell you what is already known, what questions are current in the field, and what research approaches have been tried and with what results. Your readers deserve to know that you have consulted the literature in the field, what your conclusions about the field are on the basis of your reading, and how you see your research contributing to the field and the understanding of or knowledge about the issue. More importantly, when you discuss your results later in the report, you will be referring back to this literature review to tell readers how your results compare with similar research. This is a very important task as it connects your research to the existing knowledge of the subject. At this time, reviewing the literature is all that is required. You will refer back to this literature review later in the report.

Statement of Hypothesis or Research Question

At the end of the literature review, it is possible to state your hypothesis and restate research question(s). In doing so, you transform the human issue into a limited, researchable issue. The human issue concerning youth homelessness becomes "What is the incidence of youth homelessness in Vancouver during February?," "How many housing inquiries are made each night at a youth drop-in centre?," or "Has there been an increase in the incidence of youth homelessness as a result of the deepening of the recession?" The human issue concerning marital breakdown could be transformed into hypotheses such as "Similarity of religious background and commitment is negatively related to marital breakdown," "Strength of religious commitment is negatively related to marital breakdown," or "Degree of financial stress is positively related to marital breakdown."

The hypothesis or research question is a restatement of the human issue in the form of a researchable issue.

Methodology

In this section, you describe and give reasons for your choices in the selection and operationalization of variables, research design, and sampling. The discussion of methodology must appear at this stage. It cannot appear earlier because it will only make sense if the research problem and the hypothesis have already been explained. It cannot appear later because the next section, "Description and Presentation of Data," will not make sense unless it is preceded by an explanation of the methodology. Ensure that all relevant methodological information is included, such as how your participants were recruited and selected, type of sampling procedure used, and a description of the population of interest and of the data analysis strategy. This is important information that provides readers with important context to your research and allows them to assess the appropriateness of the research method in relation to your research problem. Without this information, your report or article will not be seen as credible when compared with other research that provides accurate detail on methodology.

Description and Presentation of Data

Here you briefly describe how the data were collected and present your findings. It is important to stick very closely to a simple description of the data, leaving speculation and discussion for the next section. This section, like the last, is guided by your hypothesis, thesis statement or research question. Here you present the data that are relevant to the issues you raised and clarified before. Remember to describe all your tables and charts so that all readers can understand the underlying relationships (if any) between your independent and dependent variables. For qualitative research, it is important to tell the reader how you identified themes and the context in which they appeared. It is important to present the findings that are relevant to the hypothesis or question guiding your research in a consistent and clear manner. This means that data that is not connected to your thesis statement or does nothing to answer your research question should not be included in your report.

Conclusion and Discussion

In the conclusion, you return to the "human issue" with which you began and relate the findings of your research to this issue. You state your conclusions clearly, and then discuss the implications for the issue. The conclusion may include speculation on possible future research, plus discussion of some of the limitations of your research and its possible policy or practical implications. This is the point where the researcher returns to the literature review and asks the question "How different or similar are my findings from what is currently reported in published research on this topic?" This is a very important step, as it informs readers of the gaps in knowledge that your research fills: it connects your research to the larger research community and allows the researcher to consider limitations and future research questions based on the gaps in knowledge that cannot be filled by the findings of your study.

Bibliography

In this section, you list all the references you consulted while doing your research. Use a bibliographic format that is currently used in one of the major journals in your field. Pay careful attention to the information required for books, chapters in books, articles, and websites. Some forms of material, such as documents, may have to be codified and listed separately. If it is a term paper or thesis, consult your professor about the format required. If the report is funded, consult the funders about their style preferences. If you are submitting this as an article or a book to a peer-reviewed publisher, then you must follow the publisher's stylistic guidelines.

Appendices

Appendices are convenient places to put material that is relevant to your report but that would interrupt the flow or take too much space in the body of the report. This may include copies of questionnaires or other research instruments, letters written seeking permission to conduct the research, more detailed reports of data collected, or supporting documents. This section ought to be considered as a space to store supporting material. While this material is not essential to telling your story, it gives interested readers more information about your project.

Your research report should tell a story, or have a logical flow, so that the reader progresses from issue to issue and is always aware of how each section of the material relates to the rest. This "storyline," or logical flow, is not always clear until the end of the project. If your report does not read well, think it through again, reminding yourself of the issues raised at each stage and how these issues are related to the overall flow of your argument.

The length of a research report depends on various factors. Your professor may have set a word limit, or you may wish to publish your report in a journal that has expectations about the size and style of articles it publishes. Master's and doctoral theses have typically book-length word limits. Your funding organization may have a template to follow for submitting the report. Your stakeholders may require different information. For some projects, you may be required to produce several research reports for different audiences. The Appendix presents a full article-length research report containing a mix of qualitative and quantitative data. It is a good example of a report that does not require advanced statistical analysis yet makes significant academic and policy conclusions about an area of social life. It contains all the elements needed for a research report and is suitable for submission to funding and government agencies.

Conclusion

Congratulations! You now have the tools to start and complete a small research project. Your next step is to conduct your own research project. Start small. Large projects are complex and time-consuming, and can be difficult to manage for a first-time researcher. Once you have gained experience in small research projects, you are ready to tackle larger projects with more research questions.

The elements of a research report are similar to the elements required in published peer-reviewed journal articles, government reports, theses, dissertations, public presentations, and posters. The difference is the length or space given to each of these tasks. A thesis, dissertation, or book will allow for more elaboration, more words, and more information than a 15-minute public presentation will. The strategy that researchers use to approach these tasks differs depending on their audience. Experts usually expect jargon and more detail. Laypeople quickly get frustrated with such details. Good researchers can navigate both audiences but need to prepare different materials depending on what is expected of them.

We strongly advise students who are interested in gaining further knowledge to take as many courses in social science, quantitative and qualitative research methods, and statistics as possible. These courses will provide you with the skills necessary to analyze results from qualitative projects and large datasets and to examine questions of correlation and causation related to your research questions. This skill set will not only make you a stronger researcher but will allow you to provide more definitive answers to your questions. As well, the job market for students knowledgeable in research methods is growing as more and more businesses, universities, and research centres acquire new recruits with these types of skills.

Questions for Review

1. Why do professional researchers publish their findings? When they do, what information must the report include? Why?
2. What information must your research reports include? Why?
3. Identify the one sentence or question that provides guidance on what to include in a research report.
4. What are the ethical reasons why a research report should be submitted?

Suggestions for Further Reading

Muller, J. (2010). *Writing in the social sciences: A guide for term papers and book reviews.* Don Mills, ON: Oxford University Press.

Northey, M., Tepperman, L., & Albanese, P. (2009). *Making sense: A students' guide to research and writing in the social sciences* (4th ed.). Don Mills, ON: Oxford University Press.

Pratt, M. (2009). For the lack of a boilerplate: Tips for writing up and reviewing qualitative research. *Academy of Management Journal, 52*(5), 856–62.

Schneider, E., & Schutt, R. K. (2011). Finding information. In D. F. Chambliss & R. K. Schutt (Eds.), *Making sense of the social world: Methods of investigation* (3rd ed.). Los Angeles: Pine Forge.

Suggested Web Resources

McIntyre, E. (2015, February 7). *Research dissemination: Reporting and sharing your research* [Video file]. Retrieved April 12, 2018 from www.youtube.com/watch?v=TES_cB4pKGw

Michigan State University, Undergraduate Research Office. (2013, September 17). *How to prepare an oral research presentation.* [Video file]. Retrieved April 12, 2018 from www.youtube.com/watch?v=LzIJFD-ddoI

Schleicher, A. (2012, June) *Reporting research findings* (TED Talk) [Video file]. Retrieved April 12, 2018 from www.youtube.com/watch?v=k7GfwRnuhTU

Appendix

Final Report: The Job Search Experiences of Immigrant and New Generation Youth in Winnipeg[1]

Lori Wilkinson

Department of Sociology, University of Manitoba[2]

Abstract

Using a series of semi-structured interviews with racialized immigrant and new generation youth in Winnipeg, supported by quantitative data from government sources, this report examines the job search strategies and initial labour market entry of racialized youth. The factors that enable and constrain their labour market entry are examined with respect to the commonalities and differences with the third-plus generation. Although new and immigrant generation youth use many of the same job search strategies as those born in Canada, there are significant differences. Social networks are smaller and have less reach into lucrative entry-level positions, especially for immigrant youth. Both groups indicate that racism and accent issues are significant challenges influencing successful labour market strategies. Despite these challenges, there are benefits to being the child of immigrant parents, particularly the ability to straddle two cultures.

Introduction

A central feature of the transition to adulthood for many youth is the acquisition of employment. Despite its importance in the overall life course and the growing body of academic research on immigration, few researchers have examined the labour market trajectories of new generation immigrant youth. According to Statistics Canada (2007),[3] first- and second-generation youth make up over 16.1 per cent of the new entrants to the job market, a number that will increase as the baby boomers begin to retire. While they are a significant part of the labour market, they are also the most vulnerable. In the most recent economic recession, youth made up 31.1 per cent of the unemployed, a rate 3.5 times that of the adult population. More distressingly, their unemployment rate was a staggering 21 per cent (Statistics Canada, 2009a). When we consider the fact that 57 per cent of migrants to Canada arrive before the age of 29 years (Citizenship and Immigration Canada, 2010), the influence of migrant youth in the Canadian labour market cannot be understated. In a time of labour shortage, the need for up-to-date information on the labour market experiences of this group is warranted.

Using semi-structured interviews, we recruited racialized immigrant and new generation youth[4] from the Korean, Filipino/a, and South Asian communities in Winnipeg. These three communities represent the fastest-growing groups in the city. We address one main research question along with two sub-questions. First, what are the job search strategies of new and immigrant generation youth in Canada? Second, how do community contacts, family, and social supports influence job search strategies? And finally, what are the advantages or disadvantages of being a child of immigrant parents in terms of finding employment? These are important questions for consideration given the demographic importance of this group, particularly in terms of their contribution to economic growth in Canada.

This report begins with a brief review of existing research on new generation youth, discrimination, and employment as a way of situating our research questions. It is followed by a brief description of the methodologies used in the data collection process. The findings and their implications for knowledge and government policy are then followed by the conclusion.

Literature Review

New generation youth are those born in Canada to at least one (but typically two) immigrant parents. They are differentiated from first-generation immigrant youth (born outside of Canada) and the third-plus generation (those born to Canadian-born parents of three or more generations in the country). Membership in the new generation has been increasing alongside the increase of migration to Canada. As Table A.1 shows, the absolute (N) number of new generation youth has been increasing in the past 10 years but its proportion to the total population remains stable, averaging 13.1 per cent of the population in 2011 and 12.8 per cent in 2006.

Table A.1 • Canadian population by immigration status and year[5]

	2001		2006	
	N	%	N	%
Immigrant generation	299,672	37.4	165,174	19.6
New generation	105,099	13.1	108,278	12.8
Third-plus generation	398,151	49.5	570,990	67.6
Total	802,922	100	844,442	100

Far from being a Canadian-only problem, youth unemployment has global repercussions. The United Nations (2007) estimates that there are more than 60 million unemployed young people worldwide. In developed countries such as Canada, unemployment among young people has remained consistently high, regardless of how well or poorly the economy has performed. Historically, the unemployment rate for Canadian youth has hovered between 2.5 and 3.0 times that of the rate for adults. Recent research comparing the unemployment rates of immigrant, refugee, and Canadian-born youth reveals that the unemployment rate for newcomers is 2.5 times that among those born in Canada (Wilkinson, 2008).[6] Table A.2 shows the unemployment rates of male and female youth by immigrant status. Among the population of 15- to 24-year-olds, 19.9 per cent of recently arrived immigrant women are unemployed, as are 14.8 per cent of recently arrived immigrant males. These rates are higher than for those born in Canada but are particularly troubling for women.

The Canadian labour market is severely short of workers in many fields and professions. By 2020, it is estimated that the Canadian labour market will require one million new workers (Chrètien, 2003), with many of those vacancies expected to be filled by migrant labourers and their children.[7] Another study indicates that over 70 per cent of the growth in the Canadian economy can be directly attributed to the contribution of immigrants (Statistics Canada, 2003). Despite this apparently rosy outlook for migrants in the Canadian economy, the latest recession has had significant negative effects on the newly arrived migrant population. According to a Statistics Canada report, immigrants who have been in the country for less than five years have unemployment rates three times that of people born in Canada (Grant and Yang, 2009).

Table A.2 • Unemployment rate for youth ages 15–24 by sex and immigrant type, Canada, 2006[8]

	Male	Female
Born in Canada	12.7	9.8
Recent immigrant, 5 years or less	14.8	19.9
Recent immigrant, 5 to 10 years	16.1	15.4

For many young people, the acquisition of paid employment is one of the most important stages in the transition to adulthood. By age 24, 68 per cent of Canadian-born youth are working full- or part-time or are actively looking for work (Statistics Canada, 2006). Finding employment is also an important indicator of social inclusion given its role in physical survival, sense of identity, social integration, and civic participation. Labour market inclusion is also a good indicator of how well racialized and migrant communities have been integrated into Canadian society. Conversely, exclusion from the labour market is linked to a range of problems for young people, including social exclusion, long-term unemployment, poverty, delinquency, and low levels of self-esteem.

Canadian researchers have spent much time examining the various labour market pathways travelled by young adults but have spent very little time examining the unique experiences of new generation youth.[9] Anisef et al. (2000) and Anisef and Murphy Kilbride (2003) have conducted some of the few studies about labour market trajectories among immigrant youth. They find that accent and English-language proficiency influence settlement experiences among youth. Anisef, Sweet, and Frempong (2003) also find that age at immigration is correlated with labour market success. Those entering Canada at later ages are more likely to experience difficulty in finding work. An Australian study finds that perceived standing in the host culture also influences labour market outcomes and job-seeking behaviours (Nesdale and Pinter, 2000). For the most part, however, most existing studies on child migrants and labour market trajectories were conducted on those arriving to Canada in the 1960s and 1970s when labour market conditions were much different (Bonikowska and Hou, 2011).

Several characteristics make the job search experiences of new generation youth unique. There are advantages and disadvantages to life as a second-generation youth. The well-publicized immigrant-drive effect, one that makes parents more involved with and more demanding of their children, may have positive benefits in terms of higher education. Anecdotal evidence suggests that they do better in school as a result. High school performance is positively correlated with better labour market outcomes. There are disadvantages as well. Since changes to the Canadian immigration policy removed the last racial barriers to migration, the ethnic origin of migrants to Canada has changed. Despite the growing ethnic and racial diversity in our country, racism is still evident in the labour market. Since the number of new generation youth from racialized groups is growing, this is likely to have an effect on them (Shields, Rahi, and Scholtz, 2006). As Bonikowska and Hou (2011) and Picot and Hou (2011) discovered in their preliminary research, there is some evidence to suggest that the new generation continue to have an advantage in terms of educational and labour market outcomes when compared to other generation youth, but this finding applies only for white groups.

The influence of familial, friendship, and community ties is well known in the labour market. This is particularly true for those searching for their first jobs. Studies on youth employment in Canada reveal that family ties are a major source of job referrals (Canadian Youth Foundation, 1995; Granovetter, 1974; Yan, 2000). We know very little about the influence of newcomer networks and family ties on job attainment among new generation youth. Are immigrant communities more resourceful in terms of their use of ties to sustain employment opportunities among their youth? Given that the unemployment rate for immigrant adults is higher than average (Statistics Canada, 2004), perhaps the network ties to employment are looser.

In the United States, Portes (1995) observes that when compared to immigrant youth, the new generation has better economic outcomes. Not much is known in the Canadian context about the influence of family or community ties in terms of labour market conditions of the new generation. Bonikowska and Hou (2011) find, however, that recently arrived immigrant youth are still more likely to attend post-secondary education than other youth in Canada. These results, however, ought to be taken with caution because this study did not include migrants arriving in the most recent decade, given the unavailability of data. Picot and Hou (2011), in their study comparing the economic outcomes of new generation youth in Canada and the United States, find that although the overall economic success of the new generation is greater than for other generations, significant effects of racialization remain. New generation youth who are members of racialized groups in both countries, but particularly the United States, have lower rates of economic success than their white peers, when other factors are controlled.

Methodology

Thirty-five youth between the ages of 17 and 30 were selected using non-probability quota sampling methods. Our aim was to obtain a good number of unemployed and employed youth, both male and female, within the Korean, Filipino/a, and Asian communities in Winnipeg, to obtain a sample large enough to examine similarities and differences among the population. Youth from these three communities make up over 45 per cent of all immigrant arrivals to Manitoba (Manitoba Labour and Immigration, 2007). Youth were recruited through extensive advertisements at various employment agencies, post-secondary institutions, and listservs during the summer of 2007. Potential respondents were also identified by key stakeholders from employment agencies and various ethnocultural organizations. While the sample is small and the results cannot be generalized to the population, we are confident that we obtained a relatively representative sample of this population in Winnipeg.

In the end, our sample consisted of 8 Korean youth, 10 Filipino/a youth, and 17 youth from other Asian[10] countries. Their mean age at the time of the interview was 24 years. Semi-structured interviews, lasting on average 30 minutes, were conducted to gain information about the labour market trajectories of first- and new generation youth.

Findings

Finding Work

At the time of the interview, 11 of the youth were unemployed. Of those with work, almost a third reported they had gotten their present job "without trying." Most (40 per cent) took between one and two months to find employment. A few had more difficulties, searching for over one year. One respondent, a new generation female of Pakistani origin, reports, "I wasn't really looking; it came to me as the convenience of being a new generation. I'm not quite an immigrant youth. I do have experience being born and raised here. I am familiar with work and I don't have the obvious barriers like an accent or things like that." Her experience was similar to that of other new generation youth who generally found it less difficult to find work than their first-generation counterparts.

When asked about how they found their current job, family and friendship networks were reported as the most popular channels. These connections were vital in finding employment for many of the youth in our study. A new generation female of Korean origin reports, "My friends sometimes tell me where they are currently working. A lot of Korean people work at sushi restaurants apparently. They are always looking for Korean or Asian waitresses. They offered but it never appealed to me." Another new generation Korean female reports that she found her present job through her sister's boyfriend. While it netted her employment, the job wasn't very fulfilling so she used her connections to find other work in the retail sales industry.

Other youth replied that they had located their work by "traditional" means through applying directly to employers, through want ads posted on the internet, or through job banks. A new generation Korean female reports that she "just went to the mall and asked if they were hiring and gave them my résumé." Others used internet job banks, though one Pakistani female reports, "Right now, I look through the job bank, but from my experiences from before it is not very good at all because you send them an email and you don't get a response at all." Co-op placements netted employment for some new generation youth. It seems, however, that the era of newspaper want ads is nearly over. Only one person in our study indicated they had looked in the newspaper for employment opportunities.

We asked the youth to identify the job search strategies that they felt worked best for them. The youth, regardless of generation status, overwhelmingly reported that family and friendship networks were the most successful means of securing employment. A new generation male from Lebanon reports, "I asked everybody I know who is working or who know[s] of this type of work that I'm interested in." Others reported their church networks as highly useful in obtaining employment. A new generation female reports, "Well, sometimes if you go to church, they have businesses and stuff. They have restaurants and you can be a waitress or something." Others reported posting their résumés online or receiving referrals from former employers.

When asked if they received support from their ethnocultural community, the results were evenly split. About half indicated they did not receive assistance, while just over half did. One new generation Filipina female reports that her community did not help her. Instead, she feels she is "resourceful" and it helps that her education was obtained in Canada. Another new generation Filipina female reports that she went out of her way not to use ethnic community ties. When asked how she attained her current job, she replies, "Through my old district manager. She's an old white lady. She's nice." This reluctance to rely on ethnic or family networks may be tied to the need to form an independent identity—one that is separate from ethnicity and family.

Unlike the new generation, first-generation youth were unlikely to utilize ethnic networks. A first-generation female from Bangladesh replies, "I asked my friend for help. She is Canadian. I know my English is poor; I need practice, and I also feel nervous when talking with another person. It is good to talk to another person who is good in English." A first-generation female from Korea is cynical in her observations about how networks influence job opportunities for young people in Winnipeg. "I found it really doesn't matter what is on your résumé or where you applied or which job bank you signed on. It's who you know, and everyone knows that." Conversely, new generation youth credited their ties within the community with helping them secure employment. A new generation male from Japan reports, "Yes, definitely from my ethnic community. I work at a sushi restaurant. He [my employer] was from the same cultural centre I was from. He knew my family background. That was the reason he hired me [over] anyone else." In sum, both new and immigrant generation youth know there is a network that funnels young people into jobs in the city; the utility of the network might be different depending on your group membership.

We then asked the youth who or what they found most helpful in the job search process. Overwhelmingly, family and friendship connections were deemed most important. A new generation Indian female reports, "I think in a lot of ways, friends, because they can give you a better description of what it is like, the job itself and what it involves and whether or not you as a person qualify for that job." A first-generation Indian male replies that his most successful job search strategy involved asking "my uncles and family friends if they had any opening in their private business."

Other modes of job search strategies were reported but were deemed less helpful. A new generation Korean male indicates the internet as a valuable re-source. "Actually the Government of Canada website. Instead of me just walking by, I can know which place is actually hiring. I can actually choose what I want instead of walking from store to store." Another new generation male replies, "When you contact placement agencies they normally have a job instantly for you. . . . but you don't get [many] options there. They are pretty much the jobs that you want to quit after three months anyway." First-generation youth were likely to report that other Canadians were helpful for them. A first-generation Iranian male replies, "I found the people who are citizens of Canada or immi-grants who have been here for a while and holding jobs are more useful because they know the society better."

All participants were asked to compare their job search experiences with those of other youth. Most new generation respondents indicated that they had an easier time finding a job than those who had immigrated to Canada but a more difficult time than third-plus-generation white Canadians. A new gen-eration Korean female reports, "We already know how to interact with people here, so when we go to a job interview we pretty much know what they are going to ask us and expect of us. For the ones that just come here it is kinda hard to adapt to society so they get that cultural shock." Another new genera-tion youth, a male of Japanese origin, reports, "Because I was born in Canada, I had a better opportunity as a Canadian citizen and. . . . I was more acquainted with the culture of this country rather than people who will face language bar-riers." Even first-generation youth understand this difference. A first-generation female from Korea reports, "I noticed that since they are newer to Canada, the jobs they find are the ones that are easy to get, like restaurants or mall jobs. They don't explore any other jobs, like more complicated ones. . . . In my opinion, it is about self-confidence and the way you carry yourself. It's a new world for you. There are different cultures; you don't know what to say to people."

Factors Enabling and Constraining the Job Search

Youth were asked to identify barriers, if any, in their job search strategies. Age, lack of education/experience, racism, language, and culture were identified as constraints. Each is discussed in turn.

Age was a major barrier to employment reported by all the youth, regardless of their ethnocultural origin or generation status. A new generation female Korean states that her youth was the biggest barrier to finding employment. Employers, she states, would hire older people if they could. A first-generation male Filipino agrees. He told us that he felt he was passed over for employment because he was too young. Their statements are not different from those of non-immigrant origin.

Related to age is lack of education or work experience. Like other Canadians, the youth in our study were cognizant that education and previous work experience are valuable assets in the labour market. This is true even for those participants with professional careers. A new generation Filipina female reports, "When I was young, I did my master's right away. So, I felt like I was over-qualified because of my degree. I felt under-qualified because of my (lack of) experience. That's why I did not apply for my current job—because I had the education but didn't feel I had the experience they needed."

Racism was the next most common barrier reported by all participants. A new generation Indian female reports that her worst problem in finding a job is "being an outsider always, never fitting in necessarily. I think this is inevitable when you are being a visible minority. In general you don't always fit in." The idea of not fitting in is a theme reported by others in the study. A new generation Japanese male reports, "[P]eople will not hire me because they cannot even pronounce my name. That was one of the major conflicts I had. And a lot of people told me even when I go to church I should use my English name."

A number of the respondents identified a particular chain of restaurants as being racist. Several (unsolicited) comments about the same restaurant were repeated by respondents of all generations and ethnocultural backgrounds. According to a new generation Korean female, "If I try to get a job at XXX (*name omitted*[11]) or something like that, it would be impossible because they don't really choose Asian people and stuff like that. It's really hard. My Asian and Caucasian friends applied for a job and only the Caucasian got the job; I find that very interesting."

Some respondents, however, felt that their ethnocultural background was a benefit to finding employment. A first-generation Korean female reports that in obtaining her current employment, "It helped that I am female and a minority." A new generation Filipina relates the following story, "Now when I work at the front desk, the delivery people come in. The majority of them are immigrants. They get excited to see a minority behind the desk of this major (TV) network. So they always get into small conversations like, 'How did you get this job?' I like to think they could aim higher."

Culture was also identified as a major barrier to employment for both immigrant and new generation youth. A new generation Pakistani female reports that her culture and religion prevent her from working late hours. She says that "time constraints (are a major barrier). Like I can't work past 10 because my family is just that way. I have to be pretty much home by 10. And a lot of jobs, if you close in any retail jobs, you're in there from 10:30 to 11:00 most times. That doesn't usually play out for me." Others feel that the ethnocultural networks are not extensive enough to help them find employment. A first-generation male from Korea states, "Even though someone immigrates to Canada [five to ten years earlier], they stick to their prior culture. . . . When immigrants come here, they have no networking whatsoever." Others, such as this first-generation male from China, report, "[D]uring the interview process, the Chinese people are really humble, but here, they want to see confidence. For us, we try to balance so we won't be cocky." A first-generation female from Japan states, "In Japan, you are in a very fast pace, but here it is slow pace. I try to be fast, [but] here I do not have to be like that."

The Benefits and Challenges of Being the Child of Immigrants

We asked all participants to describe what they felt were the benefits and challenges of being the child of immigrant parents in terms of finding employment in Canada, a question that applied to both groups of youth in our study. Most participants reported that there were advantages and disadvantages to having immigrant parents. A new generation Japanese male reports that a major advantage for him is his "ability to understand different cultures because of my parents. I had a dual life, in a sense." This benefit is reiterated by first-generation respondents. A first-generation Filipina female reports, "I found all my work through the Filipino community. The network here is massive. It doesn't mean that all my contacts are Filipino; it happened that they know of someone in the community that could get me in contact with someone." Another first-generation male from Korea states that his linguistic abilities were key to his current employment: "I can speak Korean and English. [In] the sushi place my family's friends run, [they] don't speak English at all so they want me to work because I can speak both languages."

There were, however, challenges to being the child of immigrant parents. A new generation Filipina female tells us, "I find some people assume that because I look ethnic that I'm not fluent in English and that I do not have the same thinking or mind-frame [of] a Canadian person even though I am Canadian. . . . I find in interviews people will ask me 'How long have you been in Canada?' or 'How did you learn how to speak English so well?' That is the first step back for me because they do not assume I am up for the part."

First-generation immigrant youth reported slightly different challenges to having immigrant parents. Some of the first-generation respondents, with family in other countries, received financial support from them to pursue a post-secondary education. This is a common practice used among families to maximize the economic trajectories of family members. Typically, older siblings will forgo school to ensure that younger siblings are provided with additional support and guidance in attaining a post-secondary education. A female from the Philippines reports that the major problem for her was "money, of course. I paid for my education alone and worked [at] the same time. My brothers helped us in [any] way they [could]. They helped us for sure in other ways not so monetarily."

Discussion

In many ways, the job search strategies of new and immigrant generation youth do not differ from those born in Canada. All are concerned about getting a good job. Many use traditional job search strategies, such as dropping off résumés and watching want ads, though most exclusively use the internet to accomplish this. They also use family and community networks to find employment. In fact, family and ethnocultural community networks are viewed as the most productive ways of locating employment for these two groups, not substantially different from what is observed among Canadian-born youth. What differentiates new and immigrant generation youth from other Canadians is that the size and quality of their networks differ. In the United States, Leu (2009) reports that 70 per cent of American-born youth find their first professional jobs partly with the help of large family networks. The networks of first- and new generation youth tend to be smaller and less connected to well-paying jobs when compared with those of Canadian-born youth (Kilbride et al., 2004; Kunz, 2003). These small networks are an even greater impediment among racialized youth living in the United States (Perreira, Harris, and Lee, 2007).

The main barriers to employment identified by new and immigrant generation youth were age, education/experience, racism, culture, and language. Age and education/experience barriers are similar to those reported by third-plus-generation youth. Almost all youth experience difficulty transitioning to the labour market. Employers tend to prefer workers with some experience rather than those fresh out of school. Lack of experience combined with age may mean some youth are "left behind." These issues are particularly important to consider during periods of recession. Youth who enter the labour market during recessions have longer spells of unemployment and lower lifetime earnings, as much as 8 to 9 per cent lower, as a result (Mendelson, 2010; Pagliaro, 2010). As Grant and Yang (2009) have reported, immigrants as a group had some of the highest rates of unemployment during the 2008/09 recession. That, combined with being young, may adversely affect the employment and income trends of new and immigrant generation youth over their lifespan.

Racism, culture, and language issues, however, produce slightly different experiences for the new and immigrant generations. Although racism is also experienced by the third-plus generation, the degree to which it is evident among the youth in this study is stark. Even though we did not directly ask any of the participants about their experiences of discrimination (we did not want to bias the results), almost all of the respondents reported issues related to discrimination when looking for work in Winnipeg. Accent issues were troubling to youth in our study, as both newcomers and immigrants were questioned about their ability to speak English. Some, particularly those from the new generation, experienced situations where employers were surprised that their English skills were superior! Their comments are based on a widely held misconception that racialized persons must be foreign born and lacking in English skills. This is a very subtle type of racism where colour determines who is viewed as a "legitimate" Canadian. These undercurrents of racism, as expressed through employer comments about language and accent, can be central in individuals' perception of self-worth and belonging in society. As Kilbride (2004) and her colleagues point out, the assumption that racialized Canadians have significant language deficits or speak with an accent has a detrimental influence on immigrant youths' feelings of belonging in our society. Our findings certainly echo this sentiment and even go a bit further. Issues related to accent and presumed language deficits follow young people well into the second generation. In short, the study shows that there is significant covert racism that may partly determine economic outcomes among new generation youth that have not been adequately considered until now. It is worth mentioning, however, that first-generation youth were more likely to personally experience issues related to language and racism than new generation youth. New generation youth in this study are more likely to discuss racism and language issues as something they observe rather than personally experience.

Being a child of immigrant parents has benefits and challenges. The benefits of having immigrant parents are first noted in the ability to straddle two cultures. Knowledge of both the heritage and Canadian cultures is seen as a significant benefit among the youth in our study. The ability to "fit in two worlds" is one they feel can help them overcome some of the challenges related to racism and language issues. In our increasingly globalized labour market, employers are beginning to recognize the importance of diversity in their work force (Ely and Thomas, 2001). Similarly, bilingualism is also seen as an advantage of having immigrant parents. Again, the economic benefits of speaking more than one language may be seen in higher wages in certain professional occupations (Coomer, 2008). Bilingualism, however, also has its downside. As the participants in this study point out, the language and accent issues "haunt" them throughout the job search and promotion process. A recent study of immigrant youth and school-to-work transitions finds that those unable to speak one of Canada's two official languages were significantly less likely to find work in their first four years in the labour market (Wilkinson et al., 2010). In the same study, participants revealed the problems related to their accent and finding employment. In this way, bilingualism may be both a blessing and a curse.

Another challenge faced by immigrant youth in particular is what is called the "family investment strategy." Chronicled in existing research as a strategy where immigrant wives take menial paid employment upon arrival in order to support their husbands in acquiring a new language and upgrading their job skills (Baker and Benjamin, 1997), the family investment strategy has meant that women are more likely to become "stuck" in low-waged employment in the long term. Frequently, reskilling and language learning among men takes longer than anticipated. The longer women remain outside the profession in which they were trained, the less likely they are to find work in this field in the long term. This phenomenon is seen among some of the young migrants in this study. Struggling families opt to send the youngest to post-secondary education while older children enter the labour market as soon as possible.

Their labour is needed to economically assist the family and to offset the costs of educating its younger members. This means that older children are not given the same opportunities for post-secondary education as their younger siblings, which may cause resentment. Younger children may also feel extreme pressure to excel in school as a result of the sacrifices their family has made for their education.

Conclusion

This study has outlined the job search strategies of immigrant and new generation youth. Like Canadian-born youth, this group's job search strategies mirror significantly those of other youth. Perusing want ads and hand-delivering résumés have given way to job search and résumé submissions by the internet. This is hardly surprising given the extent to which the electronic world has entered into our homes and schools. Although immigrant and new generation youth use family networks to find employment, the extent and quality of these networks is not as great as they are for those born in Canada. More unexpected are the roles that racism, language, and accent play in the process of finding work among this group. Youth from both groups perceive significant levels of covert racism in their search for employment. This perception of racism has important consequences for a multicultural society such as Canada's. If there is a significantly marginalized group of people in any society, the health of that country may be jeopardized. Lack of citizenship engagement, wide-scale discontent, and periodic social unrest may be consequences if the marginalization of groups of people becomes entrenched in social consciousness. In extreme cases, this may decrease economic productivity and may lead to political instability, as was seen in France in the riots led by mainly young immigrant men during the summer of 2008. There, generations of North African youth were marginalized from social and economic life and their discontent culminated in a summer of riots protesting crime and diminished economic opportunities. Australia has seen similar discontent among the immigrant and racialized youth of that country.

For all the questions answered by this study, there remain many more. First, what has become of these youth? Did they find better work after the study was completed? Were their career ambitions fulfilled? Did their perceptions of racism change over time? Would the findings from Winnipeg apply to other Canadian cities? Could our observations be validated in other countries? These are important questions that future research must address in order to understand the employment trajectories of new and immigrant generation youth. What this study has done is to help question the assumptions that academics, policy-makers, and practitioners have made about newcomer and new generation youth and the seamless transition to work. The results from this research clearly reveal that this group faces many barriers and challenges to finding employment. Understanding how these issues may affect their strategies and outlook in the long term ought to be a guiding principle of future research.

Notes

[1] This project was made possible by a grant received from the Prairie Metropolis Centre of Excellence for Research on Immigration and Integration.

[2] Research assistance provided by Fadi Ennab, Janet Nowatski, and Heather Noga, undergraduate students at the University of Manitoba, is gratefully acknowledged. Joyce Cabigting-Fernandes and Bong-Hwan Kim provided assistance with recruitment of participants for this study.

[3] This figure is based on calculations of the author.

[4] Second-generation youth are children with at least one foreign-born parent commonly acknowledged as the children of immigrants. Following recent convention, we now refer to second-generation youth as *new generation youth*, as the term moves away from the idea of "once an immigrant, always an immigrant."

[5] It was not possible to disaggregate the unemployment rates of first-, second-, and subsequent generation youth in that study.

[6] Source: Statistics Canada, 2004; Statistics Canada 2009b.

[7] It should be noted that another source of labour has been largely ignored. Indigenous Peoples are the fastest-growing segment of the Canadian population, but few have examined the potential of this group. It is not the purpose of this article to examine the potential contribution of Indigenous Peoples, but it is noteworthy that when asked about the segments of the population that help fill labour market shortages, a group of Manitoba businesspeople mentioned Indigenous Peoples only 5 per cent of the time.

[8] Source: Statistics Canada, 2007.

[9] Betcherman and Lekie (1997), Baldwin (1998), Gabor et al. (1996), and James (1993) provide interesting overviews of the Canadian-born youth population but do not examine new generation youth.

[10] Five are from the People's Republic of China, three from Pakistan, and nine from other Asian countries.

[11] According to various ethics legislations (i.e., your provincial, professional organization, and the *TCPS2*), you are required to mask the identity of particular individuals, businesses, or organizations unless they have provided written consent to be identified in your research.

References

Anisef, Paul, and Kenise Murphy Kilbride, eds. 2003. *Managing Two Worlds: The Experiences and Concerns of Immigrant Youth in Ontario*. Toronto: Canadian Scholars' Press.

Anisef, Paul, Paul Axelrod, Etta Baichman-Anisef, C. James, and Anton Turrittin. 2000. *Opportunity and Uncertainty: Life Course Experiences of the Class of '73*. Toronto: University of Toronto Press.

Anisef, P., R. Sweet, and G. Frempong. 2003. "Labour market outcomes of immigrant and racial minority university graduates in Canada." In M. Ducet, ed., *CERIS Working Paper*, 45. Toronto: Joint Centre of Excellence for Research on Immigration and Settlement—Toronto.

Baker, M., and D. Benjamin. 1997. "The role of family in immigrants' labour market activity: An evaluation of alternative explanations." *American Economic Review* 87, 4: 705–27.

Baldwin, Bob. 1998. "Intergenerational equity: The objectives of policy." In Miles Corak, ed., *Labour Markets, Social Institutions and the Future of Canada's Children*, 175–9. Ottawa: Statistics Canada.

Betcherman, Gordon, and Norm Leckie. 1997. *Youth Employment and Education Trends in the 1980s and 1990s*. Working Paper No.W-03. Ottawa: Canadian Policy Research Networks.

Bonikowska, A., and F. Hou. 2011. *Reversal of Fortunes or Continued Success? Cohort Differences in Education and Earnings of Childhood Immigrants*. Analytical Studies Branch Research Paper Series. Ottawa: Statistics Canada, Social Analysis Division.

Canadian Youth Foundation. 1995. *Youth Unemployment: Canada's Hidden Deficit*. Ottawa: Canadian Youth Foundation.

Chrètien, Jean. 2003. "Immigration and multiculturalism: Lessons from Canada." *Progressive Politics* 2, 2: 22–9.

Citizenship and Immigration Canada. 2010. *Facts and Figures 2008: Immigration Overview*. Ottawa: Department of Citizenship and Immigration Canada.

Coomer, N. 2008. "Bilingualism, wage differentials and the minimum wage: Three essays in the economics of labor and health." PhD diss., Department of Economics, North Carolina State University.

Ely, R.J., and D.A. Thomas. 2001. "Cultural diversity at work: The effects of diversity perspectives on work group processes and outcomes." *Administrative Science Quarterly* 46, 2: 229–73.

Gabor, Peter, Steven Thibodeau, and Santanita-Manychief. 1996. "Taking flight? The transition experience of native youth." In Burt Galaway and Joe Hudson, eds., *Youth in Transition: Perspectives on Research and Policy*, 79–89. Toronto: Thompson Educational Publishing.

Granovetter, M.S. 1974. *Getting a Job: A Study of Contacts and Careers*. Cambridge, MA: Harvard University Press.

Grant, T., and J. Yang. 2009. "Immigrants take brunt of recession, recover less quickly." *Globe and Mail*, 27 July.

Kilbride, K. Murphy, P. Anisef, E. Baichman-Anisef, and R. Khattar. 2004. "Between two worlds: The experiences and concerns of immigrant youth." http://ceris.metropolis.net/Virtual%20Library/other/kilbride2.html, accessed 10 May 2004.

Kunz, J.L. 2003. *Being Young and Visible: Labour Market Access among Immigrant and Visible Minority Youth*.Catalogue RH63-1/581-08-03E-PDF. Ottawa: Human Resources Development Canada.

Leu, J. 2009."Labour market mobility in a global economic downturn." Paper presented at the 14th International Metropolis Conference, Copenhagen, Denmark, 14 September.

Manitoba Labour and Immigration. 2007. *Manitoba Immigration Facts: 2006 Statistical Report*. Winnipeg: Manitoba Labour and Immigration.

Mendelson, Rachel. 2010. "When reality bites." *Maclean's*, 9 April.

Nesdale, D., and K. Pinter. 2000. "Self-efficacy and job-seeking activities in unemployed ethnic youth." *Journal of Social Psychology* 140, 5: 608–14.

Pagliaro, J. 2010. "Students fight for summer jobs." *Maclean's*, 6 May.

Perreira, K.M., K.M. Harris, and D. Lee. 2007. "Immigrant youth in the labor market." *Work and Occupations*, 34, 2: 5–34.

Picot, G., and F. Hou. 2011. *Seeking Success in Canada and the United States: The Determinants of Labour Market Outcomes among the Children of Immigrants*. Analytical Studies Branch Research Paper Series. Ottawa: Statistics Canada, Social Analysis Division.

Portes, A. 1995. *The Economic Sociology of Immigration: Essays on Networks, Ethnicity, and Entrepreneurship*. New York: Russell Sage Foundation.

Shields, J., K. Rahi, and A. Scholtz. 2006. *Voices from the Margins: Visible Minority Immigrant and Refugee Youth Experiences with Employment Exclusion in Toronto*. CERIS Working Paper 47. Toronto: CERIS.

Statistics Canada. 2003. *Annual Labour Force Survey Statistics*. Ottawa: Minister of Public Works and Government Services.

———. 2004. *The 2001 Census of Canada*, Public Use Microdata File for Individuals. Ottawa: Statistics Canada.

———. 2006. "Youth in transition survey: Update of the education and labour market pathways of young adults." *The Daily*, 5 July.

———. 2007. *Selected Demographic, Cultural, Educational, Labour Force and Income Characteristics (830), Mother Tongue (4), Age Groups (8A) and Sex (3) for the Population of Canada, Provinces, Territories, Census Divisions and Census Subdivisions, 2006 Census—20% Sample Data*.

———. 2009a. *The 2006 Census of Canada*. Public Use Microdata File for Individuals. Ottawa: Statistics Canada.

———. 2009b. *Annual Labour Force Survey—August 2009*. Ottawa: Statistics Canada.

Tomkowicz, Joanna, and Tracey Bushnik. 2003. *Who Goes to Post-secondary Education and When: Pathways Chosen by 20 Year Olds*. Ottawa: Statistics Canada.

United Nations. 2007. *World Youth 2007: Young People's Transition to Adulthood—Progress and Challenges*. New York: United Nations.

Wilkinson, L. 2008. "Labor market transitions of immigrant-born, refugee-born, and Canadian-born youth." *Canadian Review of Sociology/Revue canadienne de sociologie*, 45, 2: 151–76.

———, S. Lauer, R. Sin, A.K.T. Tsang, and M.C. Yan. 2010. *The Labour Market Transitions of Newly Arrived Immigrant Youth: A Tri-Provincial Study. Final Report*. Ottawa: National Metropolis Project and Statistics Canada Research Data Centres.

Yan, M.C. 2000. "Coping with unemployment: Some lessons to learn from a group of unemployed ethnic minority youths." *Canadian Social Work Review* 17, 1: 87–109.

Glossary

accidental quota sampling A participant selection strategy that involves some selection of participant characteristics. For instance, a researcher who sets up a booth in a shopping mall selects the first 10 female and the first 10 male shoppers to participate in her study. The sample is a quota because the researcher identifies the importance of interviewing an equal number of males and females. The sample is accidental because the respondents are not screened using other characteristics, and simply the first 10 of each group are selected based on a first-come, first-served basis.

accidental sampling A strategy to select research participants by using informants close to the researcher, typically used in qualitative studies. This procedure allows the investigator to approach potential respondents without worrying about personal relationships and individual characteristics. For instance, a researcher can set up a booth in a shopping mall and ask shoppers to test a new hand lotion. This sample is accidental in that it contains only shoppers who are at that particular shopping mall on the day the study occurs and contains only the people brave enough to approach the booth and agree to participate in the study. It is also known as haphazard sampling.

action/cultural framework A way of making sense of qualitative data. In this framework, researchers must gain extensive knowledge of the culture of the group with whom they are working prior to collecting and analyzing data. This can be done by consulting published sources of information about the group, visiting its website, obtaining pamphlets or informational material, and consulting experts.

bar graph A visual representation of the effect of an independent variable on a dependent variable. The graph appears as a series of bars that align along the x-axis (horizontal axis). Also known as a histogram. See Figure 11.1, for example.

bracketing A way of thinking that helps researchers separate their own experiences and opinions from those of the people they are studying. When a researcher is interviewing or writing about others, it is important to keep one's thoughts and opinions separate from what the participants say. Your job as a researcher is to share participants' experience and not obscure the research with your own biases.

case study A type of research design that is concerned with the situation of a single person, group, town, institution, or nation. Put another way, the case study treats the entity as the unit of analysis (see *unit of analysis*). An example of a case study could be a study that examines the organizational structure of the Hospital for Sick Children in Toronto. The purpose of this study is to understand how this institution is organized. It is not intended to compare this hospital with others.

categorical variable See *nominal variable or concept*.

cluster sampling A procedure that involves identifying elements by groups. Elements from all groups are randomly selected to participate in the study. For example, the city of St John's, Newfoundland, could be identified easily by federal electoral boundaries. There are just two federal ridings in St John's: St John's East and St John's South–Mount Pearl. In a cluster sample, we could identify 50 voters from St John's East and 50 from St John's South–Mount Pearl.

comparison study The purpose of a comparison study is to compare two or more entities on similar variables. The study of obesity rates among immigrant children and Canadian-born children would be an example of a comparison study.

concept An idea or a symbol that stands for something, or that represents a class of things or a general categorization of an impression of something. At the start of a research project, key concepts must be defined (see *conceptualization*).

conceptualization The point in the research design where major concepts such as the independent and dependent variable are identified and formulated. It is the process of creating clear, consistent, rigorous, and systematic definitions for concepts. The conceptualization process differs in qualitative and quantitative methods. In qualitative research, the definition of the concept is derived from the data collected. In quantitative research, the definition of the concept is developed prior to data collection.

confidentiality A concept that signifies that the information provided by participants in a research project will remain anonymous and not attributed to them in any way. The goal of researchers is to present research results in a way that maintains the anonymity of all respondents while ensuring that data released publicly cannot be used to identify any individual or group involved in the research project.

constant A type of variable that has no variation. A professor may ask a question on a test and 100 per cent of the students provide the correct answer. As a result, there is no variation in the response because all of the students provided the same answer—which statisticians refer to as a constant. Similarly, a survey may ask a question to respondents and all of them respond with the same answer. While this rarely happens, constants are troublesome and ought to be avoided. This problem can be resolved by asking questions that have a variety of different possible answers, such as those using a Likert scale. See also *variable, Likert scale.*

content analysis A type of data collection that involves the examination of various forms of communication—usually in written form. Researchers access the written data and prepare codes and themes as they review and re-review the material to come up with a better understanding of a phenomenon.

cross-tabulation A reference to the creation of a table that includes the effect of one independent variable on one dependent variable. See Table 11.5, for example. It is a term used in quantitative research.

datum (singular), **data** (plural) Latin; neutral past participle of *dare*, "to give." A thing given or granted; something known or assumed as fact and made the basis for reasoning or calculation.

decolonizing research Research designed to correct the historic tendency of marginalizing, disadvantaging, and harming Indigenous persons in the research process. It has long been acknowledged that many widely used research practices are embedded in a Western, racist way of thinking. The decolonization movement in research recognizes the history of abuse experienced by Indigenous persons at the hands of researchers. Today, we work together with Indigenous Peoples to recognize and centralize their voices in all research.

deductive approach A method of inquiry used by quantitative researchers. In this approach, researchers design their project by building on existing theories and research to test new assumptions and build new knowledge about a topic. The idea is to collect empirical data to test existing theories. It is also known as the "top-down" approach to research in understanding social life.

dependent variable (or **concept**) The main topic of interest in a research study. It is known as the "effect" or result variable. It is typically called "dependent variable" in the research language.

empirical Based on, guided by, or employing observation and experiment rather than theory. From the Greek word *empeirikos*, meaning "experienced, skilled." It generally refers to a statement or a belief that can be tested using observable facts.

equity A concept that encourages researchers to consider their participants as equals in the research process. This means treating participants with respect and listening to their requests and concerns.

ethics An honourable code of behaviour in research. It is also a concept that encourages researchers to "do the right thing" with regard to the treatment of their participants. This means treating research participants with respect and dignity, and treating the information they provide with the utmost confidentiality and care. Almost all professional organizations have a code of ethics, outlining what constitutes acceptable conduct in the field.

experiment (or **experimental design**) The most scientifically rigorous type of research design. It involves isolating the research subjects to conditions that control all other factors except the independent and dependent variables of interest. In the experiment, the value of the independent variable is changed in order to measure its unique effects on the dependent variable. Participants in experiments must have several characteristics in common (which are dictated by the research question). For instance, in a study of heart disease incidence, participants are separated by sex, social class, and other aspects deemed important to hold constant (see *constant*) in order to observe the "true" relationship between the independent and dependent variables. True experimental conditions are difficult to achieve in social science research. Psychologists are most successful at implementing this approach.

facilitator Person or persons who organize and conduct focus groups. See *focus groups*.

field notes A collection of research observations, including an account of the methodology used and steps taken in conducting the research project. These may be recorded in a physical notebook or in an electronic file. They are essential documents in any research project as they provide a written, preferably daily, record of research activities.

focus group A type of group interview where 4 to 12 participants with similar characteristics meet and discuss issues related to the researcher's topic of interest. The focus group is run by one or two facilitators who direct the group conversation. Facilitators usually have an interview guide provided by the researcher which lists a short number of topics or questions that must be discussed during the focus group. Like unstructured interviews, the questions or topics need not be addressed in the order they appear in the interview guide. The facilitator's job is to ensure the focus group does not end before the topics of the interview guide are discussed in sufficient detail.

frequency The distribution of cases on a particular variable. For example, in a study of 100 Canadians, the frequency of males in the sample is 54 while the frequency of females is 46. Frequency distributions are important information to present in research studies so readers have an idea of the demographic characteristics of the sample.

generalization A statement that attempts to broadly describe the characteristics of large groups. For example, "men are physically stronger than women" is a generalization. This does not mean that all men are stronger than all women; it is an overall observation. In qualitative research, generalization is not an objective. The idea is to uncover individual life experiences, while in quantitative research the purpose is to identify trends that can be used to describe a larger population.

Gus-wen-tah A Haudenosaunee word referring to a two-row Wampum belt to signify that an agreement between two parties has been made. The concept recognizes that research involving Indigenous Peoples must be reciprocal, and that researchers and Indigenous participants must collaborate as equals on all research projects. It is also a way of recognizing the important contributions that Indigenous Peoples have made and will make in research on health, culture, society, and other concerns.

hypothesis A statement that can be empirically tested. It is phrased in a way that can be supported or falsified. For example, the statement "men suffer higher rates of cardiac arrest than women" can be verified or rejected based on the observation of evidence that either support or refute the statement.

independent variable (or **concept**) Generally referred to as the "cause" of the dependent variable. It explains or predicts the dependent variable. This term is usually expressed as "independent variable" in the research literature.

in-depth interview A qualitative research method that involves asking general questions of participants in order to obtain personal reflections and experiences regarding the phenomena of interest. Researchers use an interview schedule rather than a survey as a guide to topics important to the study. Interviewers encourage participants to talk about their experiences rather than answering direct questions as a way of encouraging a conversational tone during the interview. This approach is meant to elicit more authentic information than that obtained using structured interviews, which are deemed to be too artificial and too biased (as personal bias sometimes alters the shape of the question). A major benefit of in-depth interviews is the ability for the interviewer to probe respondents for additional information, an activity not possible in structured interviews.

inductive approach A qualitative process of social inquiry that starts with observations from real-life settings (or derived from talking to individuals) and then uses this data to create new theories. It is known as a "ground-up" approach.

informed consent Consent given by potential participants based upon a clear appreciation and understanding of the facts, implications, and consequences of an action. To give informed consent, the individual concerned must have adequate reasoning faculties and be in possession of all relevant facts regarding the purpose and outcomes of the research project. For example, persons with diminished intellectual capacities (such as people with serious brain injuries) and children are not able to provide informed consent.

interview A research design that involves asking questions of research participants. It can take several forms: structured interview, semi-structured interview, and unstructured interview. Qualitative researchers prefer semi- and unstructured interviews, whereas quantitative researchers always use structured interviews to collect information.

interview guide (or **schedule**) A list of questions that will be asked to participants in a qualitative interview. The questions need not be asked in the order in which they are listed, nor must the interviewer ask the questions exactly as worded. The interviewer's job is to ensure the questions are answered at some point in the interview process, but allowing participants to use their own words as much as possible.

joint exploration A way of conducting research that allows the participation of non-researchers as part of the research process. For example, a community organization that assists the research team in developing the interview guide, identifying and recruiting participants, and interpreting the results is part of the research team. Other common partners include municipal, provincial, and federal departments, non-governmental organizations (such as the Red Cross/Red Crescent or Amnesty International), and philanthropy organizations such as the Winnipeg Foundation.

Likert scale Refers to the responses appearing after a question on a survey. Typically, the Likert scale has five responses: 1–strongly disagree, 2–disagree, 3–neither agree nor disagree, 4–agree, and 5–strongly agree.

line graph A graph on which the intersection of continuous level independent and dependent data are plotted on a graph for each individual case, and a best-fit line is drawn through the points. An example is shown in Figure 11.8.

longitudinal comparison research design Involves repeated measurement of phenomenon across two or more groups or cases over a period of time. Using the National Longitudinal Survey of Children and Youth and the New Canadian Children and Youth Study (see *longitudinal*

research design) to compare the obesity rates of immigrant and Canadian-born children between 2001 and 2008 would be one example of such a comparison design.

longitudinal research design Involves the repeated measurement of a phenomenon over a period of time. The purpose of longitudinal research is to address questions of change over time. The New Canadian Children and Youth Study, for instance, follows the same 4300 immigrant families over a period of 8 years and measures changes in health behaviours, academic performance, and mental health of children ages 5 to 18 years.

marginal total The number indicating the sum of all cells in a single row or column. It provides information about the total sample and is important information for a quantitative research table.

maximizing benefits The idea that any research conducted should maximize the benefits and minimize the harm to participants. While there is usually no benefit to an individual to participating in a study, once the research has been published and disseminated, the outcome should make elements of life for the group more positive than negative.

mean A statistical calculation that depicts the average score of a variable. The mean or average is calculated by summing the scores of each individual on the selected variable and then dividing that number by the total number of individuals in the study.

measuring instrument The tool that is used to collect data in your study. For surveys, the measuring instrument would be the questionnaire. For an unstructured or semi-structured interview, the measuring instrument would be the interview guide.

minimizing harm The idea that all research must be conducted in a way that does not harm participants. If harm is a possible outcome, then researchers must provide participants with information regarding the potential for harm and the opportunity to not participate or to end their participation in any research project. Participants should not be physically, psychologically, or emotionally harmed as a result of participating in research. This is a central ethical concept for all researchers.

multi-stage cluster sampling A variation on cluster samples that involves several stages of random sampling of groups or clusters prior to the selection of participants. See *cluster sampling*.

negative relationship A connection between two quantitative variables that is in the opposite direction (see *positive relationship*). For example, your results might indicate that as years of education increase, income decreases. Because education is going up and income is going down, we call that a negative relationship.

nominal variable (see *concept* or *categorical variable*) A level of measurement. It is a type of factor that has many different categories but the categories are equivalent to one another. In other words, the different categories of the concept can be considered the same "value." For instance, men are not higher in value than women—they are simply a different category. Similarly, one ethnic group is not superior to another—it is simply a different ethnic group. In the research literature, this term is most commonly called "nominal variable."

non-participant observation A qualitative form of data collection that occurs when the researcher observes activities associated with the research population but does not actively participate in them.

non-random sampling A procedure that involves the selection of participants using non-random means. It is a sampling procedure that is used extensively in qualitative research as the purpose of most studies using this paradigm is to understand a phenomenon in great detail without needing to generalize the findings to a larger representative population. Also known as non-probability technique.

observation A way of collecting data that involves close monitoring of events, individuals, environments, or phenomena.

operationalization The procedure undertaken to turn a concept into a variable; developing concrete definitions of concepts in an attempt to make a concept measurable. In quantitative research, operationalization of variables must take place prior to data collection. In qualitative research, operationalization comes as a result of data collection so that individual participants' meanings can be incorporated into the definitions.

participant observation A qualitative research technique in which the researcher observes and participates along with the study subjects. This technique aims to reduce the distance between the researcher and the study participants. When the researcher interacts in various social situations and participates as part of the group studied, it is believed that the observations and conclusions drawn are more "authentic" than those drawn from quantitative research, given that the researcher in this case is more distant and objective. This subjective, in-depth immersion in the situation can yield rich, diverse data that contextualize situations and environments that quantitative research are unable to produce.

phenomenologism/phenomenology A qualitative research method that believes every individual perceives the world differently. For this reason, researchers using a phenomenological approach interview a very small number of people, but produce very rich, descriptive reports of the issue of interest. The data collection process is iterative; as the researcher collects more and more data, their focus and output change, meaning interviews conducted early in the project may contain very different questions from the ones asked of participants at the end of the project.

photojournal An increasingly popular method of qualitative data collection. Participants are supplied with disposable or digital cameras and asked to take pictures of their lives and events over a short period of time. The photos are uploaded and participants are asked to reflect on them and describe their significance. The photos and commentary are used to produce evocative and highly engaging multi-dimensional reflections of the research topic, and they are a rich source of data.

photovoice A qualitative method of collecting data, particularly among people whose voices are largely marginal. Participants are given cameras to take photos of their everyday lives. Afterwards, they are asked either to complete a questionnaire for each photo (sometimes producing beautiful photo albums) or to meet with a research team to construct a narrative about the photo. This provides visual evidence that enhances the data collected by the survey. These photos and the information collected about them form an important part of the knowledge that researchers gain from underprivileged groups.

pie graph Displays the frequency distribution of a single variable. This type of graph is appropriate for categorical (nominal) variables. See Figure 11.5, for example.

plain language statement Another term for a consent form. It is an effort made by researchers to explain the purpose and outcomes of a research project without using technical language or disciplinary jargon. The intent is to provide clear information and details about a research project so that the participant can decide whether or not to consent to participate.

positive relationship A connection between two quantitative variables (see *negative relationship*). In the case of a positive relationship, both variables may move in the same direction. For example, you might observe that as number of years of education increases, income also increases. Since both variables are increasing, we call this a positive relationship.

positivist approach/positivism The idea that the only valid evidence is that which can be derived from empirical, objective observations. Positivists attempt to build a body of knowledge using theories. Theories are tested and altered based on repeated research. Repeated observation will prove or disprove theory. Positivism is in direct contrast to realism.

primary research The act of collecting new data. These are data that have not existed in other forms prior to the research project (see *secondary research*).

privacy A concept that signifies that information about an individual research participant should never be shared. Individuals generally have the expectation that their information will be used for legitimate research purposes and will not be shared with others. Most provinces have legislation intended to ensure the privacy of its citizens.

purposive sampling Some established researchers believe that their expertise in a particular topic can help them identify "typical" cases worthy of study. The researcher selects cases she feels best represent the phenomena of interest and these people participate in in-depth investigation. This strategy is appropriate for qualitative studies. It is less commonly known as judgmental sampling.

qualitative research design A method of research that is typically concerned with the collection of data that exclude numbers. It can include personal accounts, feelings, observations, images such as photos and drawings, and personal beliefs. Proponents of this research design believe that numbers oversimplify our understanding of complex human phenomena. A nurse conducting a study of the experience of postpartum depression among new mothers would likely use a qualitative research design where she could ask mothers to tell her about their personal experiences. This data provides personal details about the daily lives of mothers with postpartum depression and is helpful for uncovering the personal and family experiences in a way that cannot be fully understood using numbers. It is a powerful method of giving "voice" to the participants in a research study. Typically, the sample size of qualitative research designs is small, sometimes fewer than 20 people. Qualitative research designs include unstructured interviews, focus groups, participant observation, and ethnographies.

quantitative research design A method of data collection that focuses on assigning numerical values to social science research questions. This research design is most interested in answering questions of *how often* and *how much*. The data collected can be numbers, percentages, or statistics. Epidemiologists used hospital databases to identify the characteristics of patients who were admitted to the ER after suffering a stroke. They discovered that patients under the age of 60, those who sought treatment less than 24 hours after the onset of symptoms, and those who were female were more likely to survive than those without these characteristics.

questionnaire Also referred to as a survey. A list of questions that are answered by respondents participating in a quantitative research design. The questions may be read and responded to by the respondent on paper or on computer (online or through programming on laptops provided). The questionnaire may also be administered by an interviewer who reads the questions as worded on the survey and records the responses provided by the respondent.

random sampling A way of selecting participants for research that employs an equal probability for each entity in the target population to be selected for study. Sample selection strategies that involve an equal probability for all individuals to be selected are a "gold standard" in quantitative research.

reliability   Refers to the ability of a concept to provide the same results after repeated measurements. Consistent measurements, those that provide similar results with similar populations, are said to be reliable measures of a concept. For example, researchers are able to accurately identify sufferers of post-traumatic stress disorder in repeated surveys, which means the questions asked are reliable.

representativeness   The quality of the sample that allows the researcher to take the findings from the small number of observations and apply it, with some certainty, to the description of a larger group of similar entities with the same characteristics. For example, a sample is representative if it reflects the characteristics of the population it is supposed to represent. A study of Canadians' voting preferences is representative only if the characteristics of the sample reflect those of the larger voting population (i.e., this sample must exclude those under age 18, non-citizens, and institutionalized or incarcerated persons).

research ethics board (REB)   A committee, usually consisting of research experts and sometimes graduate students and members of the public, that reads and reviews all proposed research projects at a university or institution. Research ethics boards are tasked with pointing out ethical errors or potential errors in research projects prior to the beginning of the research. The boards are meant to assist researchers in identifying ethical problems that might negatively affect the participant and/or researcher. Most members will have been trained in the *Tri-Council Ethics Policy* of the Government of Canada. Every publicly funded university in Canada must have at least one research ethics review board.

research objective   Used when a hypothesis is not desirable or possible, this is an important aspect of qualitative research. In qualitative research, the goal is not to prejudice or guess the results of the study like we do when using hypotheses in quantitative research. Instead, we list some information or objectives we would like to achieve at the end of the study. In qualitative research, the research objective is a statement that does not identify the direction of a relationship between two variables or concepts. It is a type of statement that is also desirable for some descriptive research projects. This is a particularly useful way to organize research on a previously unknown topic. For example, early studies on cyberbullying would pose research objectives such as observing the patterns of cyberbullying rather than examining the causes of cyberbullying (a topic that would be researched later once more information about the nature of cyberbullying was understood).

researcher bias   The propensity for investigators to select participants who are similar to them (i.e., have the same characteristics) or to include only participants in the research study who exemplify their beliefs. For instance, a researcher who studies political attitudes and who supports the NDP would be biased if she selected only participants who support the NDP.

sample   A small group of people used in a social science study to represent the characteristics of a greater population. Scientists select samples of populations to provide estimates about certain population attributes in order to develop or refine theories, provide guidance for treatment, or learn more about various social and health phenomenon. For example, a business owner may select a sample of 20 customers out of her database of 1250 customers and ask them to rate the quality of her newest product. The 20 people selected represent a sample of her customer database. The procedures for selecting the sample are different for qualitative and quantitative research methods.

scale   A series of questions on a survey that have been designed and tested to provide valid and reliable measurements of a particular concept. Scales measuring varied concepts such as post-traumatic stress disorder, consumer habits, anxiety, and other issues are commonly used and may require permission from the original authors before they are used in your study. Scales provide a reliable measurement of these concepts and allow you to compare the results of your survey to those of others who have used the scale.

scattergram   A type of graph that identifies the intersection between the independent and dependent variables for single cases on a graph. It is appropriate for continuous level independent and dependent variables. See Figure 11.7.

secondary research The act of conducting research by using available data. Examples include analyzing administrative or government records; performing a statistical analysis of someone else's publicly available data; or combining data into a new dataset. In secondary research, the researcher does not do any additional data collection (see *primary research*).

semi-structured interview A type of qualitative research design that consists of a semi-directed conversation between the interviewer and participant. The interviewer has an interview guide consisting of a small list of questions or topics that must be discussed during the interview. The order of the topics is dependent on how the conversation between the interviewer and participant flows. The interviewer's job is to ensure that all the relevant topics have been discussed and to probe for information resulting from new topics that are mentioned by the interviewee.

simple random sampling A procedure where every element has an equal and non-zero chance of being selected to participate in the study. A researcher has access to an electronic database of students attending Nipissing University. He wants to conduct a study of student satisfaction and, with the permission of campus administration, he selects respondents at random, perhaps using a random number generator, to identify students to complete his survey. Simple random sampling is the "gold standard" of quantitative sampling procedures but it is typically very difficult to obtain. It may also be used in conjunction with other sampling procedures that use multiple steps to achieve a more random selection of participants.

snowball sampling A procedure that takes information from the first 3 to 10 selected participants to create a larger sample. These initial "seeds," as the first selected participants are called, are asked to provide names and contact information of other potential participants to the researcher. The researcher then uses this information to contact these "friends" for the study. These new recruits in turn may be asked to provide names and contact information of other potential respondents. The idea is that the larger the snowball gets, the closer the sample begins to mirror certain characteristics of a random sample. This is not a valid procedure for quantitative research (with the exception of

respondent-driven sampling—a complex statistical procedure used to numerically identify the length of relationships between recruits obtained in snowball samples), but it is frequently used in qualitative studies.

stratified random sampling A technique that attempts to randomly select participants from each group. A researcher wants to know if there are differences in length of hospitalization among patients recuperating from knee-replacement surgery. The researcher may first take a random sample of hospitals in Canada and randomly select five for the study. From the five participating hospitals, a sample of 100 knee-replacement patients from each is asked to participate, resulting in a sample of 500 patients from across Canada.

structured interview A form of quantitative interviewing where the researcher asks a series of questions from a list. The questions must be asked in the order in which they appear on the list and the researcher must ask the questions exactly as worded. The idea is to provide the same research conditions for all participants, regardless of who interviews them.

systematic matching sampling A procedure that assigns participants to study groups that are homogenous on all but the attribute under consideration. Medical studies typically do this. Participants are assigned to one study group based on similar characteristics, such as sex, age, and ethnic group. Each group is different. For example, one study group consists of European females aged 18 to 24 years, while another consists of African females ages 18 to 24 years. Still other groups vary in terms of ethnic group and age group. The purpose is to study the effects of a new contraceptive pill. The exposure to the new contraceptive pill or the placebo is determined using random sampling assignment. When randomness is not built into the strategy, this must be considered a non-random/non-representative procedure.

systematic sampling When elements in a population are arranged in a list, a systematic sample is obtained when every nth element is selected. For example, say you have a list of 10,000 patients with arthritis who live in Alberta. You are interested in obtaining a sample of 100 patients to study a new exercise regime designed to alleviate chronic pain among arthritis sufferers.

If we take 10,000 (the total number of arthritis patients) and divide it by 100 (our desired sample size), we get 100. Next, we randomly select one respondent numbered between 1 and 100. This is our start point. Say that random number is 42. Our first respondent will be individual #42 on the list, the next will be the individual numbered 142, and the next case will be 242. If we take every 100th person on this list, we will obtain a sample of 100 participants. This is a quantitative sampling procedure and is not to be confused with systematic matching sampling.

theory   A set of ideas or beliefs that are used to explain a phenomenon or social problem. Human capital theory suggests that students who work hard, get good grades, and go to post-secondary institutions to get occupational training will attain good-paying, rewarding jobs as a result. This is a theory of how higher education is linked with occupational attainment.

triangulation   A method of combining the results of two or more methods. In this method, a single researcher tries to answer a research question using multiple methods. Each method provides different information that helps to provide a more complete answer to the research question.

typical actions framework   A qualitative method of data analysis that focuses on daily actions of a particular group. By collecting information about the daily activities of participants, the researcher has a better idea of lifestyles and interpersonal interactions within the research study group.

unit of analysis   The object of study. Social science research typically studies the individual. Sometimes, however, the unit of analysis might be a larger group such as a family, a business, or an organization. Awareness of the unit of analysis is significant in both qualitative and quantitative research.

units of measure   The format the data collected by a survey takes. A unit of measure would be kilograms if we were collecting data on a person's weight. Hours would be the unit of measure if we were asking someone about how many hours they studied for their research methods test. If the question were about the temperature, Celsius would be the unit of measure.

unstructured interview   A type of qualitative interview that lacks a questionnaire. Researchers enter the interview with no pre-recorded questions or preconceived notions about how the participant might respond. Instead, the goal here is to introduce the topic of study and encourage the participant to use her or his words and ideas as much as possible. The role of the interviewer is to encourage the participant to share their thoughts and to ask for clarification when necessary. Interviewers are given an interview guide, a list of topics that must be discussed in the interview. Participants are encouraged to speak freely about subjects of interest as a way of reducing researcher bias that creeps into directed questions. In this way, researchers hope to obtain a more authentic version of events or more legitimate observations by participants in their own words. This form of interviewing gives participants the most power to determine the content of the final product.

validity   Refers to whether or not the variable accurately represents or measures the concept of interest. There are many different forms of validity including face validity, construct validity, external validity, internal validity, criterion-related validity, and content validity.

variable   According to the *Oxford Dictionary*, a variable is "an element, feature, or factor that is liable to vary or change." In social science research, a variable is a concept that can take on more than one value. For instance, participants in a health survey may be asked if they have ever been diagnosed with diabetes. This question is followed by three choices: yes, no, I don't know. The three choices constitute the variability of the variable "diabetes diagnosis." The variable is an extension of a concept—giving the concept characteristics that can be measured and are observable. See also *constant, independent variable* (or *concept*), and *dependent variable* (or *concept*).

vulnerable person   A term used to describe someone who, owing to such circumstances as having diminished mental capacity or being under the age of consent (17 years of age or younger), is unable to provide consent to participate in a research project. In these instances, a guardian or parent must provide the consent for the individual to participate. It is also advisable to have the person sign an assent form, which is much like a consent form but is not legally binding.

Index